RHETORIC IN THE HUMAN SCIENCES

EDITED BY
HERBERT W. SIMONS

Ⓢ SAGE Publications
London · Newbury Park · New Delhi

First published 1989

SAGE Publications Ltd
28 Banner Street
London EC1Y 8QE

SAGE Publications Inc
2111 West Hillcrest Drive
Newbury Park, California 91320

SAGE Publications India Pvt Ltd
32, M-Block Market
Greater Kailash — I
New Delhi 110 048

British Library Cataloguing in Publication data

Rhetoric in the human sciences. – (Inquiries
in social construction series).
1. Philosophy of social sciences
I. Simons, Herbert W.   II. Series
300'.1

ISBN 0-8039-8178-3
ISBN 0-8039-8179-1 Pbk

Library of Congress catalog card number 88-62376

Typeset by AKM Associates Ltd, Ajmal House,
Hayes Road, Greater London
Printed in Great Britain by Billing and Sons Ltd, Worcester

Contents

To Aunt Bea and Uncle Leo

Preface

Each Spring since 1980 Temple University's Department of Rhetoric and Communication has held a conference on some central theme related to the general topic of discourse analysis. This book is a product of the 1986 conference on Case Studies in the Rhetoric of the Human Sciences. Another product of the conference, *The Rhetorical Turn: Invention and Persuasion in the Conduct of Inquiry*, is soon to be published by the University of Chicago Press.

As with other books in the Temple series this one has taken on its own separate identity. All of the conference papers were revised for the volume, some of them quite extensively. Four essays were added so as to round out the volume, two of them authored or co-authored by conference participants. Together these essays should provide a fair indication of the concerns motivating those involved in the current "rhetoric of inquiry" project within the human sciences, of the kinds of applications that are being made of rhetorical theory to diverse subjects, and of the possibilities for bringing rhetorical concepts and principles to bear upon new and as yet uncharted areas of inquiry.

Interest in rhetoric is quite fashionable these days, a reflection in part of widespread dissatisfaction with foundationalism in philosophy, and of the rejection of other objectivist orthodoxies in the various disciplines. But there is also a sense of optimism about the new movement, the conviction that rhetoric can provide a much-needed bridge between disciplines. The distinguished law professor, James Boyd White, has said: "Rhetorical analysis provides a way of addressing the central questions of collective existence in an organized and consistent, but not rule-bound way. . . . Rhetoric may also provide a set of questions and attitudes that will enable us to move from one academic field to another and in so doing to unite them. . . . Rhetoric in the highly expanded sense in which I speak of it might even become the central discipline for which we have been looking for so long – which 'science' has proven not to be – by which the others can be defined and organized and judged."

These are mighty prospects for a discipline once known as the "Harlot of the Arts," but the vitality of the current movement leads me to take them seriously. White's comments were made at the precursor to the Temple conference, a major "Symposium on the Rhetoric of the

Human Sciences" held at the University of Iowa in 1984, the significance of which is attested to in part by its gavel-to-gavel coverage on Iowa Public Radio. The Iowa collection has since been published by the University of Wisconsin Press as part of its thirty-volume series on the Rhetoric of the Human Sciences along with a Temple conference product, *The Legacy of Kenneth Burke* (1988), edited by Trevor Melia and myself. At the Iowa and Temple conferences, as at other interdisciplinary conferences on the "Rhetorical Turn," the excitement over the new movement has been quite palpable and the possibilities for useful talk across disciplines clearly demonstrated.

For those unfamiliar with rhetoric as a tradition of scholarship, or who associate rhetoric with bombast and deception and thus cannot imagine anyone saying anything good about rhetoric, the introduction to this volume provides some sense of the term's historic range of meanings, and the essays by Czubaroff, Hariman, and Keith and Cherwitz provide useful beginnings as well. One hoped-for consequence of the new movement is that rhetoric will be taken up as a field of study at more and more universities, not just as an art of composition (as in all too many English departments) but also as an art of invention, judgment, and argumentation. Michael Billig's *Arguing and Thinking: A Rhetorical Approach to Social Psychology* (Cambridge University Press, 1987) does an especially fine job of introducing social scientists to the rhetorical tradition. Also highly recommended is Donald N. McCloskey's *The Rhetoric of Economics* (University of Wisconsin Press, 1985).

The 1986 Temple conference was an intense affair, featuring some 60 papers and 150 participants, many of whom had been participants at the Iowa Symposium or were contributors to the Wisconsin series. Frances Spisak and Don Stewart put in long hours helping me organize and coordinate the 1986 conference, and numerous other faculty, graduate students and office staff in the Department also deserve thanks. Special thanks go to Ronye Smaller, Diane Johnson and Linda Tilli. Richard Brown and Kathleen Jamieson served as unofficial consultants on the project and Bruce Gronbeck, John Lyne, Donald McCloskey, Allan Megill and John Nelson gave good advice on both my conference and book-publishing efforts.

The conference was made possible by grants from the Research Board of the Speech Communication Association and from the Faculty Senate Lectures and Forums Committee at Temple. But it remained dependent on the generosity of the participants and of their home institutions for support. Thier generosity continued throughout the review process for the books. Two of the conference participants, Kenneth Gergen and John Shotter, invited me to join the series they were putting together on Inquiries in Social Construction. I am grateful to them for the overall direction that they have given to the book project, and I am delighted that their series went to the London arm of Sage Publications.

Among the joys of working in the "rhetoric of inquiry" area is that one gets to interact with scholars from a wide array of disciplines. Recently at a conference at Iowa on Argument in Science, I had the opportunity of meeting a number of British sociologists of science, including Malcolm Ashmore, Barry Barnes, Harry Collins, Trevor Pinch, and Steven Woolgar. The similarities between the rhetoricians of science and the sociologists of science were striking, extending even to parallels in the divisions within each group. Yet until the Iowa meeting they had not interacted. Hopefully this book will help increase the flow of intellectual traffic across continents and between groups.

Notes on Contributors

Herbert W. Simons is a Professor of Rhetoric and Communication at Temple University and founder of the Temple Discourse Analysis Conference Series. He has guest-taught seminars on the Rhetoric of the Human Sciences at Maryland and Massachusetts and at the East–West Center in Honolulu. He is also a member of the Board of Advisors to the Project on the Rhetoric of Inquiry (POROI) at Iowa. His recent books include *Persuasion: Understanding, Practice, and Analysis; The Legacy of Kenneth Burke* (co-edited with Trevor Melia); *Form, Genre, and the Study of Political Rhetoric* (co-edited with Aram A. Aghazarian); and *The Rhetorical Turn: Invention and Persuasion in the Conduct of Inquiry* (in press).

Linda Brodkey is an Associate Professor of English at the University of Texas at Austin. She has published articles in *College English* and *Written Communication* and a book, *Academic Writing as Social Practice*. She is currently working on the rhetorical representation of adults in law and education.

Victoria Chen is an Assistant Professor in the Department of Speech at the University of Florida, Gainesville. Her research interests include the development of intercultural communication theory and the analysis of social reality lived by persons who are enmeshed in bicultural systems, for example, Asian Americans.

Richard A. Cherwitz is a Fellow to the Ben F. Love Regents Professorship in Communication and Director of Graduate Studies at the University of Texas in Austin where he specializes in rhetorical theory and argumentation. He is a co-author with James W. Hikins of *Communication and Knowledge: An Investigation in Rhetorical Epistemology* and editor of *Philosophical Perspectives on Rhetoric* (in press).

Jeanine Czubaroff is an Assistant Professor in Communication Arts at Ursinus College. She has studied, lectured on, and written about the controversy surrounding B.F. Skinner for the past decade. Her analysis of his rhetoric recently appeared in the *Journal for the Experimental Analysis of Behavior*.

Steve Fuller teaches at the Center for the Study of Science in Society at Virginia Polytechnic Institute, and is Executive Editor of *Social Epistemology: A Journal of Knowledge, Culture and Policy*. He has written many articles in a wide variety of areas in the human sciences and has recently completed a book, *Social Epistemology*. He was the principal organizer of the 1988 Sociology of the Sciences Yearbook conference, which was devoted to the relevance of cognitive psychology to the study of scientific reasoning.

Alan G. Gross teaches at Purdue University's campus in Hammond, Indiana. He has been interested for some time in rhetoric of science, a subject on which he is now completing a book. He has published articles in his field in *Quarterly Journal of Speech* and in the *Journal of Technical Writing and Communication*.

Robert Hariman is an Associate Professor of Speech Communication at Drake University where he teaches and writes about rhetorical theory and political discourse. His essays have appeared in the *Quarterly Journal of Speech*, the *Journal of the History of Ideas*, and *Rhetorica*.

Tamar Katriel is a Senior Lecturer in the School of Education at the University of Haifa, Israel. Her research is in the areas of semiotics, pragmatics, and sociolinguistics. She is the author of *Talking Straight: 'Dugri' Speech in Israeli Sabra Culture* which won the 1987 SCA book award.

William M. Keith is an Assistant Professor in the Department of Communication Arts at Western Washington University. He does research on argumentation, and is interested in the connections between formal semantics and pragmatics and communication theory.

Jenny L. Nelson is an Assistant Professor in the School of Telecommunications at Ohio University, where she teaches courses in media theory and criticism. Her dissertation was a semiotic phenomenology of televisual experience. She continues to conduct qualitative audience research, with an emphasis on gender, transcription, and temporality.

W. Barnett Pearce is Professor and Chair of the Department of Communication at the University of Massachusetts, Amherst. His most recent book is *Development as Communication: A Perspective on India*, with Uma Narula, and his next book will be *Communication and the Human Condition*.

John Durham Peters is an Assistant Professor of Communication Studies at the University of Iowa. His main academic interests are in social theory and in media and modern life.

Lawrence J. Prelli is an Assistant Professor of Communication at the University of New Hampshire, where he teaches courses on rhetorical theory and criticism. He is author of *A Rhetoric of Science: Inventing Scientific Discourse* (forthcoming).

Eric W. Rothenbuhler is an Assistant Professor of Communication Studies at the University of Iowa. He is interested in communication and community, with emphasis on the ways that communicative phenomena create social solidarity, and in music, motorcycles, and mobility.

Robert E. Sanders is an Associate Professor in the Department of Communication at the State University of New York at Albany. His scholarly publications are mainly in the areas of discourse analysis, face-to-face interaction, and communication competence, including his recently published book, *Cognitive Foundations of Calculated Speech.*

Vito Signorile is Professor of Sociology/Anthropology at the University of Windsor, Ontario, Canada. His interest is in the theory of symbols as constitutive of social processes. He has published essays exploring the symbolist perspective in the works of Max Weber and Kenneth Burke, as well as several treatises on visual symbols. He is currently writing on the significance of language for a theory of human sociality.

Introduction

Herbert W. Simons

Epigraphs have a riddling quality. They are supposed to be relevant to the main text, yet taken literally, they are not. This creates a puzzle where the question is not, "What does the epigraph mean?," but instead the question is, "What is it doing here?" The solution at minimum requires the reader to infer the author's reason for heading the text with that quotation, an inferential problem that often engenders a circular reading back-and-forth between the epigraph and the main text. (Katriel and Sanders, this volume)

The Rhetorical Turn

For those accustomed to marking new fashions in the human sciences as "turns" (for example, the "linguistic turn," the "interpretive turn"), we here present news of the "rhetorical turn." Or, given rhetoric's antiquity as a field of study, and the resurgence of interest in ancient texts, perhaps we ought to be speaking of the "rhetorical return." Increasingly, scholars in a wide variety of disciplines are recasting what they are about in rhetorical terms; examining ancient rhetorical treatises for help in addressing contemporary problems; and alleging that what for so long were considered issues in philosophy or science might more profitably be addressed as issues in rhetoric (Billig, 1987; Brown, 1987; McCloskey, 1985; Nelson and Megill, 1986; Nelson et al., 1987; Simons, 1985, 1986). The project – variously known as "rhetoric of inquiry" or as "rhetoric of science" – is taking place against a backdrop of rising dissatisfaction with objectivist credos.

Significant objections have been raised in recent years to such foundationalist notions as the correspondence theory of truth, the mind as a "glassy essence," scientific language as a "mirror" of reality, and verification as well as falsification as demarcation criteria for a "true" science. At issue has been not just the status of scientific claims but of objectivity itself, whether as applied to science or to history writing, journalism, art criticism, law, women's studies, or philosophy.

These challenges to prevailing orthodoxies have prompted intensified critical attention to the language and logic of the human sciences, and ultimately to their rhetoric. There has been considerable talk of "decentering" and "de-familiarizing" scholarly texts, this so that critics might better practice what Ricouer (1977) has called a "hermeneutics of suspicion." Structuralists and formalists have been calling attention to the tropological character of language and to the influence of discursive and even prediscursive linguistic forms on both thought and expression. Poststructuralists, such as Foucault, have examined linguistic forms with a view to exhibiting institutionally imposed constraints on rhetorical choice (see Shapiro, 1986, for a useful summary of these approaches).

As can be seen, the movement to reconstitute the human sciences in rhetorical terms is not an isolated phenomenon. It has been taking place in tandem with structuralism and poststructuralism, postpositivism and critical pluralism, hermeneutics and Habermasian critical theory, each of which might be said to display its own distinctive rhetorics. Brodkey (this volume), for example, says that the dominant rhetoric of poststructuralism is that of resistance. Other important currents of thought include radical feminism, the science-as-literature project in literary criticism, the reflexivity project in the sociology of science, and the generative paradigm with which Gergen and Shotter have been identified. The Temple Conference on Case Studies in the Rhetoric of the Human Sciences had as one of its goals to explore linkages among these movements.

Perspectives on Rhetoric

As an old word, made rich but also ambiguous by a long history of inconsistent usage, the term "rhetoric" invites attention to the discursive practices of the human sciences from a variety of perspectives. Most centrally, perhaps, rhetoric is about persuasion. Thus, for example, we might wish to examine the discourse of economists, philosophers, or historians *as* persuasion; in other words, as discourse that is in some sense akin to what such prototypical persuaders as editorialists, advertisers, and politicians do. Correspondingly, we might wish to characterize a given economic theory, or philosophy, or historical account as *a* rhetoric (for example, poststructuralism's rhetoric of resistance). Such an exercise involves "perspective by incongruity" (Burke, 1969) insofar as science, philosophy, history and the like have traditionally been considered outside the province of rhetoric.

Fleshing out the ties between rhetoric and persuasion a bit more, we can say that rhetoric is the form that discourse takes when it goes public (Elshtain, 1984); that is, when it has been geared to an audience, readied for an occasion, adapted to its ends (Bryant, 1953; Gusfield, 1976). Rhetoric is thus *not* "pure" information-giving, "pure" logic, "pure" aesthetics, or "pure" expression, though it need not be false to fact, illogical, unaesthetic, or inauthentic. We might say that it is "extra-factual," "extra-logical," and the like – that it relies on something *more* than fact or logic or beauty or feeling to accomplish its ends (Simons, 1986). And indeed it must, for the province of rhetoric is the nonprovable, the contingent, the realm of judgment rather than certainty (Czubaroff, this volume; Perelman and Olbrechts-Tyteca, 1969).

Rhetoric is thus a pragmatic art; its functions those of symbolic inducement (Fisher, 1987; Burke, 1969). The rhetor, said Burke, exploits the "resources of ambiguity in language" – a wonderful phrase, to which I would add, in this television age, the resources of the nonverbal; of the paralinguistic. And I should add too that rhetoric is not just an individual practice: that there are rhetorics of organizations, of social movements, of professions, and of scientific schools and disciplines. With but a bit of casuistic stretching, we might conceive of the products of the mass media, and even of entire cultures or cultural epochs, as collective rhetorics.

The foregoing are among the relatively neutral senses of "rhetoric," but we should by no means ignore its pejorative senses as pretense, display, deception, "mere" rhetoric. When "rhetoric" is used in reference to scientists, textbook writers, reporters, and the like, it is frequently a term of derision, a way of suggesting that they have violated principles held high in their professions. Understandably, therefore, communicators of all stripes attempt to distance themselves from the "rhetoric" label if they can get away with it. Likewise, entire professions represent themselves as being "above rhetoric" even as they use rhetoric (in the more neutral sense) to legitimate themselves (Simons, 1986).

The chief objection to rhetoric over the ages has been that it deals in appearances which may be bogus or counterfeit. Although the ancient Greeks were aware that the appearances created by rhetoric could help shape or reinforce perceptions of the truth, they were also concerned that the persuader or rhetor might bend truth to effectiveness; hence Plato's characterization of sophistic rhetoric as an art of making the worse appear the better reason.

While Plato was primarily concerned with rhetoric as a perverter of truth, others have complained that it perverted human relations, transforming natural relationships built on warmth, spontaneity, and direct expressions of feeling into manipulative contexts for advantage over others.

Still another variant of the complaint that rhetoric deals only in appearances has been the charge that it is mere symbolism, tokenism, the selling of the sizzle rather than the steak. From the perspective of the hard-nosed economist or political scientist, rhetoric offers only symbolic satisfactions while material incentives, brute force, and the like, do the "real" talking in society.

Implicit in these criticisms of rhetoric are conceptions of the real as alternatives to rhetoric (Simons, 1986). The first, which I have associated with Plato but which persists in various objectivist credos, identifies the real with the true and holds open the possibility that one may arrive at the truth through reason and investigation. The second, a creature of romanticism, identifies the real with the natural, as manifested in expressions of genuine feeling. The third identifies the real with the powerful – with real rewards and real punishments as opposed to mere symbolism.

From the perspective of the rhetorician, these conceptions of the real might better be described as *ideologies* of the real. Indeed, the radical or deconstructionist critique of realism holds that there is only rhetoric; no external ground of the literal; nothing to be discovered (for example, de Man, 1978).

But not all rhetoricians are deconstructionists; far from it. Indeed some, like Keith and Cherwitz (this volume), hold that the discipline of rhetoric can work hand-in-glove with objectivist philosophy, while others, such as Czubaroff (this volume), look to rhetoric as a rational, albeit nonalgorithmic, alternative to objectivism.

Hence we come to the eulogistic senses of "rhetoric," its use as a "god" term. The study of rhetoric need not be confined to the tracking of effective persuasive practices; it may also be concerned with the study of what *ought* to persuade, given an ideal (wise, judicious, intelligent, etc.) audience. In *Modern Dogma and the Rhetoric of Assent*, Wayne Booth (1974) speaks of rhetoric as "the art of probing what men believe they ought to believe, rather than proving what is true by abstract methods"; as "the art of discovering good reasons, finding what really warrants assent, because any reasonable person ought to be persuaded"; and as the "careful weighing of more-or-less good reasons to arrive at "more-or-less probable conclusions – none too secure but better than would be arrived at by chance or unthinking impulse."

The eulogistic senses of rhetoric are concerned not just with quality of argument but also with how ideas should be expressed. In the very first paragraph of this introduction, for example, I labored over the question of whether one should speak of the "rhetorical turn" or the "rhetorical return." The question of choice of metaphors is but one small example of the tropological concerns of rhetorical study, and its application to an essay about the new movement is an example of the movement's self-questioning, self-reflexive character. Like the foregoing epigraph about epigraphs, rhetoric about rhetoric cannot avoid doubling back upon itself; cannot avoid its own rhetoricity. This adds another dimension to all rhetorical analysis.

Each of the foregoing conceptions of rhetoric has proven heuristically productive; they have advanced consideration of issues even if they have not resolved them. In such ongoing debates as between objectivists and relativists, postpositivists and antipositivists, foundationalists and antifoundationalists, monists and pluralists, rhetoric has emerged, not as a single perspective, but as a way of reconceiving the debates themselves – linking them, for example, to Greco-Roman conceptions of rhetorical invention, or to neosophistic conceptions of style and impression management. Here and abroad there has been what Geertz (1980) referred to as a "refiguration of social thought," a shift from craft and technology imageries to metaphors and analogies drawn from the humanities. In the new metalanguage of the human sciences, behaviors, cultures, entire historical epochs might be viewed as texts, scientific data as symbolic constructions, scientific descriptions and theories as narratives, mathematical proofs as rhetorical tropes, the ongoing activities of scientific communities as conversations.

In these examples the rhetorical tradition serves as an inventional resource, a storehouse of codified ways of seeing, thinking, and communicating that may be tested for their goodness of fit to the matter at hand, and which once applied to particular cases provide exemplars for subsequent analyses. In the dialectical enterprise of viewing disciplinary questions in rhetorical terms, rhetoric itself may be permitted to function as an "essentially contestable term" (Gallie, 1964), the varying conceptions of rhetoric arranged for presentation, as in an orderly conversation (Burke, 1969). What the conversation is apt to disclose is that the controversies besetting other disciplines are a bit like those concerning rhetoric itself. The popularity of the "rhetorical turn" in the human sciences is due in no small measure, I believe, to a widespread recognition among scholars in diverse disciplines that rhetoric's disputes are their disputes; that the objectivist presuppositions on which their fields depended no longer can be defended; that what they are engaged in is more akin to persuasion than to proof; that, as Billig (1987) put it, they rely more upon the "open fist" of enthymematic argument than on the "closed fist" of formal logic.

About this Book

As indicated in the Preface, this book is one of two stemming from the Temple Conference on Case Studies in the Rhetoric of the Human Sciences. The chapters are roughly divided between those dealing with the role of rhetoric in the making (or unmaking) of a science, those concerned with discursive practices in the various disciplines, and those essaying the uses and limits of the rhetorical turn. Few would question rhetoric's significance in what Czubaroff, citing Toulmin, calls "strategic scientific debates." In the emergent, preparadigmatic stage of a science, Thomas Kuhn has said, persuasion rather than proof is king. As Gross shows, for example, the very concept of scientific invention as the product of an individual's effort emerged in the early eighteenth century as the product of rhetorical invention. Similarly, at the point of paradigm clash, advocates of alternative models are apt to talk past each other, unable to agree on substantive assumptions or even on regulative norms and criterial values, and thus likely to use rhetoric as a weapon by which to denigrate their opponent's ethos (see, for example, the chapters by Czubaroff and by Prelli), and as an instrument of reality construction (see Peters and Rothenbuhler).

Clearly, rhetoric has important functions to perform in the making of a science, but it would be a mistake to assume that its role has ended at the point at which disciplinary practices have become normalized or routinized. In fact, Katriel and Sanders suggest that the conventions surrounding the use of epigraphs in scientific writing are themselves rhetorical. The same must surely be said for the metaphorical concepts that scholars in the human sciences routinely ontologize (see, for example, Nelson), or for their terminological borrowings from higher status disciplines (my chapter on psychotherapeutic placebos).

Most of the chapters in this volume focus upon the social sciences. Their subject matter includes media studies, psychotherapy, verbal acquisition in children, animal language, statistics, and cultural anthropology. Together they tell us a good deal about forms of scholarly writing – about scientific theories, research reports, book reviews, ethnographies, and scholarly exchanges. Their objects of analysis range from a single trope (Nelson on the "consumption" metaphor) to a recurring rhetorical form (Katriel and Sanders on the epigraph), and from the production of messages to their reception (Brodkey on multiple readings of a single text). Each of these chapters introduces concepts having applications far wider than the cases that they cover. Each advances consideration of questions, even if they do not resolve them. And each of them explores connections between rhetorical theory and related lines of thought.

Thus, for example, we find explicit connections in the Prelli and Gross chapters between the rhetoric of science and the sociology of science. Prelli introduces the concept of scientific *ethos*, arguing that what Merton alleges to be the norms and counternorms of scientific communities are invoked so strategically that they might better be viewed as rhetorical *topoi*. Gross also builds on Merton in exhibiting the relevance of rhetorical theory to rival claims of scientific originality by Newton and Leibniz over the invention of the calculus.

In these and other essays, faint echoes of the ancient sophists can be heard – cautioning against universalist standards of judgment, inveighing against applying algorithmic logics to questions of value, insisting that discourse about the world is always in part discourse about ourselves. Yet, as Stephen J. Gould (1987) has argued, the Protagorean thesis that man is the measure of all things does not necessarily imply human superiority; only that in our science and mathematics, as in all else, discourse creates features of the world rather than simply providing independent proof of their existence. Variants of this constructionist position find repeated expression in this book, beginning with Peters and Rothenbuhler's assessment of our mass-mediated culture and culminating in Hariman's avowedly polemical critique of a professional ethic that, he says, "is the dominant apparatus of power shaping our rules for determining truthfulness and probity."

The trope of tropes in these essays (as in the rhetoric of inquiry project generally) is that of irony; its message of messages that things are not what they seem; its lesson of lessons (if there be one), that there is a covert, ideological text in everything that is communicated – hence, that we had best attend self-reflexively to our own tropologies, our own ways of constructing the world. Thus we find Pearce and Chen a bit surprised that there is no escape from the problems of rhetoric – not even in the antipositivist writings on ethnography of two anthropologists whom they have long admired for their sensitivity to the lessons provided by rhetorical analysis. Somewhat more cynically, we find Peters and Rothenbuhler turning to the tinsel of Hollywood and to the blips and blobs on our television screens for evidence of what our worlds are "really" like. And we have Nelson compounding that irony with her own ironic reading of the concept of television consumption:

> Taking the digestive metaphor to its logical extreme, to consume is to embody. The phenomenological concept of embodiment entails the twin modes of expression and perception. The etymology of "consumption" suggests a double valence which renders the person as both subject and object, consumer and consumed. To eat, use up, devour or absorb, suggests that the significance of consumption lies not in *what* is consumed, but in the bodily *act* of "using up" or "digesting" something. "You are what you eat" implies that consumers become, through the very process of consumption, one of the producers contributing to their own transformation.

What are the limits of rhetorical analysis? What is rhetoric's relationship to knowledge, truth, and reality? What directions should the "rhetoric of inquiry" project take?

The contributors provide different answers to these questions. Signorile's debunking of efforts to rescue the statistical concept of equiprobability from the jaws of subjectivism is perhaps most representative of the deconstructionist influence on the human sciences these days, although my own chapter also betrays deconstructionist influences. On the other hand, Fuller radiates hope for a principled jurisprudence; he challenges Stanley Fish's claim that theory has no consequences, and in so doing seeks to undermine the antitheoretical foundations which Fish has provided for the Critical Legal Studies movement. Likewise, Czubaroff makes a case for the applicability of argumentation theory to what Toulmin calls "strategic" scientific debates. As regards paradigm clashes, for example, she would but supplement Toulmin's jurisprudential model with a model of rhetorical rationality geared to the deliberative assembly.

Of the various contributors, Hariman and Keith and Cherwitz clearly have the most to say about where the "rhetoric of inquiry" project should be headed. Keith and Cherwitz see the need for a "disciplining" of the "rhetoric of inquiry" project, while Hariman sees the need for nothing less than an undoing of the disciplinary structure that constrains rhetoric itself. In the current university structure, Hariman argues, rhetoric is damned if it is considered a discipline and damned if it isn't. But rhetoric may also lead the way to the needed transformation of our university culture:

> Rhetoric conceived of as a tradition of inquiry is itself highly problematic. The important point here is that they are good problems . . . If we are to think about rhetoric as a way of thinking, we must think of it in terms of its problems, especially as they are revealed in its history of suppression and marginality . . . Rhetoric's contribution to the higher learning comes in part from its condition as a marginal subject; consequently, it offers the most to one who is admitting failure. As we are in the historical moment of admitting to a failure of the human sciences (as sciences), rhetoric seems a productive commentary upon that enterprise. If we take the next step and consider the intellectual costs of the modern educational organization, rhetoric can again supply the means for reconsideration.

Alone among the contributors, Keith and Cherwitz offer a view of rhetoric that is largely compatible with the tenets of objectivism, but it is all the more valuable for that reason. Theirs is a rejoinder to "extremists" who whould push the "rhetoric of inquiry" movement so far as to replace epistemology with rhetoric, or treat rhetoric as epistemic. There is a world out there, they remind us – by which they mean something more than Peters' and Rothenbuhler's socially constructed universe. Some things are knowable and, what's more, we know that we know them. Indeed, communication fairly requires presuppositions of knowledge, including objective knowledge of language and, by implication, of the objects of inquiry. Thus, they maintain, the anti-epistemic, hermeneutic elements associated with the rhetorical turn are neither necessary nor consistent with that movement's philosophy. Rhetoric requires the possibility of genuine disagreement, but that in turn presupposes possibilities for resolution or advancement of the issues. The "extremist" rhetorical perspective leads to vicious skepticism or relativism.

Do we not have, in the conflict between Hariman and Keith and Cherwitz, further support for a view of rhetoric which I expressed earlier; as most fundamentally and most usefully a site of struggle, an arena of controversy in which we may play out the possibilities for argument on the great issues of our day?

References

Billig, M. (1987) *Arguing and Thinking: A Rhetorical Approach to Social Psychology.* Cambridge: Cambridge University Press.

Booth, W.C. (1974) *Modern Dogma and the Rhetoric of Assent.* Chicago: University of Chicago Press.

Brown, R.H. (1987) *Society as Text: Essays on Rhetoric, Reason, and Reality.* Chicago: University of Chicago Press.

Bryant, D.G. (1953) "Rhetoric: its functions and its scope," *Quarterly Journal of Speech*, 39: 404–24.

Burke, K. (1969) *A Grammar of Motives.* Berkeley: University of California Press.

De Man, P. (1978) "The epistemology of metaphor," *Critical Inquiry*, 5: 13–30.

Elshtain, J. (1984) "The rhetoric of women's studies," Paper presented at Iowa Symposium on the Rhetoric of the Human Sciences. Iowa City, Iowa.

Fisher, W.J. (1987) *Human Communication as Narration: Toward a Philosophy of Reason, Value, and Action.* Columbia: University of South Carolina Press.

Gallie, W.B. (1964) *Philosophy and the Historical Understanding.* New York: Schocken.

Geertz, C. (1980) "Blurred genres: the refiguration of social thought," *American Scholar*, 49: 165–79.

Gould, S.J. (1987) "Animals and us," *New York Review*, 25 June: 20–5.

Gusfield, J. (1976) "The literary rhetoric of science: comedy and pathos in drinking driver research," *American Sociological Review*, 41: 16–34.

McCloskey, D. (1985) *The Rhetoric of Economics.* Madison: University of Wisconsin Press.

Nelson, J.S. and Megill, A. (1986) "Rhetoric of inquiry: projects and prospects," *Quarterly Journal of Speech*, 72: 20–37.

Nelson, J.S., Megill, A., and McCloskey, D. (1987) *The Rhetoric of the Human Sciences.* Madison: University of Wisconsin Press.

Perelman, C. and Olbrechts-Tyteca, (1969) *The New Rhetoric: A Treatise on Argumentation.* Tr. J. Wilkinson and P. Weaver. Notre Dame: University of Notre Dame Press.

Ricouer, P. (1977) *The Rule of Metaphor.* Tr. R. Czerny. Toronto: University of Toronto Press.

Shapiro, M.J. (1986) "Literary production as a politicizing practice," in H.W. Simons and A.A. Aghazarian (eds), *Form, Genre, and the Study of Political Discourse.* Columbia: University of South Carolina Press.

Simons, H.W. (1985) "Chronicle and critique of a conference," *Quarterly Journal of Speech*, 71: 52–64.

Simons, H.W. (1986) *Persuasion: Understanding, Practice, and Analysis.* New York: Random House.

PART I

THE ROLE OF RHETORIC IN THE MAKING OF A SCIENCE

1
The Reality of Construction

John Durham Peters and Eric W. Rothenbuhler

[T]he question of the relationship between appearance and reality has become a particularly vexing, even obsessive preoccupation of modern men and women. We seem to have lost our way with it in a fashion and to a degree that the problematic now seems distinctive, even diagnostic of "modernity" itself. . . . Many of us, to hear us talk, even seem to doubt the existence of a "reality" itself. (MacAloon, 1984: 270)

Ritual appears in dangerous circumstances and at the same time is itself a dangerous enterprise. It is a conspicuously artificial affair, by definition not of mundane life. Rituals always contain the possibility of failure. If they fail, we may glimpse their basic artifice, and from this apprehend the fiction and invention underlying all culture. Underlying all rituals is an ultimate danger . . . the possibility that we will encounter ourselves making up our conceptions of the world, society, our very selves. We may slip into that fatal perspective of recognizing culture as our construct, arbitrary, conventional, invented by mortals. (Myerhoff, 1984: 152)

[A tragedy is] a deception which is better to cause than not to cause; to succumb to it shows greater powers of artistic appreciation than not to. (Gorgias, quoted in Copleston, 1985: 94)

In this chapter we set out a general theoretical argument about the nature of communication and discourse about it. The argument is motivated by some issues in media studies but is not limited to them. In fact, we suggest that the media, rather than ruining communication (via the manipulation of images) in fact reveal something profound about communication that was easier to leave implicit in earlier times: the constructedness of reality and the reality of construction.

The Distrust of Communication

The media are often attacked as contributing to the blurred border of appearance of reality which is often taken as a distinctive mark of the modern age. Mass communication, so goes the argument, has helped to put images in the place of facts and stories in the place of truth. Moreover, the media – precisely because they mediate experience – are taken as agents of alienation which remove us from the real experience of being present at events. We've become, so goes the plaint, a civilization that cannot enjoy attending football games without a lap television. C. Wright Mills' comment on the creation by the media of widespread "psychological illiteracy" may be taken as representative of this argument:

> Very little of what we think we know of the social realities of the world have we found out first-hand. Most of "the pictures in our heads" we have gained from these media – even to the point where we often do not really believe what we see before us until we read about it in the paper or hear about it on the radio. The media not only give us information; they guide our very experiences. (1956: 311)

In this chapter, we argue that the distinctions between image and reality, and first-hand and second-hand experience, mislead our attempts to understand communication – in any of its many forms. More particularly, we argue that the fears that media blur truth and error and remove people from real experience misunderstand the symbolically constructed aspects of truth and experience (cf. McGee and Nelson, 1985). These two fears are closely related, and are entrenched prejudices of the western intellectual tradition, though we will keep them separate, initially, for analytic purposes. The one concerns truth, that is, the accuracy of representations of the world; the other concerns authenticity, that is, the quality or intensity of human experience usually attributed to immediacy. The enemy of one is images, which re-present and hence get in the way of an unmediated vision of things; the enemy of the other is distance, which removes perceivers from the full experience of being there. Ultimately, these two issues reconnect in the problem of mediation, as we will see. The fears for the corruption of truth and authenticity are expressions of a complex of intellectual attitudes we call the distrust of communication, which is built into both popular and academic discourse about mass media, communication, and the social use of symbols generally.

Origins of Distrust: A Sketch

Perhaps the more fundamental of the two strands of distrust is the fear of images. This fear starts from the distinction between reality and our representations of it. These representations are copies or images and are not the real thing. Though Plato is more commonly recognized as the founder of the distrust of images it is Moses who begins western iconoclasm – the destruction of images. In contrast to the human-made idols that adorned temples in the ancient world, Moses called Israel to follow the real and living God, a reality beyond all representation. The great innovation of Judaism was to form a religion not based on the worship of images but of a reality deeper and beyond them (Goux, 1978).

Plato participated in a similar denigration of images, in his belief that sensory experience is a play of shadows behind which lies the reality of "forms" which are eternal and universal. The task of the philosopher – which is also the task of the human being as such for Plato – is to pierce the veil of images in order to contemplate the forms that animate and undergird the world of appearances. His criticism of the arts is consonant with his metaphysics: poetry, drama, and the plastic arts all come under his attack because they are "imitations of imitations." Painting, for example, makes copies of things as they appear to the eye, not as they really are in their underlying forms (see Plato, 1960, Book 10). Hence the arts and other products of human labor may only serve to lose people more deeply in the cavernous labyrinth of appearances rather than guiding them toward the light. Though Plato's conception of reality – the forms that undergird all phenomena and give the universe intelligible order – is not what most people today think of when they complain about the distortion of reality by images and symbols, he along with Moses nonetheless provided the West with a distrust of symbols as "mere" derivative shadows of "reality."

The distrust of symbolic representations recurs in a more familiar guise in empiricist doctrines of the seventeenth and eighteenth centuries, and after. Nothing, according to empiricism, is in the mind that did not first enter via the senses. In contrast to Plato, empiricism takes sensation as the royal road to knowledge rather than as a distraction from it. Nonetheless, there is a similar suspicion about the bewitching power of sensation, and more particularly, about the products of human symbol-making.

Language is a prime object of empiricist criticism. In the writings of such classic empiricist thinkers as Bacon, Hobbes, and Locke, one finds long tirades against the power of language to create ideas that are not really so. Language was seen as in need of the discipline (mathematical, preferably) which had proved to be so fruitful in natural science. Galileo and Newton were the empiricists' heroes; they showed how the unprejudiced observation of nature could advance the race farther than the squabbles and disputes that seemed to prevail in the realm of culture. They sought to substitute observation for argument, sensations for symbols (as if the meaning of sensations did not depend on symbolization). While helping modern science shake off medieval ideas and institutions, empiricist thought also served to institutionalize the misleading contrast between things which really exist and things which are the products of human invention – particularly such symbolic products as narrative rather than tangible things such as technology. Thus discourse, symbols, art, and narrative were placed in the unsavory company of falsity, deceit, illusion, and error. At best they were necessary evils, mere vehicles and clumsy tools. At worst they were sophistry and illusion, worthy only to be committed to the flames (as David Hume suggested for all books that lacked abstract reasoning about quantity or number).

Hume's philosophy gives us an even more specific articulation of the distrust of communication. His skepticism was both the fulfillment and annihilation of British empiricism. He agreed that nothing was in the mind save that derived from sensation, but then asked the question, how can I know the origin of sensations? Being an empiricist, he could only know the origin of sensations via sensations, and hence could never knowingly arrive at their origin. He concluded that he had no way of knowing whether sensations originate in the external world (as they seem to), his own fancy, or gods or demons (Hume, 1978). In a philosophical economy whose only coin is sensation, skepticism, taking the form of a radical distrust of all sensations, inevitably emerges. Hume's fear was that what had been taken as the real (that is, the world as revealed through sensation) might only be a by-product of the fabricated (that is, the power of imagination). Once more we see the distinction between reality and appearance undermining faith in knowledge. As William James (1890: 351) complained, Hume's error was not one of insight but of attitude – the discovery that the world has no ultimate grounding is not a scandal but a discovery worthy even of celebration (see below).

The eyes and ears were considered particularly vulnerable to deception by the empiricists, since they are removed from the things they perceive. Classic empiricism separated primary qualities (such as mass, shape, and number) which supposedly exist independently of a person to perceive them, from secondary qualities (such as color, intensity, sound) which only occur in the eyes and ears of the beholder. That is, touch is immediate, while what the eyes and ears perceive is always mediated. As Bertrand Russell, an heir in many ways to British empiricism, put it:

> It is touch that gives us our sense of "reality." Some things cannot be touched: Rainbows, reflections in looking-glasses, and so on. These things puzzle children, whose metaphysical speculations are arrested by the information that what is in the looking glass is not "real." Macbeth's dagger was unreal because it was not "sensible to feeling as to sight." (1925: 2–3)

This strand of empiricist thought – which is by no means restricted to professed empiricists but has become part of the English language – is another potent source of distrust of the electronic media, which deal in sound and sight, not touch.

Lewis Mumford's critique of the division of primary and secondary qualities anticipates the direction our argument will take:

> "I think," said Galileo . . . "that if ears, tongues, and noses were removed shapes and numbers would remain, but not odors, nor tastes, nor sounds." But why did he halt his hypothetical surgery with ear, tongue, and nose? What would become of shape and numbers and motion if the eyes and hands and brains were removed, too? Absolute entities that exist by themselves are only plausible figments of the human mind: all that can be called "real" is the outcome of a multitude of sustained transactions and interrelations between the human organism and the environment. (1970: 62)

Distrust of Communication in More Contemporary Forms

Besides Moses, Plato, and the empiricist tradition – which are perhaps better thought of as articulate examples of this distrust than the actual propagators of the doctrine – there are more immediate sources of the distrust of communication in the institutionalized ideologies of the news media. Canons of objectivity in the press are articulated in terms of moving beyond opinion and speculation to the truth. In its emergence, the ideal of objectivity in the media was explicitly connected to empiricist rhetoric about the separation of human fabrications from the real world of objects.

In Walter Lippmann's *Public Opinion* (1922), for instance, the argument is explicit that symbols are the products of emotion and cannot be trusted and that needs and desires intrude on the mapping of reality and on the unclouded spectatorship of the facts. While some might suggest that the notion of objectivity is a noble ideal even while acknowledging its unattainability, the point here is that even nominating it as an ideal is clearly founded on the belief that things are separable into the real and the fabricated (cf. Carey, 1982), and that it is possible to see the real with an eye innocent of symbols or interests.

Lippmann's *Public Opinion* illustrates a classic case of the distrust of communication (and is a text which displays many of the attitudes we wish to attack; see Peters, 1986). Lippmann gives us all the imagery with which to criticize the media for failing to provide accurate images of reality. His most well-known chapter from the book, "The world outside and the pictures in our heads," sets up the classic contrast between reality (the world outside) and the images and symbols we make about it (the pictures in our heads; the epigraph for the book is taken from Plato's story of the captives in the cave). His book is often taken as a definitive critique of the ideal of objectivity in journalism, but the virulence of his nostalgia for an immediate access to the facts only underscores the notion that knowledge ideally is unclouded by images. He starts this chapter with a story of Frenchmen, Englishmen, and Germans who lived on an Atlantic island to which the mail was brought only once every sixty days. Because of this communication lag, the news that World War I had begun reached them six weeks late. Lippmann comments: "For six strange weeks they had acted as if they were friends, when in fact they were enemies" (1922: 1). But this is indeed a stranger kind of fact than Lippmann acknowledges. He is saying that an abstract declaration of war between symbolic entities called nations supersedes the concrete community that these people had enjoyed. Is it stranger that they lived as friends when their nations were enemies, or that they became enemies upon reading a few words in something called a newspaper? Lippmann chooses the latter as the less strange fact.

Thus, while he wants to suggest that knowledge must not settle for mere images, his text describes a world in which "facts" are increasingly alien to the experience of concrete individuals. His urging that journalism – like all other agencies of social representation – turn to the facts ironically appears at a moment when the classic priority of reality over symbols is superseded. His call exhumes a rhetoric – one of the purgation of images and the quest for the real – precisely at the point of its exhaustion in terms of descriptive relevance (but not cultural power). Lippmann's own iconoclasm paradoxically coincides with the discovery that in the modern world reality is defined by symbols – might we say, that reality *is* symbolic.

The Construction of Reality and the Reality of Construction

We want to argue against two things. First, the hard and fast distinction of symbol and reality, narrative and truth. Second, the aroma of scandal that often accompanies such claims. We make no claims to being avant-garde, shocking, naughty, or daring in refusing to take the distinction between symbol and reality as important or even interesting. We do, however, wish to attack those who accumulate academic capital by marketing new arguments designed to shock the ranks of "positivists" that still supposedly infest the halls of academe (cf. Rorty, 1984). Just as the street criminal is too productive a worker in our society to be utterly stamped out (he sustains the law, prisons, police, burglar alarm installers, crime beat reporters, and prime-time TV writers), so the positivist, with his adoring attachment to a reality apart from everything human, has sustained a major part of the academic criticism industry for the past decade (supporting Marxist, hermeneutic, and deconstructive criticisms, for instance, since he takes the political as the neutral, the made as the given, and the exercise of will as apparent truth).

We suggest a more fruitful division of intellectual labor: let us do away with both the positivist's horror (who believes in reality) and the debunker's glee (who believes in constructions) and come to terms with what we as a species have made and are making. The symbolic, performative, and discursive production of reality is ordinary – a given of human society and experience. (We just happen to live in a society that has maintained a Victorian silence around reality-production, as if it were taboo.) The question then becomes not to simply establish that society – and communication – are made but to describe and explain how they are made and how they work. In other words, the question is not one of truth but of form.

We want to suggest that human society is best characterized by its being made. In it facts and fictions coexist as siblings, separated only by the relative density of interconnections to other human productions, and not by any essential underlying (ontological) difference. The terms *fact* and *fiction* etymologically are related: both are things that are made. Hamlet, for example, is a fiction in that he hooks onto the total accumulation of humanly produced reality in a few places – Danish myths, Shakespeare's text and its many children. Richard III, in contrast, is more densely connected to a specific era and place – his status to facthood is simply his denser "intertextuality" with the made artifacts of human labor (castles, history books, wars, and so on). We will give an extended example of this viewpoint which we hope will clarify the theoretical logic.

An Example: Media Events
The media's standard fare are events that have no anchorage in the world of directly experienceable fact. Such phenomena as wars, droughts, the balance of trade, the unemployment rate, the national debt, and the weather are things that have real effects on people's lives but exist as representable totalities only via the mass media. Moreover, many events exist only in media. Precisely where, for instance, did the third Nixon–Kennedy debate in 1960 take place? Kennedy was on the East coast, and Nixon on the West. Where does the MacNeil–Lehrer News Hour take place when MacNeil is in New York City, Lehrer in Washington, and interviewed guests in Los Angeles and Boston? The location of such events are in the broadcast texts alone.

The standard response to the discovery that some events seem to exist "merely" in texts, symbols, or images is one of scandal: Boorstin's illuminating study, *The Image* (1961), is one well-sung lament in a much larger chorus of mourners at the funeral of reality. Worries about the "implosion" of reality in the media (Baudrillard, 1980) are reflected at the popular level in such films as *Capricorn Two*, whose plot concerned the staging of a supposed moon landing (a media event par excellence) in the Arizona desert, and at a more sinister level, in the belief that the Holocaust never took place. In most academic and popular talk, the implosion of events into images is expressed as a Humean skepticism about the ultimate reality behind the "sensory images" (for example, of the moon) provided by our social sense organs, the media. The possibility of scandal rests on the distinction between reality and symbols, as if symbols were not real and reality were not symbolic.

Certainly telecommunication creates new kinds of social forms and new kinds of relations between humans and symbols. But to judge these as if their approximation to truth were all that mattered is to miss the point. Take, for instance, the analysis by Dayan and Katz (1985) of the marriage in Britain of Prince Charles and Lady Diana. Dayan and Katz argue that what we have been trained to see as the "real" event – the marriage – is actually a prop for the televised event. The essential insight of media events studies (along with much "post-modern" thought) is to deny any hierarchy of reality to fictions. The marriage in the Cathedral and the marriage in the living room are both equally real – which is to say they are both equally fictions, that is makings, with the word *fiction* taken in its aforementioned etymo-logical sense. There is simply no privileged rock bottom out there somewhere that we can appeal to in order to find out what really happened. Certainly the marriage in the Cathedral and on the television screen have different structures of participation (the home audience cannot kiss the bride, but the Cathedral audience cannot drink pop and eat pretzels), but their difference is not a matter of realness, only of form.

The disappearance of the rock bottom grounding where one can sort out more accurate representations from less accurate ones (see Rorty, 1979) leads to a weighting of televisual fictions over those of immediate presence – an inversion of the long Platonic prejudice. The on-the-scene public at media events – which is supposedly the "real" audience – are coached in their performance. They are props that provide a role of consecration to the event. Their job is to be seen seeing; they constitute a spectacle of the spectators. They testify to the television audience that there is reality to what it sees; their presence on the scene assures the real audience – at home – of the reality of the event. There is a price for being present. The eye-witness spectators witness only what happens. The television audience witnesses The Event – a packaged presentation of the actions of the event, the well-performed roles of excited and awed spectators, and the pedagogics of broadcast journalism.

This example is intended to make a more general theoretical point. The media have not changed the nature of communication – somehow distorting its fidelity, say. Rather, they have made its workings more apparent. They have shown that communication does not operate as a second-order approximation of reality; rather, it constitutes, it produces, reality. Some will reply that it is reference to reality that anchors communication and keeps it from being mere fantasy, mere illusion and invention. But these people have a too simple model of communication. They conceive of communication as being *about* something, not *being* something. Communication is taken to be second-order: it is the sharing of experiences, which are already made and are directly from the world. Successful communication, in this view, is parasitic on the bona fide and accurate experience of the communicators. At best, communication – the social use of symbols – offers nothing more than vicarious experience.

In this view, however, the possibility of communication as experience is ignored. This model suffers from the classic empiricist desire to ground experience in things rather than in symbols, in nature rather than culture, in objects rather than human labor. As recent philo-sophers have argued (for example, Arendt, 1958; MacIntyre, 1984) human experience can be considered *qua* experience only when it is told as a story. And even as communication researchers have argued (Lazarsfeld et al., 1948) perception is often a function of the community and commitments of the perceiver). Hence even the most bodily, individualized and personal forms of experience of the world (one's senses) are socially constructed. Experience is not something raw and dumb that gives our words their meaning; rather, our words give meaning to our experiences. As Kenneth Burke suggested, inverting the empiricist privilege of sensation over symbols, "things are the signs of words" (Burke, 1966: 359–79). Experience of the real world is always already symbolic, as is experience of others (com-munication). The experience of social life is the communicative enactment of symbolic structures just as communication is the meaningful experiencing of social life.

Responses to Objections

We recognize that there are several forms of resistance to this kind of thinking. We wish to examine several objections to it in order to show how this conceptualization of communication without scandal and without separable reality explains all that older ideas did, and more.

Distance

A first objection has to do with the complaint that one loses the direct authentic experience of things – the capacity to verify – when one admits that symbolic texts are as real as the things they claim to be "about." This objection is usually couched in the language of nearness and farness, with nearness being the sign of authenticity – of direct, first-hand, unmediated experience – and distance leading to obstacles and alienation. This objection comes from the second strand of the distrust of communication: the complaint that reality is increasingly "mediated" and hence regrettably remote from human experience. This view is a late version of the empiricist conception that touch is somehow more authentic and direct a sense-organ than vision and hearing – that which, as Russell says, most gives us our sense of reality.

Debunkers of symbols often use a language of touch and closeness to project an image of a reality more real than that made by symbols. Even those most sensitive to the workings of symbols sometimes grow uneasy when distance intervenes. While the position we elaborate here owes much, implicitly at least, to the work of Victor Turner's school (see, for example, Turner, 1982; Moore and Myerhoff, 1975; MacAloon, 1984) some of those authors are suspicious of signification at a distance. To be sure, Turner and his colleagues are highly sensitive to the roles of artifacts and ritual performances as media of realities. Artifacts can be richly evocative symbols allowing transport to other realities or times. The artifacts of a celebration are its sentiment. More than mere remains they continue to embody the celebration itself as distantly in time as their meaning can still be read (Turner, 1982). Similarly, though in a different mode of analysis, Csikszentmihalyi and Rochberg-Halton in their book *The Meaning of Things* (1981) have shown that the artifacts present-to-hand in our everyday life are the media of much of its meaning; we read the meaning of our selves and our times in our things.

Though these communication systems, like those that Innis (1951; 1972) discussed, have both temporal and spatial aspects, Csikszentmihalyi and Rochberg-Halton and Turner's school are more sensitive to time than space. Their interest in artifacts as symbols is predominantly as preservers of meaning. Shils (1981) also emphasizes artifacts as transporters across time. But communication systems can carry us across space as well. Mosse (1975) discusses statuary, architecture, festivals, and parades as the symbols of nationalism, the mediators of nationalistic mass participation. These symbols can be read as providing integration across time as the preservers of a national heritage and across space as a focus of attention and objects of pilgrimage.

MacAloon's discussion (1984) of the spectacle of the modern Olympics, for instance, seems to regard symbolic performance primarily as a route from one reality to another, from one sense of time to another, but not from one place to another. Symbolic performance may be a medium of communication, but not at a distance. He rejects the possibility of a mediated festival out of hand: "There may be media festivals, but a festival by media is a doubtful proposition. Festival means being there; there is no festival at a distance" (MacAloon, 1984: 270).

Such dismissals betray a craving for the immediacy of touch as the guarantor of social reality. They suggest a hunger for real social participation and contact. They want a mutual presence of people that can be guaranteed by something other than communication – by touch perhaps. They want people to be able to touch each other non-communicatively so as to guarantee their mutual social presence – to assuage their post-empiricist skepticism that others might be nothing but a figment of the imagination. Pinch me, they say, as if fearful they are dreaming. They want muscular social contact and a muscular society.

How, then, to explain the confluence of planning and anticipation, civil-religious attitudes, and celebratory activities around the television sets of millions accompanying the broadcast of the Olympic games (Rothenbuhler, 1985)? One argument is that the broadcast is a symbolic performance, different in form but no less real than the Olympic events. This broadcast symbolic performance is engaged via living room celebrations – friends are invited over, food and drink are served, comparisons of the live drama unfolding on television are made with the dramas elsewhere in life, and understandings are formed of each. This is no less real a form of participation than that of the spectator in the stands or the competitors on the field. Each is participating fully and completely in a constructed reality. (See Rothenbuhler, 1985 and 1988, for the full argument and evidence.)

Presence
Closely related to the privilege of touch as the bedrock of reality is the belief in the possibility of being present to things without the intervention of symbolic or perceptual media. Derrida (1967) has argued that the western tradition has deluded itself in its quest for presence, specifically the presence of speech as opposed to the distance – the mediation – of writing. The tradition has supposed that the problem of communication, for instance, is simply the encoding of consciousness (an unproblematic origin) into language (a problematic set of masks). In contrast, he argues that consciousness exists only in language itself, not outside of it. Hence there is no hope of immediate access to another (or one's own) mind or consciousness; rather, one gets symbols chasing symbols. At times Derrida's readers will get vertigo staring into the yawning abyss, but the important point for us

here is that it's silly to search for an "origin" or "center" that somehow stands outside us and yet orders and justifies our practices (Derrida, 1972). Further, it's silly to give speech or presence priority over writing or distance.

Hence the difference between mass communication and face-to-face speech is not in terms of "mediation" so much as structural possibilities. There is a formal continuity to such modes of symbolic exchange. When one person is face-to-face with another, different possibilities of turn-taking, interruption, and clarification appear than in letter-writing, for instance, but one mode is not more "direct" than the other. One can say things in letters that one cannot say face-to-face, as much as vice versa. Writing, as Derrida argues, is not a mere derivative and approximation of speech. Questing for the more real, as for the more authentic, makes no sense. Such concerns drop out once one acknowledges the make-it-up-as-you-go character of human life (though "reality" and "authenticity" are among the things made up by people). No wonder, then, that one of Derrida's chief values is play: an activity whose accomplishment requires a recognition of the artificiality and arbitrariness of the particular rules in question and yet the willingness to suspend disbelief in them in the deeper name of the game. His exposure of the futility of quests for immediacy need not be taken as a fiendishly intended paralysis of our ability to act; it can be read as a means to help us play better. There is no more need to be shocked by the exposé of the constructedness of things human.

Hence communication ought not to be separated into the mediated and the direct; rather, we should be sensitive to the variety of forms and the structures of possibilities inherent in each.

The Invention Taboo
The metaphor of mediation – which suggests obstacles to vision – should be replaced with the more profound insight that all social reality is a creative product of human labor, both symbol-making labor and other kinds. We have been taught to treat this as scandalous – to complain about the invention of tradition, for instance, as if not all traditions were invented. This is the tone of Hobsbawm and his colleagues in *The Invention of Tradition* (Hobsbawm and Ranger, 1983).

No social process could be more important than the invention and maintenance of tradition. But *The Invention of Tradition* focuses exclusively on traditions fabricated largely by British elites to eternalize their rule. While the book takes a muckraking delight in exposing the recency of supposedly venerable English traditions, it does so in a way that makes "invented traditions" seem more worthy of denigration than other kinds of traditions. And yet no author gives an example of an uninvented tradition – there are none. To go around exposing the dirty little secret that some traditions are invented while remaining silent about the rest is an intellectual move that threatens, ultimately, to liquidate all traditions, since no tradition can escape the "charge" of being invented and continually reinvented. The discussion should have been grounded in the first place in the establishment of criteria by which some traditions can be singled out as more worthy of critique than others.

This book is one example of what MacIntyre (1984) calls "unmasking" – the revelation that constructions underlie what passes as objective, timeless, or self-evident. We look forward to a climate in which the exposé of artifice has no rhetorical clout, simply because nobody pretends to unproblematic realities. The observation that humanity is the reality-making species need no longer be whispered for fear that it shock innocent ears; the only scandal is how long we believed that we did not make reality.

Politics
Those committed to social change may wonder at our account. Are we saying that all traditions, all human constructions, are fine as they are? That we should abandon critique as a tool to attack the all-too-abundant lies in the world? Others may charge us with providing the rulers with an excuse to blame the oppressed for their oppressed condition: their lack of creativity in making realities. Some may accuse us of making the constitution of society a spectacle of aesthetic performance rather than an ethical imperative to take sides. But the reality of construction ought not to conjure up only images of lone artists in garrets; institutions, states, classes, and genders are all constructions of the most real sort, competitors with iron and stone for hardness and durability.

Unmasking is an indispensable *moment* of discovery in both politics and science. But how many more times will we have to hear that the emperor has no clothes – especially when neither does any of the rest of us? The question now is, what are we going to do about it: wallow in the despair and titillation of so much naked flesh or get busy with some programs of political reconstruction and scientific discovery? (Stripping the emperor somehow has more drama than clothing the masses, but which matters more?)

To say that reality is made by humans does not mean that there are no standards of justice. Neither does it mean that one cannot sort out the humane from the inhumane constructions. As John Dewey (1927) seems to imply, once you accept the human-madeness of things, democratizing access to the means of reality-production becomes the fundamental political problem. A construction is worthy if all who dwell in it can join in its making. The *participation* of all becomes the criterion. Thus the traditions that Hobsbawm and his colleagues unmask are not suspect because they are invented, but because they were invented by a few for the "benefit" of the many. That humans construct realities does not mean the paralysis of a change-oriented politics; rather it animates and clarifies it.

Science
Just as the human construction of reality does not mean that there are no criteria of justice in the political realm, neither does it mean that anything goes in knowledge. The discovery that knowledge too is part of the reality made by men and women need not afflict us with skepticism, nor does it entail relativism. We can discard the false choice between fidelity to an unmade reality and total chaos. But how then can we account for the achievements of science, attained largely through a willingness to posit an external knowable reality?

An example of this view – that the disappearance of the Truth (with capital T) is not grounds for mourning but for celebration (since it gives us the right and responsibility to set about making fruitful realities) – can be found in American pragmatism. William James (1981: 117) argued, for instance, "Truth grows up inside of all the finite experiences. They lean on each other, but the whole of them, if such a whole there be, leans on nothing." Culture is such a mutually supporting system without foundation. But James by no means advocated the unthinking happy-go-lucky belief that anything is true that we want to be. He argued that the world, though made, is nonetheless resistant to our intentions. Our truths must be, he said, veri-fied: that is, made true. Most of what we make does not get made into truth, since it doesn't work, it doesn't help support the house of culture. A wide range of post-pragmatist philosophy of science has argued that one can abandon a belief in an unmade world and still require that theories be tested (for example, Quine, 1952; Kuhn, 1970; Hacking, 1983). Hence we are in a better position to understand what generates the achievements and misfortunes of that cultural genre called science – without being in the position of rejecting it because we have caught it partaking of the symbolic.

Conclusions

If all of this skepticism is illogical – even if deeply rooted in our intellectual heritage we, nevertheless, should know better – why do we still distrust communication?

We distrust media events and other symbolic performances because we so often see behind the bloody things. The sleek machine turns over and shows us its dirty, greasy undersides.

As Myerhoff points out in one of the epigraphs with which we begin, every performance of a ritual, the telling of every myth, is a danger. No matter how necessary a symbolic performance may be for the preservation of meaning or the integration of action, it is symbolic. The articulation of signifier and signified that lies at its heart, is ultimately arbitrary (though only for the observer and not the participant in that culture's games). If the performance is not such that it pulls all witnesses into its reality, that arbitrariness is in danger of being exposed. With that exposure, the "naturalness" of the performance crumbles. Everything in our tradition has trained us to be shocked and heartbroken at this crumbling.

But that shock is not motivated by a rational skepticism of our senses, nor an interest in understanding the dynamics of cultural performance. Rather, it is a reaction of disappointment upon discovering that the world is not real in the way the authorities we trusted said it was. But we should have known better for theirs too was a symbolic performance and we have known what symbols were all along. The time in which the exposé of artifice can count as grounds for world-weary disillusionment has gone.

The discovery that all the world is symbolic doesn't call for a rejection of the world, but a more appropriate understanding of how it works. That journalism is a symbolic performance doesn't mean that they've been lying to us all along and should never be trusted again. It means we can read of, and resist, Reagan's scandals with the knowledge that many of these same actors were central in the Watergate ritual dance. How will the drama unfold? What will be the profits and losses for the American polity? The answers to those questions depend more on the meanings of the situation than on some purported reality lurking behind them – the meanings of the situation are its reality.

The distrust of communication reigns supreme even in the disciplines most sensitive to the reality of construction. Let us forget the snickering whispers, the pointing fingers; let's stop trying to pull the rug of substance out from under each other – though it is a lot of fun. It is as if in calling each other merely ideological, or merely rhetorical, or merely scientistic we had exhausted the meaning of each other's actions – as if exposing the artificiality of the game were more interesting than playing it.

Few of the readers of this book will dispute the claim that communication – the social production of significance – is central to the human sciences, if not perhaps *the* central issue. What is an appropriate symbol for a vision of the human sciences that bases itself explicitly on the playful fabrication of realities? Consider Hermes, the god of communication. In contemporary culture, Hermes is well-known as the Olympian being whose winged sandals whisk him from god to god, bearing messages of good and ill. Indeed, the predominant image of communication in the modern world concerns the transmission, rather than construction and interpretation, of symbols. One thinks of the rhetorics and theories that have grown up around telecommunications (lightning lines, the annihilation of distance, etc.).

Less well known is Hermes the god of invention, cunning, commerce, and thievery, the patron of both travelers and the rogues who may waylay them, the conductor of the dead to Hades, the prodigious liar and trickster, and the being who lends his name to *hermeneutics*. By making one being the god of communication, lying, invention and trickery, the ancient Greeks recognized the family resemblance among the polymorphously perverse forms of human conduct: they are all the offspring of human artfulness. The Greeks saw that communication is not only a matter of conveying information; it is a matter of the construction of culture in the widest sense. Let us embrace the whole Hermes – not only the messenger of the gods but the clever fellow who displays the fruits and foibles of human creativity in all their glorious raucousness. Rather than Locke and Hume – those skeptical distrusters of human constructions who Cherry (1955: 45) once nominated as the twin patron saints for students of communication – let us make Hermes, this jack of all trades, our patron saint.

References

Arendt, H. (1958) *The Human Condition*. Chicago: University of Chicago Press.

Baudrillard, J. (1980) "The implosion of meaning in the media and the implosion of the social in the masses," in K. Woodward (ed.), *The Myths of Information: Technology and Postindustrial Culture*. Madison: Coda Press. pp. 137–48.

Boorstin, D. (1961) *The Image: A Guide to Pseudo-Events in America*. New York: Atheneum.

Burke, K. (1966) *Language as Symbolic Action: Essays on Life, Literature, and Method*. Berkeley: University of California Press.

Carey, J. (1982) "The mass media and critical theory: An American view," in M. Burgoon (ed.), *Communication Yearbook 6*. Beverly Hills: Sage. pp. 18–33.

Cherry, C. (1955) " 'Communication theory' – and human behavior," in *Studies in Communication*. London: Martin Secker and Ward. pp. 45–67.

Copleston, F. (1985) *A History of Philosophy*. Vol. 1, *Greece and Rome*. Garden City, NY: Image Books. First publ. 1946.

Csikszentmihalyi, M. and Rochberg-Halton, E. (1981) *The Meaning of Things: Domestic Symbols and the Self*. Cambridge: Cambridge University Press.

Dayan, D. and Katz, E. (1985) "Electronic ceremonies: television performs a royal wedding," in M. Blonsky (ed.), *On Signs*. Baltimore: Johns Hopkins University Press. pp. 16–32.

Derrida, J. (1967) *De la grammatologie*. Paris: Minuit.

Derrida, J. (1972) "Structure, sign and play in the discourse of the human sciences," in R. Macksey and E. Donato (eds), *The Languages of Criticism and the Sciences of Man: The Structuralist Controversy*. Baltimore: Johns Hopkins University Press. pp. 247–72.

Dewey, J. (1927) *The Public and its Problems*. New York: Henry Holt.

Goux, J.-J. (1978) *Les iconoclastes*. Paris: Seuil.

Hacking, I. (1983) *Representing and Intervening: Introductory Topics in the Philosophy of Natural Science*. Cambridge: Cambridge University Press.

Hobsbawm, E. and Ranger, T. (eds) (1983) *The Invention of Tradition*. Cambridge: Cambridge University Press.

Hume, D. (1978) *A Treatise of Human Nature*. 2nd edn. Ed. L.A. Selby-Bigge. Oxford: Clarendon Press. First publ. 1739.

Innis, H.A. (1951) *The Bias of Communication*. Toronto: University of Toronto Press.

Innis, H.A. (1972) *Empire and Communications*. Revised M. Q. Innis. Toronto: University of Toronto Press.

James, W. (1890) *Principles of Psychology*. New York: Holt.

James, W. (1981) *Pragmatism*. Ed. B. Kuklick. Indianapolis: Hackett. First publ. 1907.

Kuhn, T.S. (1970) *The Structure of Scientific Revolutions*. 2nd edn. Chicago: University of Chicago Press.

Lazarsfeld, P. F., Berelson, B., and Gaudet, H. (1948) *The People's Choice*. 2nd edn. New York: Columbia University Press.

Lippmann, W. (1922) *Public Opinion*. New York: Macmillan.

MacAloon, J.J. (1984) *Rite, Drama, Festival, Spectacle: Rehearsals toward a Theory of Cultural Performance*. Philadelphia: Institute for the Study of Human Issues.

MacIntyre, A. (1984) *After Virtue: A Study in Moral Theory*. 2nd edn. Notre Dame: University of Notre Dame Press.

McGee, M.C. and Nelson, J.S. (1985) "Narrative reason in public argument," *Journal of Communication*, 35: 139–55.

Mills, C.W. (1956) *The Power Elite*. New York: Oxford University Press.

Moore, S.F. and Myerhoff, B.G. (eds) (1975) *Symbol and Politics in Communal Ideology: Cases and Questions*. Ithaca: Cornell University Press.

Mosse, G.L. (1975) *The Nationalization of the Masses*. New York: American Library.

Mumford, L. (1970) *The Pentagon of Power*. New York: Harvest.

Myerhoff, B.G. (1984) "A death in due time: construction of self and culture in ritual drama," in J.J. MacAloon (ed.), *Rite, Drama, Festival, Spectacle: Rehearsals toward a Theory of Cultural Performance*. Philadelphia: Institute for the Study of Human Issues. pp. 149–78.

Peters, J.D. (1986) "Reconstructing mass communication theory." PhD dissertation, Stanford.

Plato (1960) *The Republic and Other Works*. Tr. B. Jowett. Garden City: Doubleday.

Quine, W.V.O. (1952) "Two dogmas of empiricism," in *From a Logical Point of View*. Cambridge: Harvard University Press. pp. 20–46.

Rorty, R. (1979) *Philosophy and the Mirror of Nature*. Princeton: Princeton Univ. Press.

Rorty, R. (1984) "Deconstruction and circumvention," *Critical Inquiry*, 11 (1): 1–23.

Rothenbuhler, E.W. (1985) "Media events, civil religion, and social solidarity: The living room celebration of the Olympic Games." PhD dissertation, University of Southern California.

Rothenbuhler, E.W. (1988) "Live broadcasting, media events, telecommunication, and social form," in D.R. Maines and C. Couch (eds), *Information, Communication, and Social Structure*. New York: Charles C. Thomas. pp. 231–43.

Russell, B. (1925) *The ABC of Relativity*. New York: Harper Brothers.

Shils, E. (1981) *Tradition*. Chicago: University of Chicago.

Turner, V. (ed.) (1982) *Celebration: Studies in Festivity and Ritual*. Washington: Smithsonian.

2
The Deliberative Character of Strategic Scientific Debates

Jeanine Czubaroff

That critical discussion is integral to scientific developoment is, after Popper and Kuhn, generally agreed.[1] But philosophers, historians, and rhetoricians of science still have little understanding of the scientific debate which takes place among scientists who disagree about fundamental premises and conceptual frameworks. Notable among efforts at characterizing the reasoning and communication which occur during such disputes is Stephen Toulmin's jurisprudential or "forensic" model of argumentation.[2] Toulmin's forensic model identifies important characteristics of what he calls "strategic" scientific argumentation, especially its nonformal and historical character. Yet a "deliberative" model of argumentation better captures the rhetorical situation of strategic scientific debate and more accurately represents the policy and value reasoning at its heart. To appreciate how both these models help us understand scientific argumentation we must look, first, at Toulmin's model and, then, at the deliberative model.

Toulmin distinguishes between "codified-law argumentation" used by scientists to justify straightforward empirical and formal claims, and "common-law argumentation" used by scientists in their disputes over fundamental assumptions, explanatory frameworks, and research programs. Implicit or explicit agreement about concepts, methods, and theoretical frameworks give codified-law argumentation a formal or calculative character. Thus, an empirical question like, "What is the specific gravity of iron?" is straightforwardly answerable because physicists share a theoretical framework which carefully defines the concepts "iron" and "specific gravity," and specifies how these concepts are to be applied in nature. The framework also provides a reliable method for measuring specific gravity.

Serious problems arise when scientists do not share strategic agreements. Frequently, the discourse between opponents is strident, dogmatic, and at cross-purposes, with each side offering empirical or formal arguments which from their perspective make sense, but which are unconvincing or irrelevant to their opponents. Eventually the disputants in such strategic debates may move beyond mutually alienating polemics. For example, once the disputants in the 1950s quantum mechanics debate recognized the conceptual nature of the issues dividing them, they ceased to attack each other and engaged in a special, "common-law," style of argumentation. Says Toulmin, "Released from commitment to any codified procedure, the disputants found themselves (so to say) in a 'common-law' world, which compelled them to discuss their disagreements in terms of 'precedents', 'consequences', and 'public policy'" (p. 238).

Conceptual questions and disagreements are at the heart of strategic scientific debates. Toulmin defines concepts quite broadly as, "the skills, or traditions, the activities, procedures, or instruments of Man's intellectual life and imagination" (p. 11). Unlike empirical questions which presuppose agreement about the concepts in terms of which they are stated and which have specific, replicable answers, and unlike formal questions which concern the structure and organization of an already accepted symbolism, conceptual questions are framed with a view toward constructing "better" terminologies, nomenclatures, or explanations.

Because scientists engaged in dispute over conceptual questions must select one among a number of reasonable options, they argue comparatively in terms of precedents, consequences, and public policy. By appeal to "precedents," Toulmin has in mind appeal to "considerations of an essentially historical kind: using the theoretical experience of earlier physicists [scientists] as a precedent, in estimating the most promising lines for future theoretical development" (p. 239). The outcomes of strategic debates over conceptual questions turn on assessment of the strengths and weaknesses, range and limitations of the different conceptual and theoretical options.

Toulmin's common-law model has both legal and political implications and he uses it in both senses. He argues that when strategic disagreements arise, "a theoretical dispute in science ceases to be a matter for routine judgement and resembles rather a Supreme Court or House of Lords case" (p. 230). The question no longer requires correct application of established procedures and instead has a "constitutional" character. The "juridical task is no longer to reapply pre-existing procedures to fresh cases. Rather, the judges now have to . . . reconsider the overall justice of the accepted legal principles and constitutional provisions, as viewed against a larger socio-historical background. In the final juridical context, logic thus becomes the servant of those fundamental human purposes that are constitutive of the law itself" (pp. 239–40).

Toulmin's Supreme Court and constitutional metaphors clarify the theoretical, interpretive, and historical nature of the questions confronted in strategic scientific disputes. They fail, however, to distinguish between types of conceptual questions, some of which are not jurisprudential in character. They also fail to capture the deliberative character of much scientific debate. It is true that creative individual scientists frequently are the leading advocates in disciplinary debates, and authoritative reference groups often significantly influence the judgments of the scientific rank and file. Nonetheless, the legal model of two advocates locked in adversarial contest and concerned to influence the decision of an appointed judge or jury does not capture the broadly public, political, and deliberative character of scientific discussion and decision-making. Individual scientific debates are but moments in broad disciplinary deliberations which take place in open professional forums, including colloquia, convention panels, conferences, journals, and books.[3] Unlike legal judgment, scientific disciplinary judgment is rarely monolithic. The deliberative model of argumentation captures the intersubjective and political character of scientific communication and judgment in a way that the legal model cannot.

The branch of government traditionally associated with deliberation is the legislature. In fact, classical Greek and Roman rhetoricians carefully distinguished between forensic rhetoric and deliberative rhetoric. For them the legal tribunal focuses on resolving disputes about past facts, while the policy-making assembly focuses on making decisions about future actions. Taking a cue from them, I look at strategic scientific controversy as an instance of deliberative reason. Below, I describe the deliberative model and indicate how it illuminates the debate about the merits of B.F. Skinner's book, *Verbal Behavior*.

Strategic Scientific Controversy and the Deliberative Model

Rhetorical and dialectical traditions teach us that deliberative reasoning addresses specific kinds of questions. Dialectician Mortimer Adler distinguishes three kinds of questions – conceptual, existential, and normative[4] – which may be at the heart of a dispute. Conceptual questions, he argues, have priority over the other two because they must be resolved before existential and normative issues can sensibly be dealt with. A conceptual question is definitional and frequently requires analysis of the "nature" of the subject specified by the concept. Psychologists, for example, must decide how to define key concepts like "organism," "environment," "behavior," and "control." Broad conceptual disputes revolve around the meaning and merits of differing theoretical assumptions, explanatory models, and root metaphors. The resolution of such disputes is complicated because an indefinite number of theoretical explanations are logically possible due to the underdetermination of theory by empirical data.[5]

Adler's existential questions are comparable to Toulmin's empirical questions or the debate tradition's factual questions. Scientists frequently seek answers to empirical questions about the existence, description, or causal connection of entities and events. The concepts in terms of which factual claims are stated are, themselves, rooted in theoretical points of view. As long as these points of view are generally accepted, the empirical claims are straightforwardly factual and the argumentation which justifies them has the characteristics of Toulmin's codified-law argumentation model. Once implicit theoretical points of view are questioned, however, the controversy ceases to be straightforwardly factual.

Adler vaguely defines the third, normative, kind of question as one which calls for judgments of value rather than fact. Debate theory is more helpful. It distinguishes two kinds of normative questions – value and policy questions. Policy questions focus on actions, programs, and policies; that is on the normative question, "What shall we do?" Questions of collective action presuppose answers to value questions like, "What should we value?" and "How should we rank our values?" Adequate reasoning about value and policy questions must address specific issues inherent in each kind of question.

Just as the distinction among conceptual, empirical, value, and policy questions extends Toulmin's analysis of the questions at stake in scientific argumentation, so his theory of common-law argumentation may be clarified and extended by taking into account the debate tradition's analysis of value and policy argumentation.

Legislative assemblies typically deliberate value and policy questions. The propositions, or "motions," before these assemblies take the form of resolutions and bills. A resolution is a generalized interpretive or evaluative statement which expresses the beliefs and judgments of the assembly as a whole. While resolutions make no immediate recommendations for policy or action, they underlie particular policy recommendations. For instance, a deliberative assembly which resolves, "We deplore the racist actions of the South African government," may be expected to pass legislation limiting its government's involvement with the South African government.

The central points of dispute or "issues" inherent in a resolution are, "What is the key interpretive or evaluative term?" "What are the relevant definitional criteria for this term?"; "What broader frame of reference justifies these criteria?"; and, "Does the interpretive or evaluative judgment actually apply in the particular case under consideration?" At times, the definition of key terms is a matter of intense dispute and the debate becomes conceptual in nature.

Obviously, the deliberative assembly must know the facts of the situation in order to determine whether the judgment applies. Thus, given the resolution, "We deplore the racist actions of the South African government," the members of the assembly must agree to a definition of "racist action," must select an evaluative frame of reference, possibly from law, philosophical ethics, religion, or history, and must systematically cite evidence confirming that the South African government has acted in a racist manner. Because factual evidence is seldom decisive in debates over the definition of values and their application, authoritative judgment, historical precedents, and analogical reasoning assume greater importance.[6] In turn, the credibility of cited authorities may become a central issue.

Legislative assemblies are especially concerned with the assessment and passage of bills. A bill is a detailed, carefully worded policy proposition which states that a particular set of policies or actions should be enacted or discontinued.[7] Unlike lawyers who debate what happened in the past (for example, "Did John Doe kill Richard Roe?"), policy advocates debate what we should do in the future. This future orientation profoundly influences the character of policy argumentation. Toulmin offers few hints about scientific policy argumentation beyond indicating that precedents and consequences are involved. Debate tradition, however, tells us that presumption and burden of proof must be properly located and a number of central or "stock" issues addressed if policy argumentation is to be logically adequate.

A policy proposal advocates a change in policy. Thus, the policy resolution, "The US government should place economic sanctions on the South African government," advocates a new economic relationship between the United States and South Africa. Because policy advocates typically call for a change in current policy or the status quo, the "burden of proof" rests on their shoulders. That is, their debate obligation is to show that their alternative policy is better than current policy. As long as the opponents in a policy debate defend current policy, they have the advantage of "presumption" in the debate. Presumption specifies the figurative ground occupied by existing belief, policy, or institutions.[8] Thus, just as in American law an individual is presumed innocent until proven guilty, so in debate tradition, existing beliefs, policies, and institutional arrangements are presumed most adequate until a good or prima facie case has been made for change. If, however, in a particular debate, no advocate defends the status quo, then neither side has the advantage of presumption.

A logically sound, prima facie case on behalf of a new policy minimally argues three stock issues. First, it identifies an "ill" in the present system which creates a "need" for a change in policy. Usually, argumentation to prove need also demonstrates that current arrangements inherently cause the ills. Second, it presents the details of an alternative plan to meet the need, and third, it argues the benefits of the alternative plan. Argumentation about benefits includes arguments that the plan meets the need, overcomes the causes, and has positive side effects. Values inevitably are grappled with both at the need and the benefits stages of policy debate.

Political deliberation of value and policy propositions and scientific common-law argumentation are similar in several respects. Arguers within both contexts must choose between conceptual and value options and must compare, evaluate, and select policies and programs. In science, the values and needs involved are intellectual, and policies take the form of theoretical models and research programs. Because both political and scientific policy argumentation are concerned with defining new policies, both are focused on the future. As Toulmin puts it, scientific debate is concerned to estimate "the most promising lines for future theoretical development" (p. 239). Inevitably, scientific argumentation like political policy deliberation involves defense of conceptual, empirical, and value claims, since the terms of the new policy must be specified and defined and the interpretive and evaluative categories must be defended against other reasonable categories and their terms must be shown to be constrained by reality.

Scientific advocates, like their political counterparts, must demonstrate "need" for a new research paradigm. They may, for instance, argue that intellectual stagnation exists in a research area because current research programs are conceptually inadequate or methodologies are out of date. Or, they may point to a pressing practical need for a technology and argue that it can be obtained only after a revision of current theoretical approaches. Once the intellectual status quo is questioned, advocates have the burden of providing a more adequate "plan" or research program for the resolution of the intellectual and practical problems identified. When new scientific research programs are introduced, their purposes must be clearly stated, their conceptual frameworks delineated, and their methodologies and procedures carefully specified and justified. Finally, scientific advocates of a new research program must argue the "benefits" of their plan. In particular, they must show that the program resolves the deficiencies or inadequacies identified in current research programs. In debate theory we say they must prove "solvency," that is, show the plan meets the need. Scientific advocates also must argue for the workability of their programs and the desirability of the consequences of their programs. Values are often at stake in debate about consequences. For instance, physicists may argue that a new theory has the additional benefit of theoretical simplicity or fruitfulness. Linguists may argue that the structural model preserves the possibility of rational action in humanity.

The deliberative model, then, provides us with a conceptual framework for study of discipline-wide controversies over theoretical frameworks and research programs. The model is particularly useful for the study of scientific communication in its justificatory phase. Scientific justification takes place in an advocacy communication context which is public or intersubjective. Typically, scientific advocacy is assertive and opinionated rather than tentative and inquiring. It may be motivated by different intellectual purposes, including initial presentation of novel ideas, amendment and criticism of others' ideas, defense of one's own or others' ideas, and integration of differing ideas.

If scientists are to be effective advocates, they must understand the rhetorical nature of scientific advocacy situations and be aware of the advocacy stances they may assume. The rhetorically astute scientific advocate will take into account four dimensions of the communication situation. First, the advocate will, as far as possible, respect situational rules of communication procedure and proof. For example, the communication contexts of professional journals, panels, and conferences are each structured by distinct rules for presentation, documentation, proof, and criticism. Failure to abide by these rules may carry the penalty of being perceived as ignorant, incompetent, or irrelevant.

Second, the rhetorically sensitive scientific advocate will systematically analyze the dispute. Since, as Toulmin reminds us, each scientific controversy is rooted in the discipline's past, case analysis begins with consideration of the immediate causes of the controversy and examination of the controversy's history. The advocate will also clarify whether conceptual, empirical, value, or policy propositions are in dispute, will identify the issues logically inherent in the disputed propositions, and will prepare an argumentative case directly addressing the vital issues. When relevant, the scientific advocate will identify where presumption lies and who bears the burden of proof.

Third, the effective scientific advocate will distinguish and take into account the goals of the scientific advocacy situation and the goals of the individual scientific advocates. The central goal of scientific communication situations, like that of the courtroom, is truth determination.[9] While desire to determine the truth may be one motive of individual scientific advocates, they also may be personally and politically motivated. For instance, the advocate may wish to gain intellectual authority and power through appointment to a large university, or to attract government funding or promising new students. These political purposes may compromise or even eclipse the dispassionate drive for truth determination. Ability to shrewdly assess the political motives active in a controversy enables the advocate to anticipate the style and appreciate the personal stakes of colleagues and opponents.

Finally, the effective scientific advocate will identify and analyze the audience which is to judge the advocacy. In educational and legal debate, one's opponent is neither one's audience nor one's judge. Instead, a third party attends to the debate and decides which side "wins." Similarly, the judging audience in scientific disputes is usually a third party to the debate. Its most influential members are the individuals who make up the profession's authoritative reference group.[10]

Once scientific advocates have carefully analyzed these aspects of their communication situation, they are in a position to define their advocacy stance in the deliberation. Three stances frequently assumed within the context of strategic scientific argumentation are: (1) advocacy of a new research program; (2) criticism of another scientist's advocacy; and (3) defense of a criticized position or program.

The initiating advocate sets the stage for the subsequent argumentation since his or her argumentation responsibility is to provide a prima facie case in behalf of a new policy. Critical assessment of the concepts, assumptions, evidence, and arguments of others is at the heart of the rationality of science. Scientific critics may be disinterested and cordial, or they may wish to overcome the ideas of their opponents in order to vindicate their own ideas. In the latter case, the critic frequently assumes an adversarial stance toward the opponent. The critic's argumentation obligation is to show that the opponent's position is inadequate on at least one issue crucial to the debate. Criticism inevitably calls forth a defensive response. Like the critic, the defender may assume a disinterested and cordial or adversarial attitudinal stance. The refuter typically engages in a selective counter-attack aimed at discrediting the critic's most telling criticisms and rebuilding the criticized position.

The insight afforded by the deliberative model and the unique rhetorical character of these scientific advocacy stances may be appreciated if we look at a particular scientific controversy. The controversy surrounding the work of B.F. Skinner is classical and by now also "historic." Let us turn, therefore, to that controversy.

The year 1957 stands out, for it was in that year that Noam Chomsky published *Syntactic Structures* and B.F. Skinner published *Verbal Behavior*. These two books proposed new research paradigms for the study of language. In the years immediately following, Chomsky's work led to the formation of a new school in linguistics. Skinner's work, however, was largely ignored by his behaviorist colleagues, primarily because "it was not entirely obvious how *Verbal Behavior* might be turned into an empirical research program."[11] Nonetheless, Chomsky regarded Skinner's research program as a rival and therefore chose to criticize it publicly. In 1959 Chomsky published a critical review of *Verbal Behavior* in the journal *Language* which became so well known among academics and was regarded as so convincing that behaviorists recognized that it had to be refuted. In 1970 Kenneth MacCorquodale published the first official behaviorist refutation in the *Journal of the Experimental Analysis of Behavior*. The following analysis attempts to show that the controversy over the merits of *Verbal Behavior* was conducted largely in policy debate terms.

Strategic Controversy in Language Research: The Debate over B.F. Skinner's *Verbal Behavior*

Verbal Behavior[12] advocates a functionalist research program for the study of verbal behavior. In Chapter 1, "A functional analysis of verbal behavior," Skinner defines the research domain of verbal behavior and identifies inadequacies in traditional language research programs. Once "need" for a better research program is established, he presents his own program. In the last section of Chapter 1, "A new formulation," and in Chapter 2, he outlines his "plan," beginning with careful definition of the scope and key concepts of his analytic framework and description of the elements of an operant analysis. He sketches the benefits of the behavior analytic program in his "Two personal epilogues."

Skinner defines "verbal behavior," the subject of his research, as "behavior reinforced through the mediation of other persons" (p. 14). "The behaviors of speaker and listener taken together" compose "a total verbal episode" (p. 2). The basic datum is "not the occurrence of a given response as such, but the probability that it will occur at a given time" (p. 22). Skinner's research domain, then, is similar to that of pragmatics, a traditional field of language research.

Classical rhetoric, grammar, logic, linguistics, literary criticism, speech pathology, semantics, and psychology are the traditional fields of language research. None of these fields, Skinner says, has identified verbal behavior as its object and none has developed an appropriate method for studying verbal behavior (p. 4). In short, "What is lacking is a satisfactory causal or functional treatment" (p. 5). What is needed is a "general analysis of linguistic processes applicable to any field and under the dominion of no special interest" (p. 5). The behavioral sciences and particularly experimental psychology are best situated to provide this general analysis of linguistic processes because, "What happens when a man speaks or responds to speech is clearly a question about human behavior" (p. 5).

Psychology has failed to produce a satisfactory causal or functional analysis of verbal behavior, says Skinner, because psychologists have relied upon an inadequate explanatory model. In particular, psychologists have relied upon "fictional causes" like "ideas," "images," and "meaning," and this reliance has obstructed research progress. All fictional concepts used to account for causal relationships in verbal behavior have the same limitations, namely, they function "to allay curiosity and to bring inquiry to an end. The doctrine of ideas has had this effect by appearing to assign important problems of verbal behavior to a psychology of ideas. The problems have then seemed to pass beyond the range of the techniques of the student of language or to become too obscure to make further study profitable" (p. 6). Similarly, the semanticist scheme, revolving around such concepts as "reference" and "meaning," "neglects many important properties of the original behavior and raises other problems" (p. 9).

Skinner completes his analysis of the inadequacies of traditional language research programs by arguing that no simple repairs may be made. Referring to endeavors to modify and improve the semanticist program, he insists, "When we attempt to supply the additional material needed in this representation of verbal behavior, we find that our task has been set in awkward if not impossible terms. Observable data have been preempted, and the study of behavior is left with vaguely identified 'thought processes' " (p. 9). Indeed, these efforts are "a sort of patchwork which succeeds mainly in showing how threadbare the basic notion is" (p. 9). Traditional conceptual frameworks and programs simply will not do: "The only solution is to reject the traditional formulation of verbal behavior in terms of meaning" (p. 10).

Having established need and analyzed the inadequacies of current language research programs, Skinner presents an overview of his program. He hypothesizes that verbal behavior may be functionally accounted for in terms of the three-term contingency of operant analysis, "stimulus," "response," and "reinforcement." In addition, an adequate functional anaylsis requires new terms to describe the different kinds of verbal responses people make. Skinner classifies verbal operants in terms of their antecedent controlling variables and identifies "mands," "echoics," "intraverbals," "tacts," and "auto-clitics." These terms, he claims, cut across the traditional terminology so that no one-to-one correspondence occurs, for instance, between the functions of the "tact" and those of traditional "reference."

The functionalist program is feasible, Skinner argues, because recent advances in behavior analysis make behaviorism a precise analytic framework. In addition, the basic processes and relations characteristic of verbal behavior are now "fairly well understood" (p. 3); and, the experimental methods used in behaviorist animal research may be extended to research on humans "without serious modification" (p. 3). Skinner's claims about behavior analysis have a dogmatic tone, however, because he does not cite specific data, scholars, experimental studies, or bibliographic references to substantiate them.

Skinner alludes briefly throughout the first and second chapters to potential benefits of his research program. He is quick to suggest practical applications of a functional analysis of verbal behavior. He bids the reader keep in mind "specific engineering tasks" that confront us, and claims, "The formulation is inherently practical and suggests immediately technological applications at almost every step" (p. 12). A functional analysis of verbal behavior should also help us answer such questions as, "How can the teacher establish the specific verbal repertoires which are the principal end-products of education? How can the therapist uncover latent verbal behavior in a therapeutic interview? How can the writer evoke his own verbal behavior in the act of composition? How can the scientist, mathematician, or logician manipulate his verbal behavior in productive thinking?" (p. 3). Skinner assures us that a functional analysis of language will provide answers to questions like these.

The benefits, however, are not merely practical. In his "Two personal epilogues" (p. 456), Skinner cites other intellectual benefits. First, a behavioral analysis "reduces the total vocabulary necessary for a scientific account" (p. 456). In addition, the analysis is susceptible to empirical test and constraints and it lays to rest unimportant puzzling questions that have, to date, handicapped researchers in their efforts to make progress in the area of verbal behavior.

Within two years of *Verbal Behavior*'s publication, Noam Chomsky personally criticized Skinner's ideas at a Harvard symposium of behaviorists and then published a thirty-two-page formal criticism of the book in *Language*.[13] Chomsky recognized almost immediately the intellectual and practical implications of the disagreement between him and Skinner. At issue intellectually were the proper goals and conceptual framework for language research. At issue practically was whose research paradigm, Skinner's or Chomsky's, would appear most appealing to language researchers.

The dispute between Skinner and Chomsky centers upon the merits of Skinner's functional explanatory model and Chomsky's structural explanatory model for the study of human language. Skinner urges language researchers to treat verbal behavior as a function of environmental factors. Chomsky, on the other hand, urges language researchers to treat verbal behavior as a result of complex interactions between external stimulation and the "internal structure of the organism" (p. 27). The internal structure of the organism is a "complicated product of inborn structure, the genetically determined course of maturation, and past experience" (p. 27). Chomsky believed that natural language sentences have a "deep structure," a structure that must be described before scholars could profitably study individual verbal behavior and its acquisition. Thus, he argues, "There is little point in speculating about the processes of acquisition without much better understanding of what is acquired" (p. 55). Skinner, as we have seen, preferred to ignore the genetic, neuro-physiological, and formal components underlying human linguistic ability and set himself the immediate task of describing the functional variables responsible for an individual's verbal behavior. These programs are clearly distinct and appear to require that scientists interested in the study of human language choose between them. This pressure to choose set the stage for Chomsky's scientific advocacy.

Chomsky hints in his opening words that the intended audience for his critical review is an interdisciplinary third party: "A great many linguists and philosophers concerned with language have expressed the hope that their studies might ultimately be embedded in a framework provided by behaviorist psychology and that refractory areas of investigation, particularly those in which meaning is involved, will in this way be opened up to fruitful exploration" (p. 26). His specifically professional ambition is to convince interested linguists, philosophers, and psychologists that Skinner's behaviorist program for the study of language is inadequate while the structuralist program is promising.

Chomsky, too, recognizes the need for fresh research paradigms in the area of language research. Thus, he spends no time arguing the issue of need in his review. While he notes that he and Skinner disagree about the factors which are causally significant in language acquisition and performance, he does not provide a systematic analysis of the deficiencies of traditional language research programs. Instead, he argues: (1) Skinner's conceptual framework for the analysis of verbal behavior is incoherent and intellectually inadequate; and (2) Skinner's behaviorist research program is not currently feasible. Within the policy debate framework, these are criticisms of the adequacy of the "plan" proposed to remedy the inadequacies inherent in the status quo.

Chomsky introduces his first criticism in section two of his eleven-section essay. Three arguments emerge: (1) The basic concepts of behaviorism are either fundamentally problematic or unilluminating; and (2) the technical terminology developed in *Verbal Behavior* is no more enlightening than traditional terms. Evidence of intellectual incoherence in Skinner's conceptual framework leads Chomsky to conclude, (3) Skinner is an incompetent language researcher. Arguments about the coherence of fundamental research concepts are characteristic of strategic scientific argumentation. So, too, are claims about the credibility of the source of ideas and studies.

Chomsky develops his first criticism by considering the fundamental concepts of behavior analysis, including Skinner's "notions" of "stimulus," and "response." He concludes, "We can, in the face of presently available evidence, continue to maintain the lawfulness of the relation between stimulus and response only by depriving them of their objective character" (p. 31). Similarly, "The term 'reinforcement' has no explanatory force, and any idea that this paraphrase introduces any new clarity or objectivity into the description of wishing, liking, etc., is a serious delusion. The only effect is to obscure the important differences among the notions being paraphrased" (p. 38). The fundamental concepts of behavior analysis are not the only inadequate terms in Skinner's conceptual framework. The entire "system that Skinner develops specifically for the description of verbal behavior" is "vague and arbitrary" (p. 44) because it is based on the inadequate "notions" "stimulus," "response," and "reinforcement." The problem is that "with a literal reading (where the terms of the descriptive system have something like the technical meanings given in Skinner's definition) the book covers almost no aspect of linguistic behavior, and that with a metaphoric reading, it is no more scientific than the traditional approaches to this subject matter, and rarely as clear and careful" (p. 31). For instance, Skinner's definition of "verbal behavior" is "clearly much too broad" (p. 45); Skinner's classification of mands is "beside the point. A moment's thought is sufficient to demonstrate the impossibility of distinguishing between requests, commands, advice, etc., on the basis of the behavior or disposition of the particular listener" (p. 47); and Skinner's "mystical" (p. 47) concept of the tact is "fundamentally the same as the traditional one, though much less carefully phrased" (p. 48).

Demonstration that Skinner's conceptual framework is inadequate is the heart of Chomsky's criticism of Skinner's behavioral research program. He completes his case with the argument that, in addition, Skinner's research program is not currently workable: "Anyone who seriously approaches the study of linguistic behavior, whether linguist, psychologist, or philosopher, must quickly become aware of the enormous difficulty of stating a problem which will define the area of his investigations, and which will not be either completely trivial or hopelessly beyond the range of present-day understanding and technique. In selecting functional analysis as his problem, Skinner has set himself a task of the latter type" (p. 55). This argument raises an important question about Skinner's program, for, the most promising research program is still useless if it is not currently feasible.

The critical stance Chomsky assumes is distinctly adversarial. Like the legal advocate, his motive is to "win," to persuade his academic audience that Skinner's program is seriously inadequate. In order to be persuasive he resorts to selective, one-sided criticism of his opponent's ideas. He advances only those arguments favorable to his case and considers Skinner's ideas only in order to refute them. Also like the intensely competitive legal advocate, he assumes an aggressive attitudinal stance, appearing confident, even dogmatic, about his own position while condescending toward his opponent's position. This unconditional and aggressive tone is revealed in Chomsky's choice of verbs and adjectives. Skinner is seldom simply "in error," but "grossly in error," (p. 46); he "retreats" to mentalisitc psychology (p. 32); reminiscent of magic, he "invokes" the term "reinforcement"; the term "reinforcement" is not just "useless," it is "perfectly useless" (p. 38); things are not just "wrong" but "obviously wrong" (p. 47).

The aggressive style frequently leads advocates to attack their opponents and, in fact, throughout his review Chomsky attacks Skinner's scientific character and competence. Negative assessment of Skinner's scientific scholarship is the substance of such remarks as, "It is not unfair, I believe, to conclude from Skinner's discussion of response strength . . . that his 'extrapolation' of the notion of probability can best be interpreted as, in effect, nothing more than a decision to use the word 'probability', with its favorable connotations of objectivity, as a cover term to paraphrase such low-status words as 'interest', 'intention', 'belief', and the like" (p. 35); and, "To speak of 'conditioning' or 'bringing previously available behavior under control of a new stimulus' in such a case is just a kind of play-acting at science" (p. 39). The conclusion that Skinner deliberately uses the word "probability" in place of lower-status terms and that Skinner is merely "play-acting" at science directly questions Skinner's scientific integrity and competence.

The academic community was impressed with Chomsky's review. In 1970 Kenneth MacCorquodale, a Skinner advocate, wrote, "Skinner's book, *Verbal Behavior*, was published in 1957. Chomsky's review of it appeared in 1959. By the criterion of seminal influence in generating controversy and stimulating publication, both must be counted major successes, although the reputation and influence of the review are more widely acknowledged."[14] Indeed, Chomsky's aggressive, comprehensive, copiously documented case not only furthered the debate, for some it concluded the debate about research programs in the area of language study. Minimally, it fastened the burden of proof squarely upon the shoulders of Skinner and his behaviorist colleagues.

Strangely, Skinner never directly and publicly responded to Chomsky's critique. His only published explanation of his silence appears in a whimsical paragraph in an essay, "On 'Having' a Poem," written for the *Saturday Review of Books*. Here he explains he did not respond to Chomsky's review because "I found its tone distasteful" and because the essay was not a review of *Verbal Behavior* "but of what Chomsky took, erroneously, to be my position."[15] Skinner acknowledges, "No doubt I was shirking a responsibility in not replying to Chomsky, and I am glad a reply was supplied in 1970 by Kenneth MacCorquodale in the *Journal of the Experimental Analysis of Behavior*."[16]

The behaviorists' failure to respond immediately to Chomsky's challenge created a bad impression of Skinner and all behaviorists and was not a wise rhetorical choice. In fact, Chomsky's criticisms were powerful and the longer they remained publicly unchallenged and unrefuted, the more humanists and cognitive psychologists felt justified in concluding that they had finally silenced Skinner. The rhetorical rationale behind this judgment is straightforward: Failure to respond to telling criticism is read as a sign of confusion and fatal weakness.

Ten years passed before behaviorist Kenneth MacCorquodale published the first systematic response to Chomsky's review. The story according to behaviorists is that MacCorquodale wrote his response in 1966 and submitted the essay to the journal *Language*, feeling that was the appropriate forum for a refutation. A year passed and then the editor of *Language* returned the manuscript indicating, in substance, that, "these sorts of arguments are well known and often heard at cocktail parties."[17] Subsequently, the editor of the *Journal of the Experimental Analysis of Behavior* offered to publish the essay. It appeared in that journal as a seventeen-page essay in January, 1970.[18] While the actual audience for MacCorquodale's essay was therefore primarily radical behaviorists, clearly he conceived the essay for a broader academic audience, an audience including Chomsky and the readers of *Language*.

MacCorquodale observes in the introduction to his essay that because Chomsky's review had not been systematically replied to, many academicians have concluded that his criticisms were definitive and unanswerable. Given this climate of opinion, MacCorquodale recognizes that before he can begin systematic refutation, he must explain why for nearly ten years no behaviorist systematically and publicly responded to Chomsky's review. He lists three reasons and argues that "none of them have anything to do with the merits of either Chomsky's or Skinner's case" (p. 83). In particular, MacCorquodale notes that many stimulus-response psychologists did not feel their brand of behaviorism was touched by Chomsky's criticism, that Skinnerians concluded their position was misunderstood or misrepresented by Chomsky and thus did not feel compelled to respond to the review any more than did other behaviorists, and that "the strongest reason why no one has replied to the review is its tone. It is ungenerous to a fault; condescending, unforgiving, obtuse, and ill-humored" (p. 84). MacCorquodale recognizes that Chomsky's truculent tone confronts the behaviorist respondent with a dilemma: "It is almost impossible to respond to whatever substantive points the review might have made without at the same time sounding either defensive and apologetic, or as truculent as the review" (p. 84). These three reasons suggest an isolation among behaviorists that cost them dearly within the wider academic community, for, over the intervening ten years the review "had an enormous influence in psychology. Nearly every aspect of currently popular psycholinguistic dogma was adumbrated in it" (p. 98).

MacCorquodale begins his refutation by reminding readers that the dispute is not an empirical one, "The reader should know in advance that there were and are no directly relevant facts to be brought to bear in this discussion" (p. 84). Instead, "the disagreement is fundamentally an epistemological one, a 'paradigm clash' " (p. 84). Like all paradigm disputes, this one calls for deliberation and individual judgment.

Having explained the delay in behaviorist response and the nature of the debate, MacCorquodale devotes sixteen pages to systematic refutation of Chomsky's criticisms of the *Verbal Behavior* research program. His response is organized around what he claims are Chomsky's three criticisms, namely that: (1) "*Verbal Behavior* is an untested hypothesis which has, therefore, no claim upon our credibility" (p. 84); (2) "Skinner's technical terms are mere paraphrases for more traditional treatments of verbal behavior" (p. 88); and (3) Speech is complex behavior whose understanding and explanation require a complex, mediational, neurological-genetic theory" (p. 90).

Implicit in MacCorquodale's formulation of the first criticism is the key issue of the scientific feasibility of Skinner's functionalist program. MacCorquodale grants that "Skinner does not seem to consider [experimental test of his program] feasible" (p. 85), but he notes that other plausible scientific theories are not testable either. Thus, he argues, Skinner's situation resembles that of the astronomer "explaining tides as the resultants of many interacting attractions. No one has ever experimentally tested that hypothesis directly either, yet it is highly plausible and supported by much observation evidence which is probably the strongest conclusion we shall ever be able to make for it" (p. 85).

MacCorquodale's refutation of Chomsky's second criticism regarding Skinner's conceptual framework is more complete. He responds point-by-point to Chomsky's criticisms of the terms "stimulus," "reinforcement," and "probability." For instance, he writes, "Reading Chomsky on the subject of the stimulus here and elsewhere in his review arouses a growing suspicion that he imagines that by naming one stimulus for a verbal response we name its only stimulus, and that one stimulus somehow preempts a response" (p. 86). Similarly, responding to Chomsky's comment that, "The term 'probability' has some rather obscure meaning for Skinner in this book,"[19] MacCorquodale says, "Small wonder, since he [Chomsky] cites *Hull's* definition of probability (resistance to extinction) as Skinner's basic indicator of probability or 'strength' rather than Skinner's" (p. 88). MacCorquodale's refutative point is that Chomsky does not understand Skinner's behavior analytic framework and as a consequence his criticisms of fundamental behaviorist concepts are beside the point.

In response to the claim that Skinner's technical terms for verbal behavior are mere paraphrases for more traditional treatments, MacCorquodale insists that Skinner's analysis is no more a paraphrase of linguistic-philosophical mentalisms than modern physics is a paraphrase of pantheism. They merely converge, but from quite different directions and with quite different credentials, upon some aspects of the same domains (p. 89). Throughout his defense, MacCorquodale directly denies Chomsky's claims and suggests that failure to notice crucial distinctions, misinterpretations, and misunderstandings explain Chomsky's mistaken critical judgments. MacCorquodale's detailed list of Chomsky's mispresentations and misunderstandings is impressive and adds weight to his defense of Skinner's behaviorist framework.

MacCorquodale relies heavily on the argument of irrelevance in his refutation of Chomsky's third criticism, namely, that adequate explanation of human speech requires reference to mediating, neurogenetic, and formal factors. He acknowledges that the "missing mediator" is almost certainly the brain and nervous system but insists that this fact is irrelevant to "the question of the validity of Skinner's hypothesis" (p. 92). Elsewhere he insists that no incompatibility exists between evolutionary and reinforcement theories because "Reinforceability is itself a genetically determined characteristic; organisms are simply born reinforceable" (p. 93). MacCorquodale's point, then, is that the fundamental assumptions underlying Chomsky's research program are not in direct conflict with the fundamental assumptions underlying the behaviorist program. Behaviorists recognize similar causal factors but prefer to study a different aspect of human speech. The ramification, for MacCorquodale, is that both research programs are legitimate and scientists should feel free to work within either paradigm. This pluralistic vision explains some of the behaviorists' puzzlement over the vehemence of Chomsky's attack: Chomsky's "declaration of war has been unilateral, probably because the behaviorist cannot clearly recognize why he should defend himself. He has not hurt anyone; he has not preempted the verbal territory by applying his methods to verbal behavior; he has not used up all of the verbal behavior nor has he precluded other scientists from investigating it to their heart's content, with any methods and theories which please them" (p. 98). This tolerant, pluralistic attitude, while admirable, fails to take fully into account the politics of science. Given limited financial resources and a limited pool of researchers, advocates of different research paradigms inevitably vie for resources and personnel.

Throughout his refutation, MacCorquodale avoids "the provocation to an *ad hominem* reply" (p. 84). Though he assumes an adversarial stance, his attacks are more circumspect. In addition, his critical terms, unlike Chomsky's, do not ascribe intellectually disreputable motives to Chomsky. Instead, he lets Chomsky's style condemn itself. For instance, while responding to Chomsky's criticism of Skinner's technical terms, he declares, "This particular criticism in Chomsky's review occupies a great deal of its total space and accounts for much of its apparent thrust and its most vivid writing. It is not often that a reviewer becomes so overwrought as to permit himself (p. 38) to characterize his author as entertaining 'a serious delusion'. But there it is" (p. 90).

A full refutation not only disarms the opponent's criticisms, it restates and even extends one's own position. By and large, however, MacCorquodale concentrates on criticism of Chomsky's review and does not take time to review recent findings of behaviorist researchers in the area of language acquisition. The behaviorists' failure to respond immediately and completely to Chomsky's review and their failure to produce dramatic results in their language research played into the hands of Chomsky's aggressively persuasive style. Many members of the scientific community found Chomsky's position more persuasive.[20]

Conclusion: Rhetorical Study of Science

Strategic scientific disputes are about cosmologies and metaphysics, about research methodologies and programs, about values and goals – issues for which no simple or singular answers are available. According to post-empiricist philosophies of science,[21] a permanent methodological and theoretical plurality exists in science. Choice among alternatives requires judgment on the basis of scientific and nonscientific values and purposes. The traditional objectivist model of scientific communication is not consistent with this understanding of science. The objectivist model rests on the extensively criticized premises that correct scientific theories are directly inferable from empirical data, and may have one-to-one correspondence to the "facts"; that nonscientific values and purposes have no role in the selection of root metaphors, theories, metaphysics, or cosmologies; and that scientists can be dispassionate about their own ideas while objectively evaluating other proposals. These assumptions have been under critical attack for much of the twentieth century. The vision of scientific controversy that emerges from these criticisms is a rhetorical one.

If rhetorical critics of science cannot rely upon an objectivist model of reasoning and communication, what model of reasoning can they rely upon? The legal and deliberative models offer alternatives with some advantages. Formal legal reasoning is similar in illuminating ways to scientific reasoning about narrowly technical and empirical questions. Problematic about the legal model is its limited communication context in which two advocates locked in adversarial contest argue before an appointed jury and judge.

The deliberative model has the advantage of placing scientific reasoning and communication in a broad political and ideological context in which the voices and concerns of the larger public echo and in which the many who are present may be heard. Thus, it permits, but is not limited to, adversarial exchanges between individuals of different conviction. The model also helps us understand the policy argumentation which is a key aspect of many strategic scientific controversies.

The deliberative model also suggests lines for further rhetorical research. Rhetoricians, for instance, may scrutinize the communication rules observed in scientific conventions, journals, and conferences. They may also identify argumentation stances which are specific to the scientific professions. The rhetorical purposes, argumentation obligations, choices, and styles inherent in these stances need to be specified and compared. Eventually, rhetorical criticism of science may help us answer tough questions like, "How is the argumentation of natural and social scientists similar and how different? How much scientific argumentation is field dependent and how much field independent? What role do intellectual and social values play in scientific policy disputes? Are there distinct issues inherent in scientific theoretical and policy claims and if so, what are they?" Answers to questions like these will not only advance our understanding of the scientific enterprise; they will also contribute to our understanding of practical reason.

Notes

1   See W. O. Hagstrom, *The Scientific Community* (Basic Books, New York, 1965); Karl R. Popper, *Conjectures and Refutations: The Growth of Scientific Knowledge* (Harper and Row, New York, 1968); Stephen Toulmin, *Human Understanding*, vol. I (Princeton University Press, Princeton, 1972); and J. M. Ziman, *Public Knowledge: An Essay Concerning the Social Dimension of Science* (Cambridge University Press, Cambridge, 1968).

2   Toulmin, *Human Understanding*, p. 236. Further page references in the text are to the same work.

3   See Ziman, *Public Knowledge*, and Toulmin, *Human Understanding*.

4   Mortimer Adler, *The Idea of Freedom* (Doubleday, Garden City, NY, 1958-61), pp. 29-31.

5   Mary Hesse, *Revolutions and Reconstructions in the Philosophy of Science* (Indiana University Press, Bloomington, 1980), Introduction.

6   Maridell Fryar and David A. Thomas, *Student Congress and Lincoln-Douglas Debate* (National Textbook Co., Lincolnwood, IL, 1981), p. 43.

7   Ibid., p. 73.

8   Karyn Rybacki and Donald Rybacki, *Advocacy and Opposition: An Introduction to Argumentation* (Prentice-Hall, Englewood Cliffs, NJ, 1986), p. 17.

9   George W. Ziegelmueller and Charles A. Dause, *Argumentation: Inquiry and Advocacy* (Prentice-Hall, Englewood Cliffs, NJ, 1975), p. 148.

10 Toulmin, *Human Understanding*, p. 264.

11 This explanation was given to me by Professor Philip Hineline, current editor of the *Journal of the Experimental Analysis of Behavior*.

12 B.F. Skinner, *Verbal Behavior* (Appleton-Century-Crofts, New York, 1975). Further page references in the text are to the same work.

13 Noam Chomsky, "Review of *Verbal Behavior* by B.F. Skinner," *Language*, 35, 1 (1959), pp. 26-58. Further page references in the text are to the same work.

14 Kenneth MacCorquodale, "On Chomsky's review of Skinner's *Verbal Behavior*," *Journal of the Experimental Analysis of Behavior*, 13, 1 (1970), p. 83. Further page references are to the same work.

15 B.F. Skinner, "On 'having' a poem," *Saturday Review of Books*, 15 July 1972, p. 32.

16 Ibid., p. 32.

17 This story and paraphrase were reported to me by A. Charles Catania and Philip Hineline, both behavior analysts.

18 MacCorquodale, "On Chomsky's review."

19 Chomsky, "Review of *Verbal Behavior*," p. 34.

20 Recently, some language researchers have concluded that the functionalist and structuralist programs are compatible. See, for instance, Evalyn Segal, "Toward a coherent psychology of language," in W.K. Henig and J.E.R. Staddon (eds), *Handbook of Operant Behavior* (Prentice-Hall, Englewood Cliffs, NJ, 1977). Jack Michael's "Verbal behavior," *Journal of the Experimental Analysis of Behavior*, 42, 3 (1984), pp. 363-76, provides an up-dated review of behaviorist literature in the area of verbal behavior.

21 Mary Hesse uses the phrase "post-empiricist philosophy of science." See her Introduction, *Revolution and Reconstructions*.

3

The Rhetorical Construction of Scientific Ethos

Lawrence J. Prelli

Aristotle stressed that a central means of persuasion is a rhetor's perceived character or *ethos*.[1] To inspire confidence in claims advanced discursively, a rhetor must display the qualities of intelligence, moral character, and good will that are held in esteem by an intended audience.[2] Research on the sociology of science makes clear that scientific rhetors are also subject to the constraints of *ethos*.

The groundbreaking work on scientific *ethos* was undertaken by Robert K. Merton.[3] Merton sought to identify the binding institutional norms that constrain the behavior of scientists, and facilitate establishing and extending certified, objective knowledge of the physical world.[4] The norms of science, Merton believes, encourage behaviors that minimize distortion during systematic observation and maximize efficient dissemination of certified knowledge:

> The ethos of science is that affectively toned complex of values and norms which is held to be binding on the man of science. The norms are expressed in the form of prescriptions, proscriptions, preferences, and permissions. They are legitimized in terms of institutional values. These imperatives, transmitted by precept and example and reenforced by sanctions are in varying degrees internalized by the scientist, thus fashioning his scientific conscience or, if one prefers the latter-day phrase, his superego. Although the ethos of science has not been codified, it can be inferred from the moral consensus of scientists as expressed in use and wont, in countless writings on the scientific spirit and in moral indignation directed toward contraventions of the ethos.[5]

The scientific *ethos* binds both technically and morally. It is technically binding because it prescribes efficient procedures for securing the extension of certified knowledge. It is morally binding because it is believed to assert what is right and good.[6] The norms identified in Merton's original formulation are as follows: *Universalism* requires that knowledge claims be subjected to pre-established, impersonal criteria that render them consonant with observation and previously established knowledge. *Communality* or *communism* prescribes that research is not a personal possession but must be made available to the community of scientists. *Disinterestedness* requires that scientists strive to achieve their self-interests only through satisfaction in work done and prestige accrued through serving the interests of a scientific community.[7] *Organized skepticism* mandates that scientists temporarily suspend judgment in order to scrutinize beliefs critically against empirical and logical criteria of judgment.[8]

Merton added to his original list the norms of *originality* and *humility* when he studied priority claims in scientific discovery.[9] *Originality* is a source of esteem for one's work because through this quality scientific knowledge advances. *Humility* ensures that scientists will not misbehave at the rate that they would if importance were assigned only to originality and to establishing priority in scientific discovery.

Much research done in the wake of Merton's studies has supported his functional norms, but there has also emerged evidence that there exists in science a second set of "counter-norms" wholly incompatible with those identified initially by Merton.[10] For example, in a well-documented study of NASA "moon scientists," Mitroff identified some of these counter-norms.[11] The list includes *particularism*, which counters universalism. Scientists often regard as legitimate judgments about research reports and proposals that are based on personal criteria, such as the ability and experience of authors, rather than on the strictly technical merits of the research claims themselves. Similarly, *solitariness* opposes communality. Scientists often do exercise property rights regarding their work. From this counter-normal vantage point, secrecy is appropriate conduct and, indeed, helps scientists avoid disruptive priority disputes and ensures that they do not waste colleagues' time by rushing immature work into print. *Interestedness* opposes disinterestedness. This counter-norm promotes conduct that serves scientists' special communities of interest (for example, their invisible colleges). Finally, *organized dogmatism* counters organized skepticism. This counter-norm prescribes that scientists do not incessantly doubt their own and others' findings, but instead assent fervently to their *own* findings while doubting the findings of others.[12]

Evidence of conflicting commitments among scientists has led some sociologists to question whether the constituents of Merton's scientific *ethos* should be considered "normative" at all. This question remains unsettled, but I do not intend to address it here.[13] My contention is that when scientists resort to these common themes in discussing, justifying, or evaluating actions the alleged "norms" and "counter-norms" of science serve a *rhetorical* function, regardless of whatever other functions they might be said to serve. Specifically, the constituents of scientific *ethos* function like rhetorical *topoi* for inducing favorable or unfavorable perceptions of scientific *ethos*. Scientific *ethos* is not given; it is constructed rhetorically. Rhetors respond to, or seek to avoid creating, ambiguities and conflicts about their scientific credibility. They do this by choosing from among a range of strategic options those that are best suited to situational contingencies. What sociologists of science have been calling the "norms" and "counter-norms" of science are effectively conceived as rhetorical *topoi* that index the available range of discursive strategies for establishing negative or positive audience perceptions of scientists' *ethos*.

First, we need to recognize that attention to the constituents of scientific *ethos* becomes salient only when the discourse of one scientist is made and evaluated by others in scientific situations that are rhetorical; that is, in problematic or ambiguous situations that involve inducing adherence to ideas presented as "scientific."[14] Barnes and Dolby make the point that scientists stress the significance of such intellectual qualities as "rationality" or "skepticism" in situations that involve celebration, justification, or conflict.[15] Within such situations successfully resolving problems or clarifying ambiguities hinges partly on the perceived qualifications of the proposing thinker or researcher. What scientific qualities will be most valued can vary from rhetorical situation to rhetorical situation.

Considerations such as secrecy, communality, objectivity, and emotional commitment may or may not be situationally relevant to evaluating a scientist's professional work. The situation in which scientific discourse is being evaluated determines the relevance and salience of each such quality. This is to say that when a scientist makes knowledge claims to colleagues and implies that these claims are "scientific" it *may* be relevant, though it will not always be imperative, to weigh the claimant's objectivity or emotional involvement, openness or secrecy, skepticism or enthusiasm, and the like. In various situations *either* of such opposed qualities *may* be relevant and be judged a *scientific* virtue or vice.

The professional *ethos* of a rhetor as a scientist becomes specially relevant when there is reason to believe that his or her primary aims are tied to such "nonscientific" pursuits as securing personal celebrity with lay audiences, achieving political or religious aspirations, or perpetuating beliefs that have occult or supernatural implications.[16] Even those seeking explicitly to popularize science risk jeopardizing their *ethos* with expert audiences. They must find "common ground" with technically unskilled audiences, leaving themselves open to charges that they are pursuing objectives other than those that are properly "scientific" or "educational."[17]

In science as elsewhere, when the status of claims is problematic the *ethos* of the claimants can become pertinent. As Aristotle said, "We believe good men more fully and readily than others: this is true generally whatever the question is, and absolutely true where exact certainty is impossible and opinions are divided."[18] Then, a claimant's "rationality" or "skepticism" can become important considerations for audiences charged with adjudicating technical claims.[19] Similarly, one might dwell on a scientist's reputation, experience, and technical skill and on such grounds give problematic technical claims the benefit of the doubt.[20]

Whatever is said or done to influence perceptions of a scientist's *ethos* will arise from a finite set of values implied by the notion of "doing good science"; for example, actions or words can indicate appropriate enthusiasm, objectivity, or skepticism. Scientific values of this sort constitute themes that can be treated verbally or implied by actions; they supply scientists with persuasive means for inducing adherence to their aims and claims as scientifically "reasonable" or "legitimate."

As soon as we recognize that we are dealing here with rhetorical *topoi*, the seeming conflict between alleged "norms" and "counternorms" dissolves. The themes having to do with scientific *ethos* are not law-like or even "rules"; they are lines of thought that bear on a scientist's credibility in this or that rhetorical situation. Mulkay's description of how the constituents of scientific *ethos* actually come into play reflects their rhetorical topicality:

> In science . . . we have a complex moral language which appears to focus on certain recurrent themes or issues; for instance, on procedures of communication, the place of rationality, the importance of impartiality, and of commitment, and so on. But . . . no particular solutions to the problems raised by these issues for participants are firmly institutionalized. Instead, the standardized verbal formulations to be found in the scientific community provide a repertoire or vocabulary which scientists can use flexibly to categorize professional actions differently in various social contexts.[21]

Topoi for building or diminishing a scientist's *ethos* are imprecise in the sense that any of the "recurrent themes" can be applied and developed in many ways. It is the abstract quality of *topoi* that makes them useful generative devices for yielding multiple specific applications. Most scientists will have some degree of commitment to such *topoi* as impartiality, objectivity, commitment, novelty, humility, and communality, and their opposites. Each scientist identifies with the *topoi* in the abstract; and then by moving in thought from the abstract to concrete applications, each can discover an array of specific arguments supportive of his or her overall position. Conflict often turns on whether one is for or against a specific *application* of a *topos*, say, humility, or whether one is for or against a *comparative ranking* of the *topoi* according to their alleged significance in a situation. For instance, there can be disagreement about whether novelty or skepticism is most important. Although the terminology of topical theory is not used, Mulkay's explanation of how "standardized verbal formulations" operate is in fact a discussion of how rhetorical *topoi* relating to scientific *ethos* are chosen:

> A major influence upon scientists' choice of one verbal formulation [what I am now calling a "topic"] rather than another . . . is likely to be their interests or objectives. It can be assumed that, for a given scientist or group of scientists, these interests will vary from one social context to another. Thus . . . when researchers were frustrated by the apparent reluctance of others to make significant findings available to them, they tended to select principles favoring communality which justified their condemnation of the others' behavior and added weight to their exhortations. In contrast, those scientists who had made the discovery were able to find principles in favor of personal ownership of results [secrecy]. In different circumstances, a person's or a group's choice of rules can be entirely reversed. Not only is it possible to vary one's choice of formulations as one attempts to identify the evaluative characteristics of different acts, but it is also possible to apply different formulations to the same act as one's social context changes.[22]

One kind of rhetorical situation in which concerns about professional, scientific *ethos* become particularly salient is marked by questions about demarcation criteria. If it were possible to draw a sharp line of demarcation between science and nonscience, there would be little ambiguity involved when classifying discursive aims and claims as "scientific" or other; hence, there would also not be any need for rhetoric to clarify the scientific standing of those aims and claims. However, whenever we seek to differentiate "science" from "nonscience" there will always be working ambiguities. In these rhetorical situations, scientists will likely choose rhetorical strategies that help them construct "boundaries" that are favorable to their own professional goals and interests and unfavorable to their competitors. For instance, researchers might make rhetorical appeals that construct "narrow" or "rigid" boundaries, inducing adjudicating audiences to distinguish their "scientific" work from the research of those they allege are unorthodox or unscientific "outsiders." In Gieryn's view, scientists engage in "boundary-work" not for the lofty epistemological reasons philosophers often cite (for example, preservation of scientific truth), but as a rhetorical means of solving practical problems that can block achievement of professional goals.[23] Scientists draw sharp contrasts between themselves and "nonscientists" to enhance their intellectual status and authority vis-a-vis the "out groups," to secure professional resources and career opportunities, to deny these resources and opportunities to "pseudo-scientists," and to insulate scientific research from political interference. We should notice, too, that researchers with "unorthodox" aims and claims will also compose rhetoric about scientific *ethos*; but they will typically seek to "broaden" or "soften" the "boundaries" of science as they are defined by defenders of scientific orthodoxy, attempting to show that they, too, are scientists and that their claims should also be taken seriously as reasonable scientific contributions.

Audiences called upon to adjudicate "boundary disputes" are often comprised of scientifically illiterate laypersons, who nevertheless have great respect for the authority of science and its practitioners.[24] When "experts" disagree about matters of public policy, the laity usually cannot decide issues on technical grounds. Rhetors will therefore seek to settle demarcation exigences by constructing "boundaries" in view of some ideal, public image of science and its practitioners. Both orthodox and unorthodox scientists will choose from among the special *topoi* of scientific *ethos* to construct public images favorable to their respective interests and objectives.

The *Topoi* of Scientific *Ethos* : A Case Study

What follows is a case study of *topoi* used to attack and defend scientific *ethos*. The case concerns Francine Patterson's and Eugene Linden's *The Education of Koko*, and Thomas A. Sebeok's review of that book.[25] In the book, Patterson explains how she taught Koko, a gorilla, to use American Sign Language. Most scientists would agree that Koko makes some kind of gestures but many also conclude that Patterson has gone far beyond her data when she claims that the animal has learned its lessons so well that it can ask questions, lie, insult, joke, apologize, and even express grief.[26] Sebeok, Professor of Anthropology, Linguistics, and Semantics at Indiana University, is one of the most outspoken critics of language acquisition studies of apes in general and of Patterson's research in particular. In his review, "The not so sedulous ape," Sebeok attacks Patterson's scientific *ethos* on the grounds that she lacks technical and communal qualities that should be displayed by "credible" scientists. Specifically, Sebeok implies that Patterson and her co-author are not "real" scientists; they are scientific "outsiders" because they display qualities of thought and behavior that are, at best, in conflict with the Mertonian "virtues" of scientific *ethos: universality, communality, skepticism,* and *disinterestedness.*[27]

Sebeok suggested that Patterson is not a "real" scientist because her technical claim-making is, in a word, "bizarre"; he repeatedly illustrated how Patterson's claims for Koko's linguistic cleverness conflict with an implied universal consensus about what is already known about the language behavior of apes. He referred approvingly to Herbert S. Terrace's conclusion, in his book *Nim*, "that there is no evidence at all that apes can either generate or interpret sentences." Sebeok buttressed this claim by arguing that Terrace's "hardly surprising" conclusion, in direct contrast with Patterson's claims, is consistent with what has been revealed by "informed" linguists, and "responsible" ethologists: "Terrace's results are . . . in perfect conformity with the long held judgment of informed linguists from Max Muller (1889) to Noam Chomsky. They accord equally well with the view of responsible ethologists, such as Konrad Lorenz, who declared, in 1978, 'that syntactic language is based on a phylogenetic program evolved exclusively by humans,' and that anthropoid apes '. . . give no indication of possessing syntactic language.' "[28] The conclusion that Sebeok would have us draw from this passage is clear. Patterson's research claims are not grounded in and consistent with established research conclusions in respectable fields of scientific inquiry. Accordingly, as a scientist, she can only be held in contempt as "uninformed" and "irresponsible."

Sebeok also criticized Patterson's research claims on the ground that she is an incompetent experimenter. Specifically, he charged that Patterson had not accounted for possibilities that the animal was behaving in response to clues given by experimenters, an experimental problem popularly known as the "Clever Hans" phenomenon. According to Sebeok, this fallacy is one "by which Koko's entire ten-year curriculum has been errantly nag-ridden. . . ." To support this contention, Sebeok appealed to authority:

> The eminent Bristol neuropsychologist, Richard Gregory, also concluded, in 1981, that apes do not exhibit either "human language or intellectual ability", and wisely admonished: "There are so many experimental difficulties and possibilities of the animals picking up clues from the experimenters, given unwittingly, that extreme caution is essential."

Sebeok repeatedly assailed Patterson's research with arguments that questioned the reliability of both her data and her interpretations of data. For instance, Patterson's competence became an issue when Sebeok challenged the interpretive claim that Koko was able to tell lies:

> Much is made of her aptitude for lying, which, according to the authors, "of course, is one of those behaviors that shows the power of language." Here, however, lurks a terminological confusion, one that, furthermore, begs the question. Many kinds of animals – the most remarkable case on record is that of the Arctic fox, *Alopex lagopus* – give, or give off, deceptive messages, in a word, prevaricate. But a lie must, by definition, be "stated," which Koko simply cannot do.[29]

From this and other instances, Sebeok would have us conclude not only that Patterson's data are suspect but also that her ability to render "scientific" judgments is highly questionable. The claims she advances cannot be accepted unless one replaces "pre-established impersonal criteria" of science with Patterson's idiosyncratic standards of judgment. In a word, the qualities of Patterson's thought and conduct lack affinity with the scientific virtue of "universality."[30]

Sebeok continued his attack on Patterson's *ethos* by drawing arguments from the powerful *topos* of *organized skepticism*. For example, Sebeok amplified both Patterson's and Linden's proclivity to minimize the importance of emotional detachment and systematic doubt in their research by associating them with proponents of a field whose scientific status has been thought questionable. They are said to be "addicted to the use of ploys familiar from parapsychology, such as that the presence of a skeptic tends to ruin experimental results." Among these "ploys" is their emphasis on emotional rapport between experimenters and animal subjects as a precondition for making successful experimental results. Sebeok quotes directly the authors' belief "that one cannot really understand the mental workings of other animals or bring them to the limits of their abilities unless one first has true rapport with them." He then asserted that the "obverse of this claim is that the intimacy between Patterson and her beloved Koko had hopelessly overclouded her scientific objectivity and judgment. . . ." In this way, Sebeok would lead us to conclude that Patterson's research claims must be technically unacceptable because her conduct resonates with an obstinate, dogmatic will to believe that Koko makes and uses language.

A scientist's professional *ethos* depends not only on how audiences perceive his or her competence, but also on how that scientist's "place" within a legitimating scientific community is viewed. To the extent that a rhetor's connection with his or her scientific community becomes confusing, so too does the legitimacy of his or her aims and claims. I have so far shown that Sebeok sought to discredit Patterson's and Linden's *ethos* by arguing that they lack the scientific "virtues" needed to make credible, technical claims. He also repeatedly challenged the authors' credibility by making their relationship with a professional scientific community seem ambiguous to the reader. Sebeok did this by using three lines of argument based on the *communality topos*. First, Patterson and her co-author do not have memberships in any legitimate research institution, so neither is a "real" scientist. Patterson had written that she was not able to analyze Koko's spoken language in detail despite an "enormous" amount of data collected. Sebeok offered this "translation": "In plain text, this citation means that since Miss Patterson's connection with Stanford University has been severed, she no longer enjoys free access to its computers." In other words, Patterson has no scientific standing because she has lost the resources of a legitimizing institution. Sebeok attacks the scientific *ethos* of Patterson's co-author, Eugene Linden, with even less subtlety. Linden is depicted as "a wrestler-turned-journalist, perhaps best known to the public for his *Apes, Men, and Language* (1974, 1981), surely the most gullible, as well as defensively emotion-laden, popular account of attempts at linguistic communication with any of our collateral ancestral species so far published. . . ." The implication here is that Linden lacks connections with legitimizing research institutions; he is, at best, a popularizer of science – and not a very credible one at that.

In addition to arguing that Patterson and her co-author do not "belong" to the scientific community by virtue of position, Sebeok "reads them out of" the community of scientists on grounds that Patterson has been unable to secure ample public funds to support her research. Sebeok was explicit: "While millions of dollars in federal funds were being squandered on the futile search for language in chimpanzees and orangutans, Patterson continued her work, without a proper institutional base, with the support of private sources, including a large, so-called 'non profit' commercial enterprise,[31] supplementing her income by minor grants from small Foundations." He further asserts that the lack of public subsidy is "one respect" in which Patterson's Project Koko differs "sharply" from other studies of ape language capacities. The reader is presumably to understand that any minimally competent student of language in primates would have had access to and used the all-too-available resources for doing the job "right," scientifically.

A third line of argument involves questioning Patterson's legitimacy as a scientist because she has failed to submit her claims for authorization by competent scientists.[32] She had success reaching popular audiences through such channels as *National Geographic* magazine, *Reader's Digest* and a documentary film,[33] but her publishing in more technical sources has been minimal, giving Sebeok warrant for asserting, "If Penny Patterson tried to publish in a scientific atmosphere, then she would be laughed out of court."[34] She was attacked as having a "warped perspective" and a "lack of receptivity to well-intentioned criticism."[35] Accordingly, the reader is left to conclude that Patterson is an "outsider" who lacks credible standing within the professional scientific community.[36]

Sebeok also challenges Patterson's and Linden's scientific *ethos* with remarks that imply they are not sufficiently *disinterested* to be pursuing "legitimate" scientific objectives with the publication of their book. "Real" scientists identify their self-interests with winning community recognition for "making contributions to the development of the conceptual schemes which are of the essence in science."[37] In contrast, Sebeok makes innuendo about Linden's "real" interests: "Her co-author's stake in this enterprise – as well as, of course, his bond of personal relationship with the gorilla – is clearly of a different order." The implication one can draw from this assertion is that Linden's primary motivations are not scientific, but are tied to making money. Sebeok asserts that Patterson's motives for conducting research amount to nothing more than a "desperate reaching out for media recognition (of which this unfortunate book represents but one example)."

My initial focus in this study has been on examining topical choices that Sebeok made when evaluating Patterson's and Linden's scientific *ethos*. At this point, I want to show how the two authors rhetorically constructed a "revolutionary" public image for science and scientists that sharply contrasts with the public image prescribed by Mertonian "normal" science. Patterson argued that objections to claims that nonhuman primates have language abilities are symptomatic of a deeper, intellectual revolution within the behavioral sciences concerned with language. After R. Allen Gardner and Beatrice T. Gardner published findings that the chimpanzee Washoe was able to use language, *Science* published rebuttals written, according to Patterson, by "the most distinguished names in the behavioral sciences." In the face of vigorous resistance by eminent scientists, Patterson claimed that the Gardners' "success" with Washoe presented "one of the most basic tenets of modern life" with an "anomaly;" there was now evidence that humans are not unique in their possession of language. She contended that the hostile reaction to these anomalous claims indicated that something like Kuhn's notion of scientific revolution was taking place in studies of language acquisition in primates.[38] Once readers embrace this revolutionary scenario, they are easily led to conclude that "credible" scientists can and do display such qualities as *individuality, particularity, dogmatism*, and *interestedness*.

Once readers agree that the Gardners have hurled fields like linguistics into "crisis" there is no warrant for esteeming *communality* as a special, scientific virtue; there is no legitimizing community consensus during periods of "crisis." Judgments about "legitimate" research institutions, "appropriate" sources of research funding, and "qualified" adjudicating audiences become partisan points of contention during "revolutionary" science. This image of non-human primate research allows Patterson to extol qualities of *individuality* as characterizing credible scientific *ethos*.[39] We are to conclude that Patterson, by following the Gardners, displays intellectual courage by making bold judgments to abandon outmoded but comfortable notions about language, and by pursuing a pioneering line of thinking even when confronted with eminent hostile opinion. Tuus, the conflict of her position with conventional knowledge is raised to the heights of scientific virtue.

Throughout the book, *universality* is minimized as an important quality of scientific thought and conduct. In revolutionary contexts, scientists cannot turn to "pre-established impersonal criteria" to settle controversy. In the case of linguistic science, they cannot rely on previously certified knowledge because, Patterson says, "there is very little that can be said about language today that is not open to question or controversy."[40] Nor can scientists settle disputes by making carefully constrained observations and using empirically rigorous experimental designs. Patterson contends: "There is much about language that does not lend itself to reduction to statistics and hard data, and some linguists have recently reacted against the rigid, formalized treatment of language. . . . This is not to justify vagueness but to illustrate that it is very difficult to speak with any confidence of 'facts' about language."[41] What scientists must do, says Patterson, is supplement the "rigid" experimental work with "interpretive" case studies.

Case studies require special interpretive sensibilities that allow researchers to achieve what I shall call, for lack of a more fitting expression, *experimental rapport* with subject beasts. The line of thought, based upon the *topos* of *particularity*, is that adequate scientific investigations of the behaviors of sentient beings require that researchers possess special abilities for developing emotional attachments with animal subjects. Patterson uses this line of thought to amplify her scientific credibility and minimize the scientific credibility of her critics. Only those scientists able to establish true rapport with the animal whose behavior is being studied will meet a necessary condition for gleaning positive evidence of language acquisition in non-human primates; those who retain rigidly objective experimental stances toward the animal will confound possibilities for discovering significant language use by the animal. Accordingly, the "best" research with primates encouraged development of rapport between scientist and animal:

> In none of these cases did the experimenter [Terrace and Premack] allow himself to develop a true, close rapport with his chimp. This was justified in the laudable name of objectivity, but given the sensitivity of the animals involved – Koko's signing is affected by even slight disruptions in her routine – it is hard not to wonder whether the different conclusions about ape language abilities reached by these scientists ultimately trace back to the different relationships between experimenters and subjects and to the persistence that has marked the efforts of those of us who have established close rapport with our subjects. If this is the case, I am reaffirmed in my belief that one cannot really understand the mental workings of other animals or bring them to the limits of their abilities unless one first has true rapport with them. Even the critics admit this possibility. What they fail to see is that the problem really is a misunderstanding of the purpose of

language. Once that misunderstanding is straightened out and we accept language as a communicative behavior, the evidence of Koko's abilities is compelling for those who want to see it.[42]

Implicit in Patterson's discussion is a view of researchers as fundamentally *dogmatic*. Scientists cannot skeptically avoid dogmatic adherence to assumptions, so the best that they can do is choose and adhere to assumptions that allow them to comprehend the full range of non-human primate linguistic ability. The choices are clear for Patterson: researchers either assume that Koko is a "dolt" and dismiss all apparently innovative and intentional linguistic acts as "mistakes," or they recognize that the animal is "a bright, playful, creative creature capable of quite sophisticated innovation."[43] "Rigid" experimentalists take the former stance, while those who supplement formal testing procedures with anecdotal, case-study material choose the latter, Patterson asserts. For Patterson, only the second alternative can yield persuasive evidence for Koko's linguistic creativity.

In Patterson's view of scientific *ethos*, credible scientists must be intensely *interested* in the consequences that their research claims have beyond the knowledge-oriented interests of scientific communities. The interested scientist addresses research claims about nonhuman primates' language abilities beyond scientific communities to expose and to falsify religious and philosophical systems that make humans the uniquely "languaging" animal. One consequence of exposing this "false" belief is an ethical challenge to humans' "rights to experiment with or harvest natural resources. . . ."[44] In sum, "virtuous" scientists are interested in the religious, philosophical and ethical implications of technical claims for society at large. They are not focused narrowly and solely on the knowledge-oriented concerns of their specialized communities.[45]

When Patterson's discourse is contrasted with Sebeok's we can see how topical selection and development can influence how situated, lay audiences will judge an individual's or group's scientific *ethos*. Sebeok constructed a Mertonian image for science, and on the basis of that image implied that Patterson and Linden were not "real" scientists because they lacked the scientific virtues of communality, universality, skepticism and disinterestedness. Patterson and Linden constructed a revolutionary image for science, and worked from that image to show that Patterson's thought and conduct displayed the esteemed qualities of individuality, particularity, dogmatism, and interestedness and, moreover, that her critics, Sebeok included, lacked those "virtues." Both Sebeok and Patterson and Linden strategically selected *topoi* in order to construct a scientific *ethos* that was favorable to securing and justifying their respective professional interests and objectives, given the constraining influences of their particular rhetorical situation.

Topoi and Rhetorical Boundaries

The case study illustrates how scientific "insiders" and "outsiders" can rhetorically construct conflicting perspectives on scientific *ethos* when responding discursively to demarcation problems. Sebeok composed a review that invoked sharp "boundaries" between science and non-science, implying that Patterson and Linden were not "real" scientists because their thought and conduct did not adhere to the "virtues" of universality, communality, skepticism, and disinterestedness. Readers are urged to dismiss Patterson and Linden as incompetent or pseudo-scientific outsiders on the basis of these "scientific" qualities and, consequently, to conclude that *The Education of Koko* must be a scientific ruse. Patterson and Linden's book created a perspective on scientific *ethos* that blurred the boundaries between science and nonscience, suggesting that credible scientists adhere in thought and conduct to virtues of particularity, individuality, enthusiasm or dogmatism, and interestedness – qualities of character that do not sharply differentiate scientists from nonscientists. I surmise that this perspective on scientific *ethos* is often created when those who view themselves as revolutionary outsiders want to challenge and to overturn the claims of orthodoxy, but more evidence is needed to substantiate this conjecture. Nevertheless, in this instance both the rhetoric of insiders and outsiders was addressed to the laity which was left with the task of deciding what qualities credible scientists do and do not have.

Sebeok and Patterson and Linden put forward contrasting public images of credible science and scientists. Sebeok depicts science as a unique intellectual activity characterized by a high degree of consensus and agreement about what "counts" as science. "Normal" scientists – those possessing a credible scientific *ethos* – will adhere to Mertonian standards of thought and conduct. Only pseudo-scientists or eccentrics working at the lunatic fringe will neglect those standards. Patterson and Linden portray science as characterized by dissensus and disagreement. "Revolutionary" rather than "normal" scientists possess qualities that are virtuous given that image. In revolutionary circumstances, Mertonian vices are shaded into virtues. Both public portrayals are *idealizations* of science and scientists. Specifically, linguistic science is neither as "normal" as Sebeok implies through his review, nor is it as "revolutionary" as Patterson and Linden would have their readers believe. These idealized visions of science and scientists can be explained only partly by the rhetors' need to address a scientific laity that is incapable of following the relevant technical arguments. I say "partly" because even scholarly commentators cannot agree about whether the actual scientific endeavor is best characterized by consensus or dissensus.[46]

The best explanation is that neither idealized vision can alone prescribe situationally transcendent and uniformly applicable standards constituting *the* scientific *ethos*. Science is both consensual and divisive, cooperative and competitive; and scientists can possess both "normal" and "radical" qualities. The alternative public "faces" of science underscore the point that scientific *ethos* is a *rhetorical* construction. Contrasting images of scientific *ethos* show that either of the opposed qualities of universality or particularity, communality or individuality, skepticism or enthusiasm, and disinterestedness or interestedness can be shaded into a scientific virtue or vice. Rhetors often include among compositional decisions those concerning which strategies are most useful for constructing a scientific *ethos* that can best advance their professional interests, given the problems they must face and the constraints of their audience and situation.

It may be that the demarcation exigence and the standard kinds of rhetorical strategies that "insiders" and "outsiders" use in response are generalizable. For instance, demarcation exigences emerge when mainstream scientists argue that parapsychology or "scientific" creationism are not "real" sciences and that their practitioners are not "real" scientists. Analysis of these disputes shows that critics of parapsychology and creationism turn to the kinds of *topoi* Sebok used to construct perspectives on scientific *ethos* in their rhetorical situations.[47] This suggests that the *topoi* identified in this study are among the standard and finite sets of themes that scientists choose from when composing discourse in response to demarcation exigences.

When scientists address ambiguities about what it means to think and to act like scientists they will turn to those kinds of arguments catalogued by the *topoi* related to scientific *ethos*. However, scientists also respond to technical kinds of exigences, and topical analysis of discourse can reveal the kinds of arguments scientists use when trying to resolve those exigences as well. For instance, scientists encounter ambiguities about the scientific significance of evidence or of the constructs that they use to articulate and apply theory. Ambiguities about the intrinsic or comparative scientific value of evidence and theory constitute a special *kind* of technical exigence which demands that scientists choose the right kind of *topoi* to make an effective rhetorical response. What some commentators call "good reasons" for making scientific judgments might actually function like rhetorical *topoi* that are specially useful for making arguments in response to problems of *scientific* "value" or "significance." A preliminary list would include the scientific "values" of accuracy, consistency, scope, simplicity, and fruitfulness.[48] Future case studies can with profit focus on revealing the kinds of *topoi* that scientists use when responding to this and other kinds of situational exigences.[49] This might lead to the compilation of topical inventories, organized according to the kinds of situational exigences that scientists confront. As these lists are amended and refined, rhetorical critics can use them heuristically to distinguish the kinds of topical choices rhetors *could* have made from those that they *did* make, and to assess the comparative persuasive efficacy of the rhetors' choices given the *kind* of situational exigence they were seeking to resolve.

The "rhetoric of inquiry" is itself a rhetorical effort at heralding a demarcation crisis in the human sciences; it seeks to indict the present "boundaries" among substantive fields of inquiry as largely artificial and points to the need to redraw or traverse those boundaries in fruitful ways. Scientists must confront concerns about professional *ethos* when addressing demarcation exigences; so too, must scholars conducting research on the "rhetoric of inquiry." However, before we go too far in our rhetorical "boundary-work" we must first clarify what the present boundaries are. Does each field of inquiry have its own technical expectations and substantive concerns which prescribe for its practitioners special "virtues" of professional thought and conduct? What does it mean to think and to act like, say, a poet, sociologist, physicist? Do the "habits" that artists and scientists display show that the "two cultures" are converging or diverging? Topical analysis provides the field-independent methodological approach that allows us to cut across the currently fragmented areas of substantive inquiry and provide answers to these and other questions. By answering such questions, we can become more self-reflective about what it means to be a member of a particular academic community and discern better whether the "boundaries" we invoke to demarcate ourselves from members of other communities are desirable for intellectual or practical purposes, or are merely artificial.

Notes

1   Aristotle, *Rhetoric*, tr. W. Rhys Roberts (Random House, New York, 1954), 1356a5.
2   Ibid., 1378a5–19.
3   Robert K. Merton first published his views on the scientific *ethos* in his essay "Science and the social order," *Philosophy of Science*, 5 (1938), 321–37. A more systematic rendering of his ideas appeared in the essay, "Science and technology in a democratic order," *Journal of Legal and Political Sociology*, 1 (1942), pp. 115–26. I am using the reprint of this essay, "The normative structure of science," in Robert K. Merton, *The Sociology of Science: Theoretical and Empirical Investigations*, ed. Norman W. Storer (University of Chicago Press, Chicago, 1973), pp. 267–78.

Unless otherwise indicated, all references to Merton's articles will be to this useful compilation.

4   Merton, "Normative structure of science," p. 270. In Merton's view, extending certified knowledge is the institutional goal of science.

5   Ibid., pp. 268–9. Merton's scientific *ethos* is the sociological complement to the epistemological position known as the "standard view." For a critique of this philosophical position which grounds Merton's sociology of science see Michael Mulkay, *Science and the Sociology of Knowledge* (Allen, London, 1979).

6   Merton, "Normative structure of science," p. 270.

7   I am relying on Barber's interpretation of disinterestedness. Storer amplifies this idea by explaining that it encourages pursuit of "science for science's sake." See Bernard Barber, *Science and the Social Order* (1952; reprinted Greenwood, Westport, 1978), p. 92; and Norman W. Storer, *The Social System of Science* (Holt, New York, 1966), p. 79.

8   For Merton's discussion of the norms see "Normative structure of science," pp. 270–8. Disinterestedness, universalism, communality and skepticism imply that *emotional neutrality* toward ideas and actions is a scientific virtue. Although Merton did not raise objectivity to normative status, other commentators have discussed emotional neutrality as a scientific value. See Barber, *Science and the Social Order*, pp. 88–9; and Storer, *Social System of Science*, pp. 79–80.

9   Merton, "Priorities in scientific discovery," in *Sociology of Science*, especially pp. 293–305.

10   For examples of research strongly supportive of Merton's normative structure of science see Jonathan R. Cole and Stephen Cole, *Social Stratification in Science* (University of Chicago Press, Chicago, 1973); Jonathan R. Cole, *Fair Science: Women in the Scientific Community* (Free Press, New York, 1979); Jerry Gaston, *The Reward System in British and American Science* (Wiley, New York, 1978); Barber, *Science and the Social Order*; and Storer, *Social System of Science*.

11   See Ian I. Mitroff, *The Subjective Side of Science: A Philosophical Inquiry into the Psychology of the Apollo Moon Scientists* (Elsevier, Amsterdam, 1974).

12   Particularism, solitariness, interestedness, and dogmatism each imply that *emotional commitment* to one's ideas and actions is a necessary ingredient of science. Some commentators have gone so far as to call emotional commitment the counter-norm to emotional neutrality. See Mitroff, *Subjective Side of Science*, p. 276. For lists containing these and other norms and counter-norms see ibid., p. 79; and Ian I. Mitroff and Richard O. Mason, *Creating a Dialectical Social Science: Concepts, Methods, and Models* (Reidel, Dordrecht, 1981), pp. 147–8.

13   Stehr provides a useful overview of the central issues involved. Barnes and Dolby and Mulkay are among Merton's most vociferous critics. Gaston and Zuckerman issue strong defenses. See Nico Stehr, "The ethos of science revisited: social and cognitive norms," *Sociological Inquiry*, 48 (1978), pp. 172–96; S.B. Barnes and R.G.A. Dolby, "The scientific ethos: a deviant viewpoint," *Archives Européennes de Sociologie*, 11 (1970), pp. 3–25; Mulkay, *Science and the Sociology of Knowledge*, especially pp. 63–73; Gaston, *The Reward System*, pp. 158–84; and Harriet Zuckerman, "Deviant behavior and social control in science," in Edward Sagarin (ed.), *Deviance and Social Change* (Sage, Beverly Hills, 1977), pp. 123–8.

14   I am following Lloyd F. Bitzer's idea that rhetorical situations are characterized by exigences or ambiguities that can be solved, clarified, or modified through discourse. See "The rhetorical situation," *Philosophy and Rhetoric*, 1 (1968), pp. 6–7.

15   Barnes and Dolby, "The scientific ethos," p. 13.

16   As examples, consider some standard attacks on the scientific *ethos* of creationists
      and parapsychologists. See Thomas I. Gieryn, George M. Bevins, and Stephen C.
      Zehr, "Professionalization of American scientists: public science in the creation/
      evolution trials," *American Sociological Review*, 50 (1985), especially pp. 399–405;
      and H.M. Collins and T.J. Pinch, "The construction of the paranormal: nothing
      unscientific is happening," in Roy Wallis (ed.), *On the Margins of Science: The
      Social Construction of Rejected Knowledge*, Sociological Review Monographs 27
      (University of Keele, Staffs, UK, 1979), especially pp. 246–7.
17   On this point, see Thomas M. Lessl, "Science and the sacred cosmos: the ideological
      rhetoric of Carl Sagan," *Quarterly Journal of Speech*, 71 (1985), p. 176.
18   Aristotle, *Rhetoric*, 1356a6–8.
19   When there is ambiguity or cause for doubt about technical claims, qualities
      exhibited through presentations and prior reputation are factors of *ethos* that will
      be weighed in formation of final judgments. Consider some examples. A leading
      advocate of the molecular memory transfer hypothesis exhibited qualities through
      presentations that some thought were less than "scientific." The scientist conducted
      scientific work without being sufficiently "earnest." Another scientist, involved in
      the discovery of the solar neutrino anomaly, drew upon his established reputation
      for being careful, modest, and open with results as an important persuasive resource
      for establishing the anomalous claim. See David Travis, "On the construction of
      creativity: the 'memory transfer' phenomenon and the importance of being
      earnest," in Karin D. Knorr, Roger Krohn, and Richard Whitley (eds), *The Social
      Process of Scientific Investigation*, Sociology of the Sciences Yearbook 4 (Reidel,
      Dordrecht, 1981), pp. 177–8; and T.J. Pinch, "Theoreticians and the production of
      experimental anomaly: the case of solar neutrinos," in ibid., pp. 94–5.
20   According to Zuckerman, she and Merton found evidence for this point when they
      examined referees' reasons for recommending or rejecting submissions to the
      physics journal, *Physical Review*. Specifically, referees were more likely to endorse
      unorthodox ideas when authored by established scientists than young or rank-and-
      file scientists. Zuckerman interprets this as evidence for the influence of
      "performance-based authority" on reviewers' judgments. Unfortunately, this idea
      was not developed in Zuckerman's and Merton's article on the subject. See Harriet
      Zuckerman, "Theory choice and problem choice in science," *Sociological Inquiry*,
      48 (1978), p. 70; and Harriet Zuckerman and Robert K. Merton, "Institutionalized
      patterns of evaluation in science," in Merton, *Sociology of Science*, especially pp.
      476–91.
21   Mulkay, *Science and the Sociology of Knowledge*, p. 71.
22   Ibid., pp. 71–2.
23   Thomas E. Gieryn, "Boundary-work and the demarcation of science from non-
      science: strains and interests in professional ideologies of scientists," *American
      Sociological Review*, 48 (1983), pp. 781–95.
24   Gieryn affirms Mulkay's claim that what I am calling the special *topoi* of scientific
      ethos become especially useful when scientists address professional rhetoric to lay
      audiences. See ibid., p. 783; Gieryn et al., "Professionalization of American
      scientists," especially pp. 403–4; and Michael Mulkay, "Norms and ideology in
      science," *Social Science Information*, 15 (1976), p. 646.
25   Francine Patterson and Eugene Linden, *The Education of Koko* (Holt, New York,
      1981); Thomas A. Sebeok, "The not so sedulous ape: review of *The Education of
      Koko* by Francine Patterson and Eugene Linden," *Times Literary Supplement*, 10
      September 1982, p. 976. Unless otherwise indicated, all references to Sebeok's
      rhetoric are to this review.

26 For instance, see Laura A. Petitto and Mark S. Seidenberg, "On the evidence for linguistic abilities in signing apes," *Brain and Language*, 8 (1979), pp. 162–83. Also see the critical review of the techniques and conclusions of language experiments with nonhuman primates, including Patterson's, in Mark S. Seidenberg and Laura A. Petitto, "Signing behavior in apes: a critical review," *Cognition*, 7 (1979), pp. 177–215.

27 Most of Sebeok's review is directed toward discrediting Patterson's *ethos*, with less attention devoted to Linden's. This is appropriate given that the book is based on Patterson's research, which is presented to the reader in Patterson's voice.

28 Sebeok's appeal to Terrace's study has added rhetorical force because Terrace had initially believed that his chimpanzee, "Nim Chimpsky," was capable of creating a sentence. Terrace admitted that he had "fantasies" about what he could accomplish with his communicating chimp, including using the animal as a translator of ape communication in the wilds; but after further analysis of his data he concluded that Nim said little on his own and was merely imitating behavior in an effort to get rewards – Nim was not able to construct sentences. When those holding "heretical" opinions publicly reform their ideas their very example provides conservative defenders of orthodoxy with powerful means of persuasion; the act of reformation casts doubt on the legitimacy of heretical beliefs and renders ambiguous the authenticity of those who still hold them. Sebeok used the reformed Terrace's "true confessions" as persuasive means for questioning the legitimacy of Patterson's claims and the scientific authenticity of her motives. Terrace explained his changed views in *Signs of the Apes, Songs of the Whales* (film, produced by Linda Harrar, Nova, WGBH-Boston, PBS, 1983).

29 Sebeok sought to discredit Patterson's scientific *ethos* by asserting throughout his review that her interpretations of Koko's behavior are riddled with "anthropomorphic" (read: "unscientific") tendencies. After all, gorillas do not willfully make false statements; only humans can lie. However, Sebeok was inducing readers to make a sharp dichotomy between "anthropomorphic" and "scientific" interpretation that is not always so easily drawn. Gould suggests that there will always be anthropormorphic tendencies when humans investigate animal behavior because "we cannot write, study, or even conceive of other creatures except in overt or implied comparison with ourselves." Human entanglements with animals is a fact for Gould; what is at issue is the nature and degree of those entanglements. See Stephen Jay Gould, "Animals and us: review of *The Chimpanzees of Gombe: Patterns of Behaviour* by Jane Goodall", *New York Review of Books*, 25 June 1987, p. 20.

30 Judgments about scientists' *ethos* often overlap with considerations pertinent to appraising the technical reasonableness of research claims, or what classical rhetoricians would have called the *logos* of scientific discourse. Although closely interrelated, I believe that the arguments just reviewed are best read as an attack primarily on Patterson's *ethos* rather than as a simple critique of technical *logos*. Sebeok is trying to induce readers to doubt Patterson's *technical virtuosity* as a scientist. The *topos* of *universality* recommends the fitting line of thought: that "real" scientists willingly and capably test their claims against preestablished, impersonal standards. Patterson fails to display her technical virtuosity by neglecting two such impersonal standards: (1) the intellectual consensus among scientists regarding what is accepted and rejected knowledge; and (2) empirical observations (due to her alleged experimental incompetence).

31 I surmise that Sebeok is here referring to Patterson's Gorilla Foundation. In her

book Patterson makes a tacit but obvious appeal to the laity for financial support of the Gorilla Foundation. See Patterson and Linden, *Education of Koko*, p. 213.

32   Of the three arguments that Sebeok draws from the *topos* of communality, only this one approximates Merton's idea of intellectual communism. From Merton's perspective, Patterson's scientific conduct is questionable because she does not willingly "share" her research by publishing in legitimate journals. Merton's idea of communism makes "secrecy" a vice because it is assumed that what is not being shared with the community is *worth* knowing. However, during demarcation crises *ability* to share can become as much an issue as willingness to share. I found it necessary to reinterpret the *topos* of communality as recommending this more encompassing line of thought: that "real" scientists actively participate in the intellectual life of their community. This is the persuasive basis of Sebeok's three arguments. Patterson fails to display community participation because she lacks a credible position, fails to secure "legitimate" research support, and will not or cannot share technical claims with scientific audiences.

33   Francine Patterson, "Conversations with a gorilla," *National Geographic*, 154, Oct. (1978), pp. 438–65 (condensed in *Reader's Digest*, 114, Mar. (1979), pp. 81–6; *Koko, a talking gorilla* (a ninety-minute 16mm film by Barbet Schroeder, available from New Yorker Films).

34   Quoted in Cynthia Gorney, "Gorilla Koko hasn't convinced everybody that she can talk," *Houston Chronicle*, 4 February 1985, section 5, p. 5.

35   Another way of putting this is that she lacked "good will" toward members of relevant knowledge communities. Sebeok recounts how Patterson and Linden responded to Terrace's conclusion in *Nim* that there is no evidence showing that apes can generate or interpret sentences by hurling "such epithets as 'muddle-headed' (Patterson), 'apostate' (Linden), and worse."

36   All of these statements imply that Patterson violated a major unwritten taboo in scientific life: she appealed "to the populace at large" rather than to the "well-defined community of the scientist's professional compeers," as Kuhn had put it. Scientists are especially vigorous in their public condemnations of those who seek to gain lay acceptance for unorthodox and unauthorized claims. The ferocity of Sebeok's review provides a case in point. See Thomas S. Kuhn, *The Structure of Scientific Revolutions*, 2nd edn (University of Chicago Press, Chicago, 1970), p. 168.

37   Barber, *Science and the Social Order*, p. 92.

38   Patterson and Linden, *Education of Koko*, pp. 24–6.

39   Individuality illuminates Patterson's and Linden's arguments better than solitariness, the purported counter-norm of Merton's intellectual communism. Rather than using "secrecy" to bolster their scientific *ethos*, they instead displayed their unwillingness to sacrifice truth to the authority of tradition and its prominent spokespersons. When anti-authoritarianism is treated as a virtue it often is called *individualism*, as some Mertonian commentators have noted. This *topos* conflicts with the *topos* of communality in the sense that I reformulated that *topos* earlier. See Barber, *Science and the Social Order*, pp. 89–90.

40   Patterson and Linden, *Education of Koko*, p. 194.

41   Ibid., p. 79.

42   Ibid., pp. 210–11. Patterson is not without distinguished company when making arguments of this kind. Barbara McClintock, winner of the 1983 Nobel Prize in Medicine or Physiology, offered a philosophical vision of science based not on objective experimentation but on what she called developing "a feeling for the organism." For her, intimacy with and sympathetic understanding of the objects of

knowledge is required to have genuine scientific knowledge. Lest this application of "rapport" be dismissed merely as McClintock's philosophical speculation, let us also turn to Jane Goodall's studies of a chimpanzee colony at Gombe in Tanzania. According to Gould, Goodall's work exemplifies a scientist's internal struggles to strike the proper balance in research between emotional involvement with the chimpanzees and the need to secure "maximal distance" so that the chimpanzees' behavior does not become distorted through the scientist's intrusions. These internal struggles illustrate that rapport can have important influences on scientific research. Gould says of Goodall's work: "You can't just march off into dense foliage and find chimps; you must first make contact and build trust in order to win acceptance and establish the possibility of following in the wild" ("Animals and us," p. 24). Goodall's experience also underscores the fact that topical choices among skepticism and enthusiasm, or objectivity and rapport, are not merely arbitrary. There are circumstances in which scientists can clarify ambiguities about their professional conduct through appeals to "rapport" as a virtue comparatively superior to "objectivity." See Gould, "Animals and us," pp. 23–5; and Evelyn Fox Keller, *A Feeling for the Organism: The Life and Work of Barbara McClintock* (Freeman, New York, 1983), pp. 197–207.

43 Patterson and Linden, *Education of Koko*, p. 207.

44 Ibid., p. 25.

45 This argument is a revolutionary variation on the theme that virtuous scientists can serve special communities of interest. Patterson and Linden are virtuous not because their interests coincide with those possessed by members of an informal college, but because their interests are linked with issues that concern general society.

46 For an overview of the key points-at-issue see Larry Laudan, "Two puzzles about science: reflections about some crises in the philosophy and sociology of science," *Minerva*, 20 (1982), pp. 253–68.

47 When orthodox scientists attack parapsychology and creationism as "pseudo-science" they include among their means of persuasion efforts to discredit the scientific *ethos* of practitioners. They do this by claiming that parapsychologists and creationists do not think and act like "real" scientists. Typically the standard Mertonian arguments are adduced in support. Parapsychologists and creationists are said to be: (1) openly defiant of both the "universal" consensus on accepted and rejected knowledge and the need for empirical confirmation of technical claims (*universality*); (2) pursuing extra-scientific motives including advancement of beliefs in the supernatural (*disinterestedness*); (3) dogmatically attached to their allegedly "scientific" claims (*skepticism*); and (4) incapable of participating in the "real" scientific community, as indicated by their inability to secure visible positions, "legitimate" research funds, and publications in orthodox journals (*communality*). Parapsychologists have been far more successful than the creationists at legitimizing their scientific *ethos*, and they did this largely by emulating the Mertonian virtues. Nevertheless, like the creationists and Patterson and Linden, they also attempt to diffuse orthodox criticism by creating a revolutionary scenario for advancing their "radical" claims. However, more critical work is needed before we can safely generalize that these and other "intellectual revolutionaries," like Patterson and Linden, draw arguments from the *topoi* of *particularity, interestedness, dogmatism*, and *individuality*. On the use of Mertonian *topoi* against the creationists, see Gieryn et al., "Professionalization of American Scientists," pp. 401–3. My claims about the parapsychologists are based on Paul D. Allison, "Experimental parapsychology as

a rejected science," in Wallis, *On the Margins of Science*, especially pp. 277–88; Collins and Pinch, "Construction of the paranormal," *passim*; and Jim Palmer, "Why is science spooked by 'psi'?" *Washington Post*, 8 Mar. 1987, sec. B, p. 3.

48   Kuhn describes functional features of these "good reasons" that reflect their rhetorical topicality: "Individually the criteria are imprecise: individuals may legitimately differ about their application to concrete cases. In addition, when deployed together, they repeatedly prove to conflict with one another," (Thomas S. Kuhn, "Objectivity, value judgment, and theory choice," in *The Essential Tension: Selected Studies in Scientific Tradition and Change* (University of Chicago Press, Chicago, 1977), p. 322). Like the *topoi* related to scientific *ethos*, these technical *topoi* have evocative, inventional powers due to their working ambiguities, thus allowing generation of varied and sometimes conflicting arguments both within and across rhetorical situations. See *ibid.*, pp. 321–5.

49   For an example of how topical analysis can be applied to technical articles see S. Michael Halloran, "The birth of molecular biology: an essay in the rhetorical criticism of scientific discourse," *Rhetoric Review*, 3 (1984), especially pp. 73–4.

4

Buridan's Ass: The Statistical Rhetoric of Science and the Problem of Equiprobability

Vito Signorile

"But why does opening the box and looking reduce the system back to one probability, either live cat or dead cat? Why don't *we* get included in the system when we lift the lid of the box?"

There was a pause. "How?" Rover barked, distrustfully.

"Well, we would involve ourselves in the system, you see, the super-position of two waves. There's no reason why it should only exist *inside* an open box, is there? So when we came to look there would be, you and I, both looking at a live cat and both looking at a dead cat, see?"

A dark cloud lowered over Rover's eyes and brow. He barked twice in a subdued, harsh voice, and walked away. With his back turned to me he said in a firm, sad tone, "You must not complicate the issue. It is complicated enough."[1]

There is a conceit among apologists for the scientific faith that the body of work and thought we call science has a privileged status, commanding universal affirmation from all right-minded people. Claims to truth that compete with those of science are often derided as rhetorical sophistries, ruled more by subjectivity, bias and wishful thinking than devotion to the objective discovery of things out there in nature. In this conception, science has no place for appeals to authority, intuition, revelation, or custom. Its representative anecdote[2] is the image of Galileo accusing his enemies of not looking with their own eyes.[3] Taking rhetoric in its popular, pejorative sense, science is promoted as its antidote: If rhetoric is the disease of human cultures, science is its cure.

A growing literature is emerging which suggests that this flattering view of science is itself a rhetoric. Since Thomas Kuhn's *The Structure of Scientific Revolutions*, our perception of science has never been quite the same. We now know that scientists do their work in the crucibles of personal whim and social ideology.[4] However, one last appeal has remained to form a bulwark protecting the credentials of all scientific work. This is mathematics. When we examine the warranting procedures employed to back up scientific claims, we find a paradigm built on the presumption of mathematical certainty. By formulating its questions in mathematical terms, subjecting them to empirical procedures, and evaluating them through the application of statistical norms, it is claimed that science thus evades the dangers of rhetorical bias.

However, it is now becoming clear that mathematics itself rests on foundations less secure than formerly thought. Perhaps beginning with the later Wittgenstein, who concluded that all knowledge, mathematical included, is rooted in the "forms of life," we have witnessed significant challenges to the presumed solidity of mathematical thought.[5]

It is my aim in this essay to show that, far from the objectivity and detachment scientists believe their statistical procedures guarantee, there is, and necessarily is, a rhetorical voice which seeks to persuade us to overlook the conceptual dilemmas lying at the heart of statistical theory. We already have a sociological literature that calls attention to the ways in which the bureaucratization of statistical procedures has become entrenched in the discipline.[6] These caveats, however, do not challenge the statistical concepts themselves. Generally, it is allowed that, if "properly done," they have their place in the production of sociological knowledge.

It is time to focus on the reasoning, the conceptual structure itself, that lies behind statistical practice, and thus to uncover the warranting procedures employed to justify them. In an effort to broach this line of inquiry, I should like to investigate a notion which is central to statistical theory: equiprobability.

The Possible and the Probable

The concept of equiprobability has a curious history. Despite the caveat to be found in the celebrated fourteenth century parable of the starving ass of Buridan,[7] by the end of the eighteenth century we discover LaPlace, who shares a place with Bernoulli as a founder of modern probability theory, employing equiprobability as a foundational concept.

There are now several competing concepts of probability.[8] The theory of LaPlace, being among the earliest, has been called the "classical" conception. These concepts all divide primarily according to whether probabilities are to be considered subjective states of uncertainty or objective states inherent in the nature of reality, regardless of our grasp of it. Carnap refers to these as "$prob_1$", and "$prob_2$", respectively.[9] Hacking calls the first "epistemological" and the second "aleatory" probability.[10]

$Prob_2$, the "objective," is the type employed in the "new" physics. In quantum mechanics, probabilities are considered intrinsic properties of the material/energy world "out there." Research into subatomic events has led to the almost universal acceptance of the doctrine of quantum mechanics that these events are fundamentally governed by probability distributions. In the more accessible writings on the subject, subatomic particles are described as probability "waves."[11] In essence, reality is in a vast state of probability. To quote Capra: "The fact that particles are not isolated entities but wave-like probability patterns implies that they behave in a very peculiar way."[12] A conclusion which Einstein resisted with the well-known claim that "God does not play dice with the universe."

The classical theory was objectivist in the sense that, when playing a game of chance, there are postulated "true" probabilities inherent in the game, which exist regardless of the player's knowledge.[13] This idea was gradually generalized to states of nature, to the point that it is now the centerpiece of quantum physics.[14] In the classical version probabilities are established as proportions of all possible outcomes. The argument was founded on the treatment of possibilities and probabilities as indentical states. The *probability* of an event was ascertained by finding a method whereby the *possible* competing outcomes could be determined. LaPlace clearly formulated the strategy. In his Second Principle he states:

> But that supposes the various cases equally possible. If they are not so, we will determine first their respective possibilities. . . . Then the probability will be the sum of the possibilities of each favorable case.[15]

By summing "equal possibilities" we get probabilities. It should be obvious that, as Hacking notes, citing Reichenbach, once the notion is entertained of a possibility having an equal weight with other possibilities, the concept of probability has already entered.[16] LaPlace's examples (coin-flipping, dice-throwing) make it perfectly clear that "equally possible outcomes" are equal by virtue of their all being equally likely. Hacking traces the notion that equiprobability = equipossibility back to Leibniz (*De Incerti Aestimatione*, 1678). It appears well-honored by the time Bernoulli published *Ars Conjectandi* in 1713. Thus, it was quite well established when LaPlace wrote his treatise on probability in 1796.[17] Hacking also observes that the basic ambiguity – are we confronted with a psychological datum or a physical one? – was not surmounted by reconceptualizing probabilities as possibilities. Indeed, possibilities are even less clearly "physical" than probabilities, since the determination of what is possible is not an empirical procedure, not a physical experiment, but rather an imaginary experiment.

The classical conception of probability requires that all the possible outcomes be known, a fact that has resulted in its being referred to as an a priori theory.[18] ın this conception, it is fairly easy to see that determining whɑt events are possible is a logical procedure, not a physical one. It is accomplished by analysis, not inspection. Thus, the a priori approach can be employed only when the conditions under which the events are produced can be specified in all their essential characteristics. Only then is it possible to deduce the range of events that can, in principle, occur. Games of chance fit this requirement very well. Given an adequate description of a game and its rules of procedure, it should be possible to determine all the possible game-relevant outcomes.

Nonetheless the analysis of a game into its rudimentary components is not as straightforward as it may seem. In a famous reply to D'Alembert, LaPlace illustrated this point by discussing the case of the probability of obtaining heads in either of two tosses of a coin.[19] D'Alembert, he explains, had considered the problem as follows:

First toss	Second toss
H	No need, game won
T	H game won
	T game lost

Possible outcomes: 3

This led D'Alembert to conclude that there were two chances of winning out of three; the probability of winning is $\frac{2}{3}$.

LaPlace goes on to show that the game-situation is not thus broken down far enough into its rudimentary components, for there are, he argues, four possible outcomes. This can be illustrated as follows:

First toss	Second toss
H	H game won
	T game won
T	H game won
	T game lost

Possible outcomes: 4

By holding the second toss to be obligatory, the opportunities for winning amount to three events out of four, not D'Alembert's two out of three. Considering the full, combined string of possibilities as equally or indifferently expected, LaPlace concludes that the probability of winning is $\frac{3}{4}$.

What this shows is that the a priori method of determining probabilities is based on a complete mapping of all the basic relevant events generated by the game. Pierce calls this a "primitive sample space."[20] The probability, then, is an "objective" fact, based not on an examination of "nature," but on a rational appraisal of the game being played.[21] The principle is that all the rudimentary possibilities are to be considered equally probable. To discover these rudimentary possibilities one should break down the components of a game into all its atomic (that is, individual, indivisible) outcomes. The separate, unit, possibilities are all taken to be equally likely. As Pedoe explains:

> D'Alembert's first case included our first *two* cases. . . . It is true that one of the three possibilities in D'Alembert's system must occur, and that the possibilities are mutually exclusive. The trouble is that they are *not equally likely*. It is evident that "heads on the first throw regardless of what happens on the second throw" (our first two cases) is twice as likely as "tails on the first throw and heads on the second."[22]

Now, this presumption of equiprobability is guaranteed by the definition of the game. The equiprobability is an artifact of the game itself.[23] That is, unless its specifications are met, the game is simply not being played. In setting up his imaginary experiment, LaPlace envisions a perfect coin in a perfectly executed game: "Let us suppose that we throw into the air a large and very thin coin whose two large opposite faces, which we will call heads and tails, are perfectly similar."[24] The game is contrived to enable us to state that our expectation on any toss of the coin is indifferent, for the coin itself is indifferently "similar" on both sides.[25]

Probability and Evidence

The objectivist, apriorist, view has persisted in statistical theory through two developments: the very influential Reichenbach–von Mises definition of probability as the limit of a ratio as n (the number of cases) approaches infinity, and *sampling theory*, of which "significance" testing is an ubiquitous example.

Dissatisfaction with the foreknowledge and presumptions required by classical theories led to the conviction that a more empirical approach would mean that probabilities should be identified for what they are: measures of the degree of our ignorance. Both Keynes and Carnap have proposed definitions which take the point of view that probabilities are relative to (or conditional on) evidence.[26] Carnap considers his approach to be a compromise between the objectivist and subjectivist views, retaining what is valid in both.

Conceptually, there should be no problem seeing the principle of indifference as a feature of subjectivist views of probability. The observer's indifference is translated as the indifferent spread of the degree of uncertainty equally to all individual events capable of occurring under the conditions of the study. However, it is also applicable to the objectivist views.[27] Not unlike the presence of an omniscient observer in Newton's concept of absolute space and time,[28] the Reichenbach–von Mises approach envisions an ideal observer who selects indifferently from a limitless universe. The approach that defines probability as long run relative frequency indifferently assigns each individual selected equal weight.

Ayer has uncovered logical problems in such theories of probability.[29] For example, objectively, either an event will occur or not. It cannot, in any factual sense, *probably* occur.[30] From the viewpoint of an *omniscient* observer, one can argue, there is no doubt about whether the event will occur or not.

Furthermore, the Reichenbach–von Mises approach depends upon the Law of Large Numbers. At the heart of this law is the requirement that the long-run sequence must be varied; that is, it should be given to no systematic arrangement, it should be "random in the sense, defined by von Mises, of being indifferent to place-selection."[31] Take, for example, the selection of odd or even numbers from the set of whole numbers. If they were arranged such that all the odd numbers came first, it is obvious that an even number would never be selected regardless of the size of the sample. Although Ayer does not indicate this, such a requirement contains the principle of indifference in the absolutist sense, for it postulates an omniscient observer from whose point of view the relevant character of the distribution is already known; all available individuals are indifferently distributed for selection.

Finally, there is the contradiction entailed in the assignment of probabilities. The principle of indifference has both a narrow and wide application. Narrowly, it is applied to dichotomous expectations: either an event will occur or not. On the principle of indifference, given no other information, the expectation is split precisely between these two alternatives. The probability of the event's occurring is $\frac{1}{2}$, as is the probability of its not occurring.

In its narrow sense the principle of indifference encounters the same problem illustrated by LaPlace in respect to the assignment of initial probabilities through the determination of possible outcomes. D'Alembert, it will be remembered, assigned equal probabilities to three possible outcomes of a game in which you win if you get one 'heads' out of two tosses of a coin. LaPlace argued that this was erroneous, since there are "actually" *four* possible outcomes, which, indifferently, should be assigned equal probabilities. One of D'Alembert's outcomes, "actually" concealed two possibilities, which ought to be put on a par with the other two.[32]

In its wider application, the principle of indifference refers to the equal distribution of probabilities in the manner suggested by LaPlace's correction. That is, when one envisions a process by which a set of rudimentary events can be produced, and one has no a priori reason to expect any one of the potential events to be favored in its occurrence (a situation that is usually guaranteed by definition), every event of the set should be considered equally likely. Nevertheless, this still puts the Reichenbach–von Mises approach in a dilemma: which events are equiprobable, those already selected (which constitute the n of the formula) or all those that can be potentially selected (which constitute the n approaching infinity)? Is this not the D'Alembert–LaPlace problem once again? Methods are employed to get around such difficulties; for example, the approach that determines the probability of ranges or classes of events rather than the point probability of individual events. But they seem rather more to obscure the problems than resolve them: what do we sum in order to obtain these class-probabilities?

Although he changed his mind later, Carnap found that, in its wider sense, the principle of indifference was acceptable.[33] He did, however, see a need for restricting the classes within which the whole set of elementary events, or properties are distributed. Otherwise we would still be led to contradictions of the type discussed above. To begin with, Carnap admitted that the principle of indifference in some form was needed in order to avoid, what he called, an "unlimited arbitrariness of choice of method."[34] The question was, which system of classification of events or properties would do? In an argument paralleling D'Alembert's, Carnap opted for the subdivision of events or properties that would be warranted by the universe of discourse in which we are conducting our experiment. For example, if we are only interested in the color of a ball selected from an urn, which ball of that color is of no interest. We are indifferent. The principle of indifference applies only within the categories of color (that is our universe of discourse), not among the individual balls.

Carnap sought to escape the consequences of the principle of indifference by resorting to the concept of symmetry. There are two points to be made here. First, the fundamental notion of the principle of indifference has managed to persist in this formulation. Secondly, the image of symmetry draws on the idea of a mechanical process not subject to human whim and bias. What is being claimed is that equiprobability can be found to be a feature of the world, independent of human appraisal.

It is instructive to consider an illuminating passage from Ayer's critique of Carnap's inductive theory of probability.[35] In his discussion, Ayer cites a parable devised by J.L. Watling, in which we are following a man along a road which divides into three branches: two continuing up a hill, one going down into a valley. On reaching this fork we find that the man is now out of sight. How do we determine the probability of his having taken the valley road?

Ayer remarks that, through the use of the concept of equal possibility (the "principle of indifference," although he does not say so), we might derive two quite different probability figures: $\frac{1}{3}$ if we consider all three roads equally likely; $\frac{1}{2}$ if we apply our indifference to the hill and the valley as possible destinations.

It is more than curious that the possibility that the person might turn back is ruled out. No doubt this is because the evidence is that he couldn't have, since you should have seen him on his way back. But then, wouldn't we be using Carnap's inductive theory without knowing it? The fundamental question remains. It is the one Carnap struggled with: what *are* the primitive events in this situation? If all possible channels of decision are to be included, then LaPlace's correction of D'Alembert's solution to his coin-tossing problem is applicable here also. Just as D'Alembert should not have ruled out a second toss if his objective was achieved on the first, so must Ayer (and Watling) include the abstractly possible decision to turn back.

As noted above, hidden in Ayer's treatment is the recognition that the situation is to be treated as one of conditional probability: probability given evidence that the man had not turned back. In this sense, the method of probability determination is very much like Carnap's inductive method.[36] The principle of indifference originally applicable to four outcomes is subsequently applied to three once one of these outcomes is ruled out by evidence.

Buridan's Ass

However, were there just four possibilities to begin with? What is particularly illuminating about this example is the fact that it is strikingly reminiscent of the parable of Buridan's Ass. There is one piece of information in Watling's imaginary experiment which makes it impossible to presume equiprobability: the man has disappeared beyond the crossroads. If the alternatives – whether three or four is of no moment here – were truly of equal probability, we should expect the man to be standing at the crossroads in a state of profound indecision.

In the version which has come down to us, the parable of Buridan's Ass describes a donkey starving between two equally attractive bundles of hay. It is perhaps no surprise to those familiar with the warping ways of history to learn that "Buridan's Ass" did not originate with the fourteenth-century philosopher. It was apparently proposed as a refutation of Buridan's theory of the will, and employed the figure of a dog rather than an ass.

In his entry on Buridan in the *Encyclopedia of Philosophy*, Nicholas Rescher says of "Buridan's Ass" that

> The example is not found in Buridan's extant writings but is based on an illustrative analogy in Aristotle's *De Caelo* (295b32) that became a standard item in the Aristotelian tradition, and occurs in the form of a dog starving between equally attractive portions of food . . .[37]

Rescher goes on to say that the form of the analogy, as it has come down to us, seems to have constituted an argument against Buridan's theory of will, namely, that the will acts on rational knowledge. If it cannot choose, because of a "symmetry of knowledge," it postpones its decision until further evidence tips the scales. In a sentiment reminiscent of Keynes' complaint that "in the long run we'll all be dead" the analogy seeks to ridicule the notion that the will operates according to Buridan's model. No one can afford to wait until "all the evidence is in."[38]

Sampling and Mechanical Symmetry

Rescher claims that a modern resolution of the problem posed by the parable would employ the strategy of, what amounts to, statistical sampling. In solving the problem of choosing between two identical-looking boxes, he advocates that we "make a choice by means of a selection process that is wholly impartial between box A and box B; that is, . . . choose randomly." Further on he concludes, "This line of reasoning establishes the thesis that *in the case of symmetrical knowledge, random choice is the reasonable policy.*" Thus the problem is "solved" by employing the concepts of symmetry and randomness. We shall now see that this way of approaching the problem is not much help in our donkey's dilemma.

An important characteristic of Rescher's solution is that it requires the selector to submit to a mechanical procedure based on the most schematic features of the selection problem. The choice is no longer a human decision, but a mechanical process.

The argument in favor of a mechanical procedure catches us in a vicious circle. As mentioned earlier regarding LaPlace's description of the procedure of tossing a "very thin" coin (see note 25), we have essentially an imaginary experiment. This "experiment" defines what must prevail if one is to arrive at precise mathematical predictions. The extent to which any actual performance conforms to these require-ments is the extent to which we are warranted in our expectations. What is put forward as a purely *de*scriptive note turns out to be a *pre*scriptive process. The acquisition and operation of a machine to produce events with equal probability is itself guided by the prior requirement that it must produce such events. For instance, Hacking, describing some "exquisitely well balanced" ancient Egyptian dice he was permitted to examine, comments: "Indeed, a couple of rather irregular looking ones were so well balanced as to suggest that they had been filed off at this or that corner to make them equiprobable."[39] Thus, we fiddle with the devices until they give us the outcomes we want.

The purely imaginary (and thus prescriptive) features of probability concepts, and the necessity of thus dealing with them at this foundational level, is illustrated when Polanyi employs a variant of Rescher's probability machine. His machine is "the Brownian movement of symmetrical solids," which he describes as follows:

> A perfectly unbiased die, resting on one of its six sides, will occasionally be tumbled over by an exceptionally violent Brownian shock. We can say that the chances of the die resting on any particular side are equal. The randomness of the impacts to which the die is subject transposes the orderliness of its cubic symmetry into the identical frequency of its six alternative stable positions. Such dynamic interaction between order and randomness is a necessary and sufficient condition for the applicability of probability statements to mechanical systems.[40]

The die is, in itself, inert. Its faces will not appear spontaneously. What we know of the die is that it is "perfectly unbiased." (Is this a description or a prescription concerning the die?) Polanyi shows further on that by this he means the die is absolutely symmetrical. But it is also absolutely neutral. To get any change in its state requires a force from outside. This force, however, also needs to be "perfectly unbiased." If it were not, it would yield biased results. The name for this perfectly unbiased force is *random*. Random selection is the dynamic side of the equation. We cannot get equiprobability from symmetrical dice alone. An unbounced die, no matter how unbiased, will show the same face forever. This interaction between unbiased objects and unbiased forces yields the expectation of equal probabilities. The issue takes us to the problem of sampling, "random" sampling.

All empirical concepts of probability are based on sampling procedures. There would be no need for probability if the burden of inquiry were simply to describe what was actually encountered. The proportions actually arrived at would be just that: descriptive accounts. Ordinarily, the data at hand are considered only a sample of all possible data: one could have something different in another selection from the pool of possible data.

Sampling methods emerge as procedural guidelines aimed at minimizing the hazards of synecdoche which accompany our leap from data to generalization. Random sampling is held to be the basis for all empirical inferences.[41] Even the purely logical theories of probability and, of course, all "tests of significance," endeavor to determine the outcomes of imagined random sampling as a means of arriving at decisions.

There is the tendency to contrast random events with rational events. Random is taken to mean disordered.[42] It describes the ultimate state of entropy the universe is itching for.[43] Now, the word *random* does come from a usage in which the sense of a disordered and wild state was paramount. The Oxford English Dictionary indicates that it was borrowed from Old French, in which it meant "impetuosity; great speed, force, or violence" in riding, running, striking and the like. In English it also took on the connotations of *aimless, without purpose, heedless and careless.* Yet, as the concept is actually used in statistical reasoning, random events are far from impetuous, ungoverned, irrational or disordered.

The *Dictionary of Statistical Terms* has this to say about the concept of "random" in statistics:

> This word may be taken as representing an undefined idea, or, if defined, must be expressed in terms of the concept of probability. A process of selection applied to a set of objects is said to be random if it gives to each one an equal chance of being chosen.[44]

The authors explain that "random" is used to denote processes which are probabilistic rather than deterministic. What we discover at work here is the round-robin of using "random" to arrive at the meaning of equiprobability, and equiprobability to arrive at the meaning of "random."

Furthermore, it is important to note the determinism hidden in the effort to guarantee randomness. For, as Kendall and Buckland observe in the entry for *random selection*: "Ordinary, haphazard or seemingly purposeless choice is generally insufficient to guarantee randomness when carried out by human beings and devices . . ." Indeed, it is not considered a human process at all. As Pedoe informs us: "all we can say of the adjective 'random' is that it is used to describe behavior which fits in with the mathematical theory of probability! Human beings cannot perform in a random manner."[45] What the statistician is trying to guarantee is strict equality of opportunity. We all know that this just doesn't happen by chance.

Random processes will not bail us out. The principle of indifference is at the heart of randomization, and this principle would put us in the same predicament as Buridan's Ass.

So much for random *selection*. What of the notion of randomly *produced* events in *nature*? Here, as we have seen in the discussion of Polanyi's "Brownian movements" device, the framework is similar to that suggested by Rescher. Selection should be rendered as a mechanical procedure: consider a mechanism that will produce events on a strictly random basis, and thus avoid the biases of human "will."

To begin with, in both the case of selection from an infinite population, and the nonselective production of an event from an infinite population, events have a zero probability of occurring. This is because any finite numerator divided by infinity is zero. Therefore, even aside from the enigma of the principle of indifference, we have here the logical expectation that nothing will occur. Nevertheless, there does seem to be a consensus that the whole edifice of probability theory would benefit from being cast in the framework of a mechanical model. This lies behind Carnap's switch from "equiprobability" to "symmetry." It is common to employ concepts borrowed from mechanics in probability theory. Such concepts as *moment* and *density* are used to define and derive probability distributions. Cramér, for example, states:

> Let us conceive the axis of X as an infinitely thin bar over which a *mass* of the total quantity 1 is distributed. The density of the mass may vary between different parts of the bar . . . we may thus say that any distribution function defines a *distribution of mass* which is distributed over the axis according to the d.f. $F(x)$. This will enable us to use certain well-known concepts and properties belonging to the field of elementary mechanics in order to illustrate the definitions and propositions of probability theory.[46]

If probabilities are equivalent to mass points, then symmetric probabilities are equivalent to mass points arranged symmetrically about a center. Now, how is it possible that this arrangement, in mechanics, should lead to a balanced, *inactive* system (unless, of course, it were "pushed" from the outside), while, in probability theory, it leads to a system so dynamic that it can continue to produce events indefinitely? If, in a given system, all probabilities are "symmetric," then that system cannot be self-starting. In order for it to produce events, it must be "pushed" from outside. But this outside force must itself be "random," otherwise it can bias the outcome. In order for *it* to be unbiased, it must also come from a symmetric system, which, in turn, requires an outside force. And so we have an infinite regress.

This point, and the anomaly of the use to which statisticians put the concepts they import from mechanics, is brought out in high relief when one considers how the notion of a random play of mechanical forces affects conclusions in the field of cosmology. For cosmologists realize that random systems go nowhere.[47] In fact, the theory of entropy is a theory of complete randomness, complete equalization, a state in which the whole universe has run down, and nothing can be expected to happen any more. We can only conclude that the principle of indifference, in any of its forms, is tantamount to a principle of entropy, and cannot logically be employed to analyze or explain how systems generate events.

The Principle of Producibility

The systems of equiprobability which we ecnounter in our statistical work do, however, seem to produce these events. And this is the dilemma: conceptually, we need a system of indifference, in the absence of any other argument for the assignment of weights, but then nothing should occur. Meanwhile, actually, something does occur (a sample is actually selected, for instance). The latter fact had long masked the former. What this situation seems to require is a reconceptualization of the whole problem, in which, first of all, there should be a place for true equiprobability – recognizing that, where there is no preference there is no selection: and secondly, as Polanyi notes in *Personal Knowledge*,[48] personal commitment plays a central role in our approach to stochastic events.

Polanyi's argument is based on the doctrine that each event, or each point-probability, is as likely or unlikely as any other in the set. The claim that a given outcome, such as the arrangement of stones to shape letters and words, cannot be due to chance because the probability of this arrangement is "vanishingly small," leaves one open to the alternate claim that *any* specific distribution of these stones cannot be due to chance. This is because they all have a "vanishingly small" probability of being just so.[49]

Polanyi points out that the difference between the first and the second case lies in our interest. The meaningful arrangement is of interest, while the meaningless ones are not. Thus, to argue that an outcome of interest to us may not be due to chance is not to make a statistically significant statement, but a personally significant statement. A fact which leads Polanyi to draw attention to "our participation in chance events."[50]

We *make* events happen. We even make them happen in required ratios. We, in effect, force nature to make a choice where she would really rather not. Is this not implied in Gardner's statement concerning quantum physics, that "the photon's wave function dictates that at the *moment of measurement* nature decides to give it a plus or minus spin with equal probability"?[51] As Zukav describes it, probability functions ("waves") are generated in subatomic physical systems *until we decide to make an observation*. At this moment the wave "collapses." All potential events become zero-probability excepting one, the one that occurs, which is (has?) a probability of 1.[52] A more homely example might be: The probability "wave" of all the potential outcomes of the roll of a die "collapses" when I, in fact, roll it. The potential of all the outcomes become zero excepting the one which occurs. In this conception, left to itself, "nature" would be a lot of probability waves waiting for us to do something, to make up our minds.

Our abhorrence for the nothing-happens outcome of our experiments is well illustrated by some work on coalitions in triads discussed by Caplow. It would be instructive for us to look at Caplow's treatment of the subject from the point of view of "rational" expectations.[53] One of the conditions under which triad-generated coalitions were studied involved the equal "strength" of each player at the outset of the game – what Caplow calls the "Type I" triad. Under the conditions of the game (as devised by Vinacke and Arkoff) all of the three possible coalitions, AB, AC, BC, were equally likely. The results of the experiment included the following for Type I triads:

Coalition	Number of games observed
AB	33
AC	17
BC	30
No coalitions	10
Total	90

Caplow accepted this finding as a vindication of his expectation concerning the Type I triad: all three coalition partnerships should be equally frequent. Although he does admit that Vinacke and Arkoff could not explain why AC is under-represented, "and," he continues, "neither can we."[54] Now, if the essence of this triadic type is such that all three possible coalitions are equally attractive, likely or probable, why should we not expect all the outcomes to be ones in which no coalition takes place? Ten such cases turn up in the experiment. Are these anomalies?

Curiously, Caplow himself skirmishes with the problem later on. Analyzing coalition strategies from the point of view of players' "rational" assessment of their tasks, he comments:

> ... the "rational" strategy whereby each player considers the other two as equally unattractive partners and invites them to bid against each other for his support leads to infinitely prolonged bidding . . . *if the players demonstrate the "strict rationality" demanded of them the bidding never ceases; no coalition is ever formed and no game is played to the end.*[55]

At this juncture Caplow cites research in which this actually happened. Lieberman found that, stymied by a purely rational approach to a game, participants could reason themselves into a state of indecision.[56] Caplow's response to this conundrum is more akin to annoyance than appreciation. In an effort to point out that rationality can be unreasonable, he goes on to say: ". . . like the ass of Buridan, they must find an irrational principle of selection or remain immobile between two equal opportunities."[57]

Once we acknowledge Caplow's insight here, the situation becomes crystal clear: The overriding consideration, the "frame," to use Goffman's conception,[58] is that the game be played. And there are some situations in which we must violate the strict rules of the game in order to "play" it. This is not uncommon, for we often relax the rules in order to keep a "game" going. Purely rational moves dictated by the game are overruled by a commitment that comes from outside the game itself.[59]

We have seen how the modern concept of probability grew out of an earlier sense in which it meant "attested to," or "testimony."[60] From there the sense wandered in several directions. Thus, both *prove* and *approval* stem from the same root meaning of testimonial. By Galileo's time, the term *probable* was already migrating from meaning the "testimony" of people, to the "testimony" of the senses, to the "testimony" of nature. The catachresis was complete. Thus being depersonalized, a metaphorical use became the dominant sense. What is needed is an attempt to recapture the personal nature of probability processes, because the rhetorical voice of science, as rational, impersonal, and objective, spoken through its statistical language, masks the central role of personal involvement.

Whether we see it as a conscious sampling or a mechanical process of production, a state of true equiprobability implies only one thing: perfectly suspended action. Nevertheless, initial probability assumptions are necessary, and equiprobability – or symmetry – does recommend itself. This is especially true of null-hypothesis formulations. What's more, such schemes seem to work. This state of affairs is not unlike that which prevailed in the eighteenth century, when the "natural philosophers" of the day were confronted with Bishop George Berkeley's ironclad and devastating criticism of Newton's concept of the "infinitesimal."[61] Because Newton's new "method of the fluxions" was much too useful to be rejected by reason of a mere logical contradiction, the scientific community chose to ignore Berkeley's argument.

For our part, we see that it is necessary, in statistical analysis, to make a complementary assumption regarding producibility within the context of equiprobable expectations. Therefore, while indifference may abstractly produce probabilities and just as abstractly allow purely mathematical manipulations, no stochastic scheme can be indifferent to the need to produce one of the events in question, despite the acknowledgement that, if there is no preference, there is no selection. This state of affairs can be summed up as a principle of producibility, which states: "in a completely random system, no event can be expected to occur unless it is produced by a force from outside that system."

This is precisely what has occurred in quantum physics. It is at the heart of the claim of the new physics that ours is a "participatory universe."[62] Capra, perhaps, expresses it best, when he writes: "The crucial feature of quantum theory is that the observer is not only necessary to observe the properties of an atomic phenomenon, but is necessary even to bring about these properties,"[63]

What producibility refers to is the crucial fact that we make the a priori decision that something *must* occur in our model of sampling events, either because something already has occurred (in whatever proportion) and we are trying to account for it, or because our procedure, our interest, our personal involvement, require the production of events.

Here we clearly see the strategic presence of that personal commitment which Polanyi finds so essential to all scientific work. One important characteristic of this personal commitment is that it is largely unspecified and unspecifiable.[64] This is because, to use Polanyi's terminology, the *focus* of our commitment gathers up *subsidiary particulars* which remain necessarily subliminal while they act instrumentally in achieving our focal purpose.

This inquiry into the purely conceptual structure of statistical reasoning shows that the commitment on the part of the participants is absolutely essential to the production of the presumably "stochastic" events being analyzed. While this commitment must conform to the rational "expectations" constituted by the discourse of investigation, it is not – cannot – itself be motivated by the discourse alone, for to do so is self-immobilizing.

Notes

1   Ursula LeGuin, "Schrödinger's cat," in *The Compass Rose* (Harper and Row, New York, 1982), p. 47.

2   To borrow a term from the Burkean lexicon. See William H. Rueckert, *Kenneth Burke and the Drama of Human Relations*, 2nd edn (University of California Press, Berkeley, 1982), pp. 208–10, who describes the *representative anecdote* as "the archetypal myth, the perfect imitation of the pure essence." It should be noted in passing that this conforms quite well with Thomas Kuhn's concept of *exemplar*, which was one of the more important senses in which he used the term "paradigm." See T.S. Kuhn, *The Essential Tension* (University of Chicago Press, Chicago, 1977), ch. 12, "Second thoughts on paradigms." An informative discussion of the concept can be found in Jeffrey Barg, "On exemplars," unpublished manuscript, Department of Speech, Temple University, 1986.

3 For an illuminating challenge to this perception of Galileo (and of science in general), see Paul Feyerabend, *Against Method* (Verso, London, 1978) and Harold I. Brown, *Perception, Theory, and Commitment* (University of Chicago Press, Chicago, 1977).

4 T.S. Kuhn, *The Structure of Scientific Revolutions*, enlarged 2nd edn (University of Chicago Press, Chicago, 1970). Also see Feyerabend, *Against Method*; Michael A. Overington, "Doing the what comes rationally: some developments in meta-theory," *American Sociologist*, 14 (1979), pp. 2–12; Richard H. Brown, "Theories of rhetoric and rhetorics of theory," *Social Research*, 50 (1983), pp. 126–37; and Donald N. McCloskey, *The Rhetoric of Economics* (University of Wisconsin Press, Madison, 1985).

5 See Ludwig Wittgenstein, *Philosophical Investigations*, tr. G.E.M. Anscombe (Basil Blackwell, Oxford, 1968); David Bloor, *Knowledge and Social Imagery* (Routledge and Kegan Paul, London, 1976), especially ch. 5; and Phillip J. Davis and Reuben Hersh, *The Mathematical Experience* (Penguin, Harmondsworth, 1983), who refer to "the rhetoric found in the introduction to logic texts" (p. 356). Both books cite the mathematician, Imre Lakatos, and his discussion of the human factor in the work of mathematicians. Davis and Hersh are especially appreciative of Lakatos' argument that mathematicians at work follow neither a "Platonist" nor "Formalist" program: "The actual situation is this . . . we have real mathematics, with proofs which are established by 'consensus of the qualified.' A real proof is not checkable by a machine, or even by any mathematician not privy to the gestalt, the mode of thought of the particular field of mathematics in which the proof is located" (p. 354).

6 See, for example, Aaron Cicourel, *Method and Measurement in Sociology* (Collier-Macmillan/Free Press, New York, 1964); J.M. Skipper Jr, A.L. Guenther, and G. Nass, "The sacredness of .05," *American Sociologist*, 2 (1967), pp. 16–18; D.E. Morrison and R.E. Henkel, "Significance tests reconsidered," *American Sociologist*, 4 (1969), pp. 131–40; William Filstead (ed.), *Qualitative Methodology* (Markham, Chicago, 1970); and Joseph Fashing and Ted Goertzel, "The myth of the normal curve," *Humanity and Society*, 5 (1981), pp. 14–31. For an account of the discovery of this rhetorical voice in econometrics, see Frank T. Denton, "The significance of significance: rhetorical aspects of hypothesis testing in economics," paper read at the Conference on Rhetoric in Economics, Wellesley College, April, 1986.

7 Placed between two equally attractive bales of hay, the donkey starves to death, because neither bale is attractive enough to out-pull the attraction of the other. The relevance of this parable is discussed later in the essay.

8 See, for example, Edward H. Madden (ed.), *The Structure of Scientific Thought* (Houghton Mifflin, Boston, 1960); Rudolf Carnap, *Logical Foundations of Probability*, 2nd edn (University of Chicago Press, Chicago, 1962); I.J. Good, *The Estimation of Probabilities: An Essay on Modern Bayesian Methods* (MIT Press, Cambridge, 1968); A.J. Ayer, *Probability and Evidence* (Macmillan, New York, 1972); and Ian Hacking, *The Emergence of Probability* (Cambridge University Press, Cambridge, 1975).

9 Carnap, *Logical Foundations of Probability*, pp. 186–7.

10 Hacking, *The Emergence of Probability*.

11 See, for example, Fritjof Capra, *The Tao of Physics* (Shambhala, Berkeley, 1975); F. Capra, *The Turning Point* (Bantam, New York, 1982); Gary Zukav, *The Dancing Wu Li Masters* (Bantam, New York, 1979); and Martin Gardner, "Quantum weirdness," *Discover*, Oct. (1982), pp. 69–75.

12   Capra, *The Turning Point*, p. 87.

13   Obviously, the game itself, which generated the "objective" possibilities in the first place, is subjective in that the rules of the game are conventional and arbitrary. More precisely, the game is an *inter*subjective entity, which, if we accept the argument of philosophers of science such as Karl Popper in *The Logic of Scientific Discovery* (Basic Books, New York, 1959), pp. 44–5, is what scientific "objectivity" comes down to. We note, then, two kinds of objectivity; one which postulates the existence of things, regardless of our conception of them, the other which is (symbolically) embedded in our conception of things. Some remarks on this can be found in my "The Pythagorean comma: Weber's anticipation of sociology in a new key," *Human Studies*, 3 (1980), pp. 115–36.

14   According to Hacking, who in *The Emergence of Probability* traces the history of this process of depersonalization, the present-day concept shares a pedigree with such terms as *approval* (ap*prob*ation) and *attestation*. From Galileo to Leibniz there was a shift from "probability" as the testimony of persons to "probability" as the testimony of nature.

15   Pierre Simon, Marquis de LaPlace, *A Philosophical Essay on Probabilities*, tr. from the 6th French edn by F.W. Truscott and F.L. Emory (Dover, New York, 1951). First publ. 1796.

16   Hacking, *The Emergence of Probability*, p. 122.

17   See Ibid., ch. 14.

18   See Ayer, *Probability and Evidence*, p. 29.

19   LaPlace, *A Philosophical Essay*, pp. 11–12.

20   Albert Pierce, *Fundamentals of Nonparametric Statistics* (Dickerson Publishing Co., Belmont, CA, 1970), p. 31.

21   Michael Polanyi speaks of this purely symbolic, Kantian sense of objectivity in his *Personal Knowledge* (University of Chicago Press, Chicago, 1962), ch. 1.

22   D. Pedoe, *The Gentle Art of Mathematics* (English Universities Press, London, 1958), p. 42. What is "evident" is that two *possibilities* are considered to be *twice as likely* as one.

23   Or, in the conception promoted by philosophers of language, "constituted" by the rules of the game. See, for example, John Searle, "What is a speech-act?," in Pier Paolo Giglioli (ed.), *Language and Social Context* (Penguin, New York, 1972), pp. 136–57.

24   LaPlace, *A Philosophical Essay*, p. 11.

25   We also run into a conceptual inelegance here. First of all, by postulating a "very thin" coin, LaPlace intended to rule out any effects of the thickness of the coin on the "experiment." Secondly, the indifference of outcome is bought at the price of a contradiction, since "two *perfectly* similar" faces are both logically and practically indistinguishable. No amount of scrutiny could reveal which side was up. Furthermore, the tossing procedures themselves would have to be unbiased, independent events – a fact which LaPlace does address himself to (more on this in the discussion of "sampling," below). Because the question of "independence" is not particularly relevant to the main argument, it will not be dealt with here. It may suffice to say that the extent to which an "event" is a "significant form" is the extent to which its independence cannot be postulated. On "significant form" see Susanne K. Langer, *Philosophy in a New Key*, 3rd edn (Harvard University Press, Cambridge, 1957), ch. 8. Also, see Michael Polanyi, *Personal Knowledge*, pp. 37–40, on "significant pattern," in his discussion of probability.

26 John Maynard Keynes, *Treatise on Probability* (Macmillan, New York, 1963), first publ. 1921; Rudolf Carnap, *Logical Foundations of Probability*.

27 LaPlace had not formally introduced this principle. It was only later that it achieved the status of a conscious requirement. Carnap traces it back through Jeffreys to Keynes. Carnap, "Statistical and inductive probability," in Edward H. Madden (ed.), *The Structure of Scientific Thought* (Houghton Mifflin, Boston, 1960), pp. 269–84; Harold Jeffreys, *Theory of Probability*, 3rd edn (Clarendon, Oxford, 1961), first publ. 1939; and Keynes, *Treatise on Probability*.

28 See Alfred North Whitehead, "The first physical synthesis," in Madden (ed.), *Structure of Scientific Thought*, p. 47, and R.B. Lindsay and H. Margenau, *Foundations of Physics* (Dover, New York, 1957), pp. 73–5, first publ. 1936.

29 A.J. Ayer, "The conception of probability as a logical relation," in Madden (ed.), *Structure of Scientific Thought*, pp. 279–84; and Ayer, *Probability and Evidence*.

30 Ayer, *Probability and Evidence*, p. 55.

31 Ibid., p. 46.

32 For a general statement on his problem, see ibid., pp. 34–5.

33 "Statistical and inductive probability," in Madden (ed.), *Structure of Scientific Thought*. Madden notes that this essay was originally published as a pamphlet dated 1955.

34 *Ibid.*, p. 276.

35 Ayer, *Probability and Evidence*, p. 35.

36 And, thus, would vindicate D'Alembert against LaPlace. For the object of the game is not to toss the coin twice, but to determine whether one wins or loses. There is no interest in the second toss if the wager is already determined on the first. D'Alembert, then, could be said to be more faithful to the *evidence* than LaPlace.

37 Nicholas Rescher, "Jean Buridan," in Paul Edwards (ed.), *Encyclopedia of Philosophy*, (Macmillan/Free Press, New York, 1967). Nor is this an entirely fanciful image. In an article on "instrumental learning," Casler cites cases of induced "anxiety" in which laboratory animals would fall into a state of such deep indecision that they, as he says, "may even starve to death." Lawrence Casler, "Instrumental learning," in David L. Sills (ed.), *International Encyclopedia of the Social Sciences*, (Macmillan/Free Press, New York, 1968), pp. 131–5.

38 The issue is one that has challenged rhetoricians from the beginning. *Does* the will act solely on rational knowledge? *Should* it? *Can* it? *Mere* rhetoric has been derided as an appeal to irrational impulses, yet it has long been known that pure rationality is *unreasonable*. On the distinction between the reasonable and the rational in law, see Chaim Perelman "The rational and the reasonable," in T.F. Geraets (ed.), *Rationality Today* (University of Ottawa Press, Ottawa, 1979), pp. 213–34.

39 Hacking, *Emergence of Probability*, p. 4.

40 Polanyi, *Personal Knowledge*, p. 39.

41 Another term used is "fair" sampling. See Ayer, *Probability and Evidence*, p. 25.

42 Polanyi considers the concept to be essentially undefinable, claiming that "it is logically impossible to give any precise definition of randomness." He argues that, if randomness means unexpected (in that a prior event will not tell what the next event will be), then no definition of a random process is possible. This is because, once defined, one could then logically determine the sequence of events it produces. Randomness is achieved, he claims, through a *tacit* process, not a logically explicit one. See Polanyi, *Personal Knowledge*, pp. 33–8; 390–3. This flies in the face of the now common practice of using computer-based algorithms to generate random numbers. Wichman and Hill, who promote their own algorithm, do, however,

admit that "The random number sequences that computers produce are not truly random at all, since true randomness depends upon having a random process available. . . ." All the computer processes *recycle* at some point, and thus cannot be said to be random (Brian Wichmann and David Hill, "Building a random-number generator," *Byte*, Mar. (1987), p. 127.

43 See Norbert Wiener, *The Human Use of Human Beings*, 2nd edn (Doubleday, Garden City, NY, 1954), pp. 28–32.

44 M.G. Kendall and W.R. Buckland (eds), *A Dictionary of Statistical Terms* (Hafner, New York, 1960).

45 Pedoe, *The Gentle Art of Mathematics*, p. 37. There is a parallel between the status of the concept of probability among mathematicians and the status of ideal types in social science. For the mathematician, the meaning of probability is set by its *mathematical* properties, not properties it may have in the real world. Thus, probabilities have the property of being between 0 and 1, and further, follow a Boolean logic of operations. Just *what* in the real world might exhibit such properties is not of mathematical concern. See Pedoe, *The Gentle Art of Mathematics*, for a discussion of this point as it was played out in arguments over the eighteenth century puzzle called the "St Petersburg Paradox."

46 Harald Cramér, *The Elements of Probability Theory* (Wiley, New York, 1955), pp. 58–9.

47 On this, see, for, example, Herman Weyl, "Symmetry," in James R. Newman (ed.), *The World of Mathematics*, vol. 1 (Simon and Schuster, New York, 1956); E.R. Harrison, "The mystery of structure in the universe," in L.L. Whyte, A.G. Wilson, and D. Wilson (eds) *Hierarchical Structures* (American Elsevier, New York, 1969); and Paul Weiss, "The living system: determinism stratified," in A. Koestler and J.R. Smythies (eds), *Beyond Reductionism* (Hutchinson, London, 1969).

48 Polanyi, *Personal Knowledge*, ch. 2.

49 Ibid., pp. 33–6.

50 Ibid., p. 21.

51 Martin Gardner, "Quantum weirdness," p. 74, emphasis mine.

52 Gary Zukav, *The Dancing Wu Li Masters*, pp. 72–5.

53 Theodore Caplow, *Two against One* (Prentice-Hall, New York, 1968), ch. 3.

54 Ibid., p. 25.

55 Ibid., p. 26, emphasis mine.

56 Bernhardt Lieberman, "*i*-trust: a notion of trust in three-person games and international affairs," *Journal of Conflict Resolution*, 8 (1964), pp. 271–80.

57 Caplow, *Two against One*, p. 27. In other words, there is a kind of madness in rationally fixating on the rules of the game. A perceptive player may subtly – or even unconsciously – change systems when the one at hand gets you in trouble if you should follow its precepts to, as Kenneth Burke says, "the end of the line."

58 Erving Goffman, *Frame Analysis* (Harper and Row, New York, 1974).

59 Feyerabend makes this point in his discussion of how the game of science has been historically played. Paul Feyerabend, *Against Method*, p. 167.

60 Hacking, *Emergence of Probability*, ch. 3.

61 See Bishop George Berkeley, "The analyst," in James R. Newman (ed.), *The World of Mathematics*, vol. 1 (Simon and Schuster, New York, 1956), pp. 288–93.

62 See, for example, Gardner, "Quantum weirdness," p. 72.

63 Capra, *Turning Point*, p. 86.

64 Polanyi, *Personal Knowledge*, pp. 59–65.

5

The Rhetorical Invention of Scientific Invention: The Emergence and Transformation of a Social Norm

Alan G. Gross

In a series of masterly essays, Robert K. Merton develops the thesis that conflicts over priority in science are not, as had been assumed, the product of unfortunate personal aberrations. They constitute instead a strategic research site for sociological analysis, one that opens a path to the paradox at the heart of the scientific enterprise, the paradox of communal competitiveness: while the general progress of scientific knowledge depends heavily on the relative subordination of individual efforts to communal goals, the career progress of scientists depends solely on the recognition of their individual efforts. This paradox, and the priority conflicts it engenders, were not always a part of scientific activity; they are a historical phenomenon, one whose origin can be traced to England in the middle of the seventeenth century, a time when men deliberated about science, and changed their minds concerning the social structure most appropriate to its advance. In the seventeenth century, the social norms of science changed.

While Merton's work exemplifies the need for sociological analysis to identify the structural conditions facilitative of such changes, norms themselves emerge and gain (or lose) support in contexts in which rhetorical analysis seems not only appropriate, but necessary to avoid charges of serious incompleteness. For Clifford Geertz, it is only through the interaction of social forces and rhetoric that "ideologies transform sentiment into significance and so make it socially available" (Geertz, 1973: 207, 212–13; see also Collins, 1975; Gieryn, 1983; Gilbert and Mulkay, 1984; Gusfield, 1976; Turner, 1978, 1982; Woolgar, 1980). Working within rhetorical theory, Thomas Farrell describes the same process of transformation, one by which social consensus initially attributed by speakers to audiences produces social norms.

To Farrell this emergence, this "ability of rhetorical transactions gradually to generate what they can initially only assume appears to possess a rather magical ambience" (1976: 11). The purpose of this chapter is to dispel this "ambience," to translate magic into rhetorical analysis. The case chosen is deliberately one already subjected to extensive sociological scrutiny. This re-examination, this parallel critical excursion, by making as clear as possible the contrast between rhetorical and sociological analyses, should highlight the value of the former in explaining social change.

The facts are not in dispute. At the beginning of the seventeenth century, scientists generally worked independently, disseminating the results of their efforts by means of correspondence and an occasional book. From time to time, a scientist might show concern for the order of discovery. But such concern was not an institutional norm. By the end of the century, the situation was radically different: concern for priority in discovery had become just such a norm, with prior journal publication its criterion.

This tale of competition begins with Bacon's vision of a scientific enterprise based entirely on cooperation. The Royal Society is founded in the spirit of this cooperative vision, but neither Sprat's vigorous propaganda on the Society's behalf, nor the Society's actual early history are free from competitive strains: conflicts over priority surface early on. With the controversy between Newton and Leibniz over priority in the invention of the calculus, a controversy that comes to a head at the beginning of the following century, the competitive strain becomes so clearly dominant that it threatens to undermine the purpose of the enterprise. At this crucial point, the influence of larger social forces, of capitalism and imperialism, impinges, and shapes the conflict. After some exploration, the Society chooses dated journal publication as its criterion of priority: the reward system of modern science is in place. But the success of this criterion in managing conflict is not without cost: competition for priority misrepresents the growth of scientific knowledge, and threatens the ethos of science by shifting the concern of scientists from knowledge to its rewards.

It is the thesis of this chapter that we may without exaggeration characterize the foregoing narrative as the rhetorical invention of scientific invention: the story of the emergence and transformation of a social norm is unequivocally a tale of persuasion.

Bacon's Cooperative Vision in *New Atlantis*

That this rhetorical story begins with a work of fiction necessitates some explanation of the scope of rhetoric: *New Atlantis* (1627) is a Utopian novel, not an argument. But for Aristotle rhetoric is not about argument only: it is about *all* the means of persuasion. *New Atlantis* is a novel with a difference: it makes the claim that a society is best when founded on the advance of science through cooperation; it persuades, not through argument, but through its vivid presentation of the benefits of that society. Salomon's House is the intellectual center of the island kingdom of Bensalem. Its goals are lofty: "the knowledge of

Causes and secret motions of things, and the enlarging of the bounds of Human Empire, to the effecting of all things possible" (p. 480). In pursuit of these goals, the members of Salomon's House perform many of the functions later entrusted to the Royal Society: the members hold meetings, communicate regularly with each other, and publish their results.

At Salomon's House, science is entirely a cooperative activity, pursued according to a firm division of labor: experimenting and the making of inferences are, for example, entrusted to different groups of workers. The science of Salomon's House is, moreover, cooperative in a larger sense; it is a transnational activity, entirely free from any taint of nationalism or imperialism: "we maintain a trade . . . only for God's first creature, which was *Light*" (p. 469).[1] The reference to Deity is apposite: even science is a form of worship: "for the laws of nature are [God's] own laws" (p. 459). In Bensalem, science is an activity totally in harmony with itself, with society at large, and with God's purposes, and it is in no way subordinate to the political purposes of the state (p. 489). Although the discovery of new knowledge is not a competitive activity – there is no competition anywhere in Bensalem – discoverers are singled out for honor and reward.

In *New Atlantis*, Bacon uses metaphor to underline the highmindedness of the Utopian vision that is his persuasive vehicle. He does this by varying the distance between tenor and vehicle in his metaphors, adjusting "the difficult and elusive relationship between A and B."[2] For example, throughout *New Atlantis*, Bacon uses light as a metaphor for intellectual and spiritual illumination. In this comparison, there is no ideational distance betwen light and the creative act. It is as in *Genesis*: "God said, Let there be light, and there was light." But in this same work Bacon compares scientific communication (the tenor) to trade (the vehicle); in addition, he compares the increase in scientific knowledge (the tenor) to the advance of Empire (the vehicle). In the latter cases, however, he uses these comparisons only to increase the ideational distance between science and both trade and imperialism: the trade is in light, the Empire human.

Potential Conflict in Sprat

Before the founding of the Royal Society in 1662, Englishmen published numerous schemes for the advancement of science, schemes whose obvious parent was Salomon's House in *New Atlantis* (see Jones, 1961: 170–6, 317). Sprat's *History of the Royal Society*, published just five years subsequent to the founding of the Society, is in this tradition. It is less the history than the manifesto of that organization; as such, it is a clear embodiment in argument of the

Baconian myth that sees national and transnational cooperation as the ideal truth-seeking procedure in the natural sciences (pp. 99ff.). Sprat notes "how much progress may be made by a form'd and Regular *Assembly*" that coordinates "the joynt force of many men" of all ranks, Englishmen who "*work* and *think* in company, and confer their help to each others' *Inventions*" (pp. 28, 39, 427). These cooperative goals are not confined to England. Science prospers "when it becomes the care of united Nations" (p. 3). Cooperation so all-encompassing implies a free exchange of information across national borders: "the benefit of a universal *Correspondence*, and *Communication*" (p. 424).

But in *The History of the Royal Society* another voice is also clearly heard, a voice at odds with the spirit of cooperation:

> *Invention* is an *Heroic* thing, and plac'd above the reach of a low, and vulgar *Genius*. . . . a thousand difficulties must be contemn'd, with which a mean heart would be broken . . . some irregularities, and excesses must be granted it, that would hardly be pardon'd by the severe *Rules of Prudence*. (p. 392)

A view of invention so hyperbolic, a stance so obviously motivated by the "desire of glory" (p. 74), is incompatible with Utopian cooperation. Even more jarring to the spirit of cooperation is Sprat's transformation of discovery into a form of capital whose owner needs better protection from society: "while those that add some small matter to things begun, are usually inrich'd thereby; the *Discoverers* themselves have seldom found any other entertainment than contempt and impoverishment. . . . The fruits of their *Studies* are frequently alienated from their Children" (p. 401). In Sprat's myth, in contrast to Bacon's, the heroic and the commercial are indissolubly linked: fellows will "reap the most *solid honor*"; but they "will also receive the strongest assurances, of still retaining the *greatest part of the profit*" (p. 75).

Sprat's other, competitive, voice also reaches beyond national borders: scientific advance is an integral component of England's imperialist destiny. The English character is best suited both to science and to command, indeed, to Empire (pp. 113–15, 420). England, therefore, "may justly lay claim, to be the Head of a *Philosophical league*, above all other Countries in *Europe*" (p. 113); London, moreover, is its ideal center: "the head of a *mighty Empire*, the greatest that ever commanded the *Ocean*" (p. 87). Imperialism and science work together: scientific advance can materially aid "the advancing of *Commerce*, as the best means . . . to enlarge their *Empire*" (p. 408): "if ever the *English* will attain to the *Mastery* of *Commerce*, not only in *discours*, but *reality*: they must begin it by their *labors*, as well as by their *swords*" (p. 423).

When Sprat is praising cooperation, he uses trade and imperialism in a Baconian fashion, as vehicles for metaphors that create ideational distance between these activities and natural science, an activity whose purpose is "*to increase the Powers of all Mankind, and to free them from the bondage of Errors, . . .*[a] *greater Glory than to enlarge* Empire" (unnumbered Epistle Dedicatory):

> By their *naturalizing* Men of all Countries, [the Royal Society has] laid the beginnings of many great advantages for the future. For by this means, they will be able, to settle a *constant Intelligence*, throughout all civil Nations; and make the *Royal Society* the general *Banck*, and Free-port of the World: a policy, which whether it would hold good, in the *Trade* of *England*, I know not: but sure it will in the *Philosophy* [natural science]. (p. 64)

Indeed, in contrast with the imperialist wars of the times, the progress of science is depicted as a war of "all civil Nations" against "*Ignorance, and False Opinions*" (p. 57).[3] But when Sprat is waxing patriotic, matters are quite otherwise. England's command over the seas has as its purpose "to bring home matter for *new Sciences*, and to make the same proportion of Discoveries above others, in the *Intellectual* Globe, as they have done in the *Material*" (p. 86).

The aims mirrored in these passages are only potentially in conflict. There is no indication that Sprat – or anyone else at the time – noticed any incompatibility between the cooperative and transnational aims of the Society, and the subordination of science to the national and imperial ambitions of England: no one, it seems, foresaw the oxymoronic potential of a *transnational* society funded under *royal* auspices. In all probability, for neither Sprat nor for the founders was this subordination anything more than another argument for the social support of science, one that was, at the same time, a laudable expression of an emerging patriotism. An author can refuse intellectual engagement, albeit at the price of some coherence; but an actual social group simultaneously pursuing cooperation and competition, transnationalism and imperialism, is plainly on a collision course with itself.

From Potentially Conflicting Aims to Actually Conflicting Norms: The Newton–Leibniz Dispute

Unquestionably, in the minds of its founders, and of its first Secretary, Henry Oldenburg, the Royal Society embodied the twin virtues of cooperation and transnationalism, the essence of Bacon's vision, the burden of Sprat's argument. In Oldenburg's words: "The object of science [is] of so vast an extent, that it demand[s] the united genius of more than one nation to exhaust the subject" (Birch, vol. I: 317). To Huygens of Holland, Oldenburg wrote that "There is no doubt at all that, if we press onwards at a steady pace, maintaining a frank and regular correspondence for our mutual benefit, we shall in time see considerable progress in every branch of science" (vol. V: 583). To

René Sluse, the Flemish mathematician, he addressed the following hyberbolic peroration:

> Throw your lot in with us, as the French and Italians have done. We earnestly pray that all your people, all Germany, and the whole of the Netherlands may associate their labors with ours. (vol. III: 537–8)

Throughout his voluminous correspondence, Oldenburg's indefatigable efforts in recruiting and encouraging all scientists, English and Continental, are everywhere apparent (vol. III: 535–8; vol. IV: 419–24; see also vol. VII: 259–60 and 336–8). Indeed, so trusted on the Continent was the Society under the stewardship of its first Secretary – its last European Secretary – that Oldenburg was able to mediate, if not always to resolve, disputes, including disputes over priority, most of which were between Englishmen and their Continental counterparts.

Such disputes arose as a matter of course when the conflicting rhetorical aims in Sprat's *History* became actual social norms, real standards of behavior among the first Fellows and correspondents, men who simultaneously worked for and against each others' interests. Even during the first years of the Society, problems of scientific ownership appeared (Oldenburg, vol. II: 291, 486). And, despite the ready availability of a register of discoveries, priority disputes broke out regularly: between Hooke and Newton; Hooke and Auzout; Huygens, and Wallis and Wren; Huygens and Wallis; van Heuraet and Neile; Huygens and Hooke; Wren and Auzot; Hooke and Mercator (Westfall, 1984: 446–52; Oldenburg, vol. II: xxii; vol. V: 374–5; vol. X: xxiv, xxvi, 73; Birch, vol. IV: 58, 84–6).

Hooke and Newton, Wallis and Wren – these disputing pairs were Englishmen. In the other disputes, however, the conflict was not only between scientists, but between England and the Continent. In a letter to Oldenburg, John Wallis, the English mathematician, disowned competitive motives on the part of his fellow countrymen: "Whatever may be thought of the French or the Dutch", certainly the English are not thus given to continual pursuit of fame" (Oldenburg, vol. X: 4).[4] But his more usual views belied these Utopian sentiments:

> Onely I could wish that those of our own Nation; were a little more forward than I find them generally to bee (especially the most considerable) in timely publishing their own Discoveries, & not let strangers [foreigners] reape ye glory of what those amongst ourselves are ye Authors. (Oldenburg, vol. III: 373; vol. X: 41–3, 282; see also vol. IX: 377–8; and Newton, Corres., vol. I: 73; vol. IV: 100)

These international disputes reached their climax in the quarrel between Newton and Leibniz over priority in the discovery of the calculus.

According to the social theory favored by Victor Turner, this quarrel was a social drama.[5] In so far as they participate in such a dispute, the actors in a social drama live, not by ordinary, but dramatic time, and exhibit not everyday, but heightened responses (Turner, 1982: 9–10). Although social dramas have identifiable acts or stages, in a drama as complex and as lengthy as the calculus dispute, it would be futile to try to map these precisely onto the actual sequence of events (Turner, 1978: 79). This lack of perfect correspondence, however, does not vitiate the theory as an explanation of the text with which we are now concerned, the "Account of the Book entituled *Commercium Epistolicum*," an anonymous summary of the calculus dispute published in the *Transactions* of the Royal Society in 1715. The "Account" is clearly a form of redress, the stage at which the representatives of a society try to come to terms with the fundamental cleavages that have driven a particular social drama to crisis (Turner, 1982: 69–70, 78).

The calculus dispute came to a head in the second decade of the eighteenth century. In 1712, under the press of events, the President of the Royal Society convened an international committee to investigate the twenty-year controversy between Newton and Leibniz concerning priority in the invention of the calculus. Within fifty days, they reported in Newton's favor, condemned Leibniz, and issued in evidence a collection of documents, the *Correspondence of John Collins and Others about the Development of Analysis*, usually known by its shortened Latin title, *Commercium Epistolicum*. In 1715 there appeared in the *Philosophical Transactions* of the Society a shortened version of the *Commercium*, the "Account."

Any attempt at redress may prove unsuccessful. So it was with the "Account," and with the inquiry that preceded it. The adjudicating body, and the documents issued in its wake, were so seriously compromised as completely to undermine credibility. The "Account" asserts that "no Man is a Witness in his own Cause. A Judge would be very unjust, and act contrary to the Laws of all Nations, who should admit any Man to be a Witness in his owne Cause" (Newton, "Account": 284). But the sole author of the "anonymous" "Account" was none other than Newton himself. Nor was this his worst. As President of the Royal Society, he had personally selected the committee of inquiry, carefully stage-managed its deliberations, and thoroughly supervised its report.

This brazen behavior had implications far wider than the calculus dispute. From the middle of the sixteenth century, which saw the collapse of the Church as the transnational State, there had been no legitimate governor of the conduct between nations. It is in the century of the Royal Society, the first full century to bear the brunt of this absence, that Grotius wrote his groundbreaking *De Jure Belli et Pacis* (1625) "to see whether there were not certain common duties generally felt as binding, if not always practiced, and to set forth an ideal" (Figgis, 1960: 246). And it is in the context of this general need for international law that we should see Oldenburg's attempt to legitimate the Royal Society as a means of enforcing common duties in science – what we would call social norms. But Newton's outrageous conduct signalled the utter unravelling of Henry Oldenburg's efforts to transform the Royal Society into a transnational body capable of adjudicating scientific disputes.[6]

A failure at redressing the dispute between Leibniz and Newton, the "Account" was nevertheless successful at making vivid a vision of science diametrically opposed to that of Salomon's House, one which dramatizes the claim that science is wholly competitive and wholly national in character. The "Account" realizes this rhetorical vision by inventing two dramatis personae: Newton, who stands for honor, genius, England; Leibniz, who represents immorality, intellectual theft, foreign intrigue. Although the "Account" persuades us neither of Leibniz' guilt nor Newton's innocence, by its twin characterizations it convinces us that the differences between these men are indeed irreconcilable.

By casting the "Account" in the form of a prosecutor's summation before a jury, Newton makes this irreconcilability a given of his case: unrelenting verbal attack becomes, not a pleasure to indulge, but a duty to discharge. In the following lengthy passage – only length can adequately display his forensic skills – Newton combines historical evidence with sarcasm in a devastating assault on Leibniz' credibility:

> When Mr. *Newton* had received this Letter, he wrote back that all the said four [mathematical] Series had been communicated by him to Mr. *Leibniz*. . . . Whereupon Mr. *Leibniz* desisted from his Claim. Mr. *Newton* also in the same Letter dated *Octob.* 24. 1676. further explained his Methods of Regression, as Mr. *Leibniz* had desired. And Mr. *Leibniz* in his Letter of *June* 21. 1677. desired a further explication: but soon after, upon reading Mr. *Newton's* Letter a second time, he wrote back *July* 12. 1677. that he now understood what he wanted; and found by his old Papers that he had formerly used one of Mr. *Newton's* Methods of Regression, but in the Example which he had then by chance made use of, there being produced nothing elegant, he had, out of his usual Impatience, neglected to use it any further. He had therefore several direct Series, and by consequence a Method of finding them, before he invented and forgot the inverse Method. And if he had searched his old Papers diligently, he might have found this Method there; but having forgot his own Methods he wrote for Mr. *Newton's*. (p. 279)

Working among the Ndembu, Victor Turner discovered that their social dramas tended to widen until they coincided with their society's deepest conflicts, that crisis tended to display, and redress inscribe these conflicts (1982: 70). It is this tendency that accounts for Newton's view of the priority dispute as an element in the struggle between nations. In English, in an English journal, Newton plainly addresses an audience solely of Englishmen, an audience viewed as both judge and jury ("Account": 309, 310, 313).[7]

This tendency for social dramas to widen and deepen accounts also for Newton's conviction that the calculus dispute represents a difference over ultimate issues. Liebniz is wrong, not only as a man and a mathematician, but in every possible way and at every possible level:

> It must be allowed that these two Gentlemen differ very much in Philosophy [methods of doing science]. The one proceeds upon the Evidence arising from Experiments and Phaenomena, and stops where such Evidence is wanting; the other is taken up with Hypotheses, and propounds them, not by Experiments, but to be believed without Examination. (p. 314)

Indeed, Leibniz is mistaken even about the role of the Almighty in the conduct of the physical world (Newton, "Account": 314).

It is another characteristic of social drama that it eventually asserts its independence from its main disputants. In the case of the calculus dispute, the flames of controversy were just as likely to be fanned by others as by Leibniz or Newton; and the quarrel survived Leibniz' death. As it advanced, it deepened; as it deepened, it darkened: the motives of the opposition became automatically suspect, and all attempts at mediation failed. By the time of Newton's "Account," the dispute had been transformed into an irresolvable debate over irreconcilable ideological views, a debate that promised to renew itself in virulence any time two scientists disagreed about priority.

This tendency of the contestants in priority disputes to lose control made imperative an administratively simple solution that would reduce the frequency of such disputes, and contain within the bounds of normal civility those that actually did break out. But before we carry the story of priority to this next stage, the stage at which the institutional response approaches adequacy, we must pause to scrutinize more carefully two assumptions that Newton was careful not to scrutinize at all – that disputes over priority are disputes over intellectual property, and that they are international in character.

Priority as Property

The distance between temporal priority and a property right is metaphoric space. In the latter half of the seventeenth century, this space was traversed: metaphor became social fact. What was at stake in the calculus dispute was the ownership in perpetuity of this branch of mathematics: exclusively the invention of one Englishman, exclusively the product of the English genius for science.

This concern for the scientific ownership that priority affirms is wholly a historical phenomenon. Science is not necessarily conscious of priority; the norms of modern science are not the norms of the ancient Greek, or the medieval enterprises of that name. For example, Theodoric's medieval scientific masterpiece, *On the Rainbow*, was clearly original, a brilliant synthesis of theory and experimentation. But in medieval science originality was permitted, rather than encouraged: Theodoric's was an originality permissible because it clashed neither with the authority of Aristotle nor with the tenets of Catholic Christianity, two medieval *scientific* norms. An originality that did so clash, as Bruno and Galileo learned, would soon cause a conflict every bit as intense as that between Leibniz and Newton.[8]

Not until the middle of the seventeenth century did a concern for scientific originality take roughly its present form. In fact, so persuasive was this form that it seems natural today to speak of the *product* of scientific activity as, in some sense, the *exclusive property* of a *person*: why? In the seventeenth century, at least two notions of scientific property were broached. In Huygens' opinion, credit for a scientific discovery "ought to be equally assigned to all those who find out a thing without regard to the time [when it was done], provided that they can state firmly that they have made the discovery without any assistance" (Oldenburg, vol. V: 362). In his controversy with Leibniz over the calculus, Newton asserts his very different point of view: "second Inventors have no Right. The sole Right is in the first Inventor until another finds out the same thing apart. In which case to take away the Right of the first Inventor, and divide it between him and that other, would be an Act of Injustice" ("Account": 305; see also 308).

Neither view of scientific property is explicable without recourse to the revolution in the law of property that accompanied the rise of capitalism. New forms of enterprise, such as joint stock companies, required new law; at the same time, the commercialization of society altered the legal status of existing endeavors. From time immemorial, a plow or a book were forms of property, chattels; now, for the first time, the *idea* for a plow, or for a book, were also forms of property, very different forms, new to the law. Patents and copyrights gave inventors and authors a kind of monopoly: the rights to manufacture and to print could be exclusively owned; as property, they could be bought and sold.[9]

Both Newton and Huygens claim that priority is a right to intangible property of this new sort. It is, of course, not a legal right precisely. The right to priority in scientific discovery cannot be licensed, reassigned, or sold. But priority is precisely analogous to a property right: its proper assertion creates in every scientist the duty to acknowledge another's ownership (Hart, 1980: 257–8).

Huygens' view of a common right did not prevail. Its source was in older ideas of property, ideas in the process of being superseded; for example, the feudal notion of the shared rights of tenants to a commons was already endangered, and would not survive the eighteenth century. Newton's view, on the other hand, did survive. It clearly rode the crest of the new law of the Stuarts: the exclusive ownership of inventions and literary works guaranteed, in the first case, by the exempting clause of the Statute of Monopolies, and, in the second, by the Copyright Act (Jenks, 1949: 284–5, 289). Under the sway of such exclusivity, only collaborators, and those making a precisely simultaneous independent discovery, could share a priority right.[10]

But why did priority become a national as well as an individual property right? On reflection, we need not be surprised by the close connection between capitalism, nationalism, and its twin, imperialism. Within England, the mid-century saw both agriculture and manufacturing reorganized on competitive lines in accordance with the nascent capitalism on which the industrial revolution would eventually be built. Internationally, in its search for raw materials and markets, England was involved in a bewildering succession of wars and alliances whose only common thread was international competition, the imperial aim held in common by England and the Royal Society. At the end of this period, signalled by the Treaty of Utrecht in 1713, England's colonial rivals, France and the Netherlands, were exhausted by a half-century of warfare. England, on the other hand, was invigorated in every way by fifty years of national and commercial triumph, a vigor manifested very evidently in the rise of English science under the aegis of the Royal Society. It is no accident that in the "Account" Newton's forensic skills are animated by a set of values that were also the basis of the British Empire.

Dealing with Priority Disputes

If the possibility of strife over priority were not continuously to loom, the establishment of an administratively simple means for its determination was imperative. This means had to be persuasive; that is, it had to be acceptable to the community of scientists in the absence of a transnational adjudicating body, an International Court of Scientific Disputes. The means the Royal Society eventually adopted is still in place. Scientific discoveries became, and have remained, exclusive properties, held by a right analogous to copyright, a right at the same time personal and national; their priority was, and is, routinely guaranteed by dated journal publication, a procedure that simultaneously fixes the ownership necessary for competitive advantage, and guarantees the broadcast of ideas that the imperative to share demands. Since it simultaneously satisfies two potentially conflicting social norms, dated journal publication seems a natural and elegant resolution of the paradox of communal competitiveness (compare Zuckerman and Merton, 1973: 465).

But matters were far less clear for scientists at the time. In the first place, in the seventeenth century, the distinction between printing and publishing was very real. Publication was making public; it was the sharing of ideas. Printing was only one means to this end. Writing to Oldenburg in 1665, Adrien Auzout states the general view: "I see little difference between printing scientific matters contained in letters and showing these same letters to those learned in these matters who can copy them out when they have them on loan" (Oldenburg, vol. II: 518). Speaking of a scientific discovery, Viscount Brounckner says its author "did then communicate & publish ye same (though not in print) to my self & others" (Oldenburg, vol. X: 291). Giving a lecture was also a means of publication: Wren regards a lecture as "publication enough" (Birch, vol.I: 48). From this point of view, lectures and letters were the equivalent of dated journal publication. But, past mid-century, such earlier notions were becoming obsolete; indeed, these last two clarifications are embedded in disputes over priority.

Seventeenth-century scientists were undecided, not only on what publication meant, but on whether the broadcast of completed work was the best means of securing priority, Huygens suggested an alternative to full publication: the announcement of work in progress in anagrammatic form (Oldenburg, vol. V: 556). Oldenburg suggested an alternative to anagrams. He was confident that the temporal priority of scientific discoveries could be established by means of the registration stipulated in the founding documents of the Society (Weld, 1858: 527). He constantly advertised this option, and himself used the register to resolve a dispute (Oldenburg, vol. II: 329; vol. III: 537; vol. IV: 422; vol. V: 104, 178; vol. X: 2, 67). In 1665, he proposed to regularize the process:

> Mr. OLDENBURG made a motion in the name of some member of the society, that when any fellow should have a philosophical notion or invention, not yet made out, and desire, that the same sealed up in a box might be deposited with one of the secretaries, till it could be perfected, and so brought to light, this might be allowed for the better securing inventions to their authors. (Birch, vol. II: 24; see also 212)

But registration was not without problems. The register, of which Oldenburg was so proud, was manifestly incomplete (Sprat, p. 311;

Birch, vol. III: 514; vol. IV: 60, 464; Stimson, 1948: 66–7). And, even though the Society accepted Oldenburg's proposal, they worried that their fellows might be tempted to register even half-baked ideas. In an amendment, they insisted that any invention so registered be perfected "after about a year's interval" (Birch, vol. II: 25).

By the 1670s, the tide had turned permanently in favor of securing priority by the simple expedient of publication in the newly founded *Philosophical Transactions* (Oldenburg, vol. X: 67). By the last twenty years of the century, the trend toward regular publication became marked. In 1683, the Society passed a resolution to emphasize record keeping and putting things in writing (Birch, vol. IV: 251). By 1686, there are clear signs of a regular procedure: Papin's paper is read, registered, and published; as are papers by Halley, Hooke, Vossius, and DeVaux (Birch, vol. IV: 452, 486, 488, 527, 556, 492, 499, 550). The trend toward dated journal publication as a guarantee of temporal priority soon took full hold: by publishing in print accounts of their completed discoveries or inventions, scientists simultaneously shared their results, and established their claim to these results as theirs alone. By creating the means by which the ownership rights to its knowledge could be established, the scientific community transformed rhetoric into social reality.

Priority and Scientific Advance: The Implications of a Social Invention

If the story of priority ended here, it would be incomplete; it would omit the intellectual and social consequences of basing the reward system of science on the respective dates of receipt of rival journal articles, dates that are surrogates for originality. As a general rule, these consequences distort the meaning of scientific advance.

In the first place, this concentration on priority obscures the nature of scientific discovery. In any important case, issues of priority are likely to be beyond settlement. George Stigler, a Nobel Laureate in economics, asserts:

> When an idea is more than a technical definition or a highly specific analysis, the temporal priority is hopelessly obscure. Who first discovered [such major ideas in economics as] diminishing marginal utility, or diminishing returns, or the quantity theory, or the theory of underemployment equilibrium? I do not know, but it is common knowledge that all such ideas have long histories before they are stated by the men who made them important. (1965: 3)

Thomas Kuhn's classical analysis, "Energy conservation as an example of simultaneous discovery," gives us a detailed example of this problem in physics. Kuhn concludes:

> What we see in [the works of these scientists] is not really the simultaneous discovery of energy conservation. Rather it is the rapid and disorderly emergence of the experimental and conceptual elements from which that theory was shortly to be compounded. (1977: 72)

Secondly, a concentration on priority entails an emphasis on originality itself, an emphasis that misrepresents the nature of scientific advance. The testing of hypotheses, the accumulation of knowledge in a particular field, the refinement and elaboration of a theory – Stigler points to three important components of such advance in which originality is, at best, a minor factor. Moreover, discoveries as great as the calculus and natural selection were multiple and nearly simultaneous. Had Newton and Darwin never lived, the calculus would have been discovered by the end of the seventeenth, natural selection by the middle of the nineteenth century. How important is priority to science when such discoveries are virtually inevitable? Furthermore, even scientists to whom considerable originality is usually ascribed function for the most part in a more ordinary capacity: even Newton and Darwin spent most of their scientific lives working out the implications of their great insights.

Indeed, a concentration on priority entails an emphasis on originality that may actually impede scientific advance:

> Quite aside from the fact that much original work is mistaken, an excessive rate of production of original work may retard scientific progress. . . . [w]hen the rate of output of original work gets too large, theories are not properly aged. They are rejected without extracting their residue of truth, or they are accepted before their content is tidied up and their range of applicability ascertained with tolerable correctness. A cumulative slovenliness results. (Stigler, 1965: 14)

Finally, too great a concern with priority distorts the efforts of scientists; it encourages them to show a "concern with recognition" at the expense of a "concern with advancing knowledge" (Merton, 1973a: 338): the actual effect of a concern for priority may undermine its intended effect, the encouragement of scientific advance.

Theoretical Implications

If my analysis is correct, rhetoric is an essential component in social change, and rhetorical analysis is an essential ingredient in sociological analysis. But the complementary nature of rhetorical and sociological analyses may indicate a deeper kinship. Writing this chapter, I was struck by the ease with which I selected priority disputes as a strategic research site for rhetorical analysis. No rhetorician had gone over this ground before; but, surely, no rhetorician of early modern science could ignore this forensic Everest. By way of contrast, we may note the initial resistance among responsible scholars to Merton's recognition of these same priority disputes as a strategic site for sociological research, a resistance Merton points to with the legitimate pride of a pioneer. He quotes his fellow scholar, Charles Gillispie, writing in 1958:

> In a note . . . to Merton, I wrote that, although it seemed surprising that the phenomenon was so nearly universal an accompaniment to scientific discovery, I did wonder whether the matter wasn't a bit trivial; I don't believe I also said "unworthy" but recollect that such a dark thought was in my mind. (Gillispie; quoted by Merton, 1987: 22)

In addition, I was surprised by the ease of fit between Merton's central insight and my rhetorical analysis. In part, this ease has a source in Merton's own awareness of rhetoric as a category of sociological evidence. In his priority paper, for example, he claims that "property rights in science [consist in] the recognition by others of the scientist's distinctive part in having brought the result into being." As support for this claim, he cites texts employing metaphors in which priority is the tenor, property the vehicle: for example, "Ramsay. . . . asks Rayleigh's *'permission* [my italics] to look into atmospheric nitrogen'" (Merton, 1973c: 294–5).

That this quotation occurs, not in Merton's text, but in a footnote, is clear rhetorical evidence that, for him, sociology was the master, rhetoric the servant. Still, in my analysis of the rhetoric of Bacon, Sprat, Oldenburg, and Newton, I found so clear and complete, so serendipitous, a confirmation of the essential correctness of Merton's central thesis that more than mere confirmation seemed involved. Indeed, rhetorical analysis seemed unerring in its ability to penetrate the collective psyche of these pioneers of the social institution of modern science: patterns of figurative language in Sprat, for example, displayed Merton's conflicting imperatives at their birth, a birth of which, apparently, neither Sprat nor three centuries of readers had been aware.

Since Merton's conclusions were available to me, my rhetorical analysis cannot have the epistemological status of his groundbreaking work. My central insight concerning priority, an insight that organizes this paper, is borrowed from sociology, not earned by rhetoric. But so serendipitous a relationship between sociological and rhetorical analysis may be an instance of a more general kinship between two allied disciplinary matrices. Perhaps neither has genuine epistemological priority; perhaps social forces, like capitalism and imperialism, forces that seem so impersonal, so like natural forces, are fundamentally no less rhetorically constituted than is a concern for priority in scientific discovery. If that were so, the division of labor between rhetoric and the sociology would still hold – sociology would still deal with the structural determinants of social conditions, rhetoric with their symbolic content and style – but for methodological, not epistemological reasons.

Notes

A Scholarly Award from Purdue University Calumet materially aided in the completion of this chapter. I would like to thank Robert K. Merton for a detailed critique of an earlier version of this chapter, and Herbert Simons for his relentless criticism of later versions.

1   In the myth, Bensalem avoids imperialist confrontation with other nations by keeping its existence a secret. It has few visitors, and its collectors of scientific information, its Merchants of Light, "sail into foreign countries under the names of other nations" (p. 469).

2   The phrase is from Barnfield (1968: 53). See Black (1962: 47) for some insight into the terminology problem.

3   Black's theory, which I find convincing, makes metaphoric meaning the product of the interaction of theme and vehicle. This theory permits the Baconian use of metaphors from trade and imperialism to prepare the way for other uses, very different in meaning.

4   This is an English summary. The full text appears in Huygens (vol. VIII: 305–8).

5   On the theoretical reach of the dramatistic, Kenneth Burke is, of course, the seminal thinker *par excellence*. But Turner's life-long focus on the implications of the dramatistic in concrete social situations makes his views more immediately relevant in this instance.

6   To this day, no such body exists. A typical contemporary effect of its absence is the continuing priority dispute between American and the Soviet scientists concerning the discovery of two transuranium elements.

7   To follow the arguments in the "Account," a reader needed a knowledge of both Latin and mathematics; in that sense, Newton's audience was very specialized, and not particularily English. But my point here is that the rhetoric of the "Account" creates its own audience, a fiction of Englishmen patriotic to the point of chauvinism.

8   This is not to deny that earlier scientists might have seen some gain in asserting temporal priority for their discoveries; Galileo is a well-known example (pp. 232–3, 245).

9   For the idea of a revolution in law, I am indebted most to Tigar and Levy. Their account is avowedly Marxist, but it is not seriously distorted, as reference to Holdsworth and Jenks makes clear. For the idea of a right, I am indebted to Hart.

10   This exclusivity is also in line with the English practice of primogeniture, whereby the eldest son inherits all. This is far from the case on the Continent (Pollock and Maitland, 1968; Knappen, 1964; Smith, 1928). In Newton's particular case, such exclusivity may also have had a psychological motive: Newton was a posthumous only son abandoned by his mother and stepfather (Westfall, 1984; Manuel, 1979).

References

Bacon, Francis (1937) "New Atlantis," in *Essays, Advancement of Learning, New Atlantis, and Other Pieces.* Ed. Richard Foster Jones. New York: Odyssey Press. pp. 447–91. First publ. 1627.

Barnfield, Owen (1968) "Poetic diction and legal fiction," in Max Black (ed.), *The Importance of Language.* Ithaca: Cornell University Press. pp. 51–71.

Birch, Thomas (1968) *The History of the Royal Society for Improving of Knowledge from its First Rise.* A Facsimile of the London Edition of 1756–57. Ed. A. Rupert Hall and Marie Boas Hall. 4 vols. New York: Johnson Reprints.

Black, Max (1962) *Models and Metaphors: Studies in Language and Philosophy.* Ithaca: Cornell University Press.

Burke, Kenneth (1962) "Four master tropes," in *A Grammar of Motives and a Rhetoric of Motives.* New York: World. pp. 503–17. First publ. 1945.

Cole, Jonathan R. and Cole, Stephen (1973) *Social Stratification In Science.* Chicago: University of Chicago Press.

Collins, H.M. (1975) "The seven sexes: a study in the sociology of a phenomenon, or the replication of experiments in physics," *Sociology,* 9: 204–24.

Farrell, Thomas B. (1976) "Knowledge, consensus, and rhetorical theory," *Quarterly Journal of Speech,* 62: 1–14.

Figgis, J.N. (1960) *Political Thought from Gerson to Grotius 1414–1625: Seven Studies.* New York: Harper. First publ. 1916.

Galilei, Galileo (1957) *Discoveries and Opinions of Galileo.* Ed. Stillman Drake. New York: Doubleday.

Geertz, Clifford (1973) *The Interpretation of Cultures.* New York: Basic Books.

Gieryn, Thomas F. (1983) "Boundary-work and the demarcation of science from non-science: strains and interests in professional ideologies of scientists," *American Sociological Review,* 48: 781–95.

Gilbert, G. Nigel and Mulkay, Michael (1984) *Opening Pandora's Box: A Sociological Analysis of Scientists' Discourse.* Cambridge: Cambridge University Press.

Gillispie, Charles Coulston (1973) *The Edge of Objectivity: An Essay in the History of Scientific Ideas.* Princeton: Princeton University Press. First publ. 1960.

Gusfield, Joseph (1976) "The literary rhetoric of science: comedy and pathos in drinking driver research," *American Sociological Review,* 41: 16–34.

Hall, A. Rupert (1980) *Philosophers at War: The Quarrel between Newton and Leibniz.* Cambridge: Cambridge University Press.

Hart, H.L.A. (1980) "Definition and theory of jurisprudence," in Joel Feinberg and Hyman Gross (eds), *Philosophy of Law.* 2nd edn. Belmont, CA: Wadsworth. pp. 252–8. First publ. 1954.

Holdsworth, Sir William (1966) *A History of English Law.* 16 vols. London: Methuen. First publ. 1925.

Huygens, Christian (1888–1950) *Oeuvres complètes de Christian Huygens publiées par la Société Hollandaise des Sciences.* 22 vols. The Hague: Martinus Nijhoff.

Jenks, Edward (1949) *A Short History of English Law from the Earliest Times to the End of the Year 1938.* London: Methuen. First publ. 1912.

Jones, Richard Foster (1961) *Ancients and Moderns: A Study of the Rise of the Scientific Movement in Seventeenth-Century England.* New York: Dover. First publ. 1936.

Knappen, M.M. (1964) *Constitutional and Legal History of England.* Haden, CT: Archon Books.

Kuhn, Thomas S. (1977) "Energy conservation as an example of simultaneous discovery," in *The Essential Tension: Selected Studies in Scientific Tradition and Change*. Chicago: University of Chicago Press. pp. 66–104. First publ. 1959.

Leeuwenhoek, Antony van (1960) *Antony van Leeuwenhoek and his "Little Animals"*. Ed. Clifford Dobell. New York: Dover. First publ. 1932.

Manuel, Frank E. (1979) *A Portrait of Isaac Newton*. Washington, DC: New Republic Books. First publ. 1968.

Merton, Robert K. (1973a) "Behavior patterns of scientists," in *The Sociology of Science: Theoretical and Empirical Investigations*. Ed. Norman W. Storer. Chicago: University of Chicago Press. pp. 323–42. First publ. 1968.

Merton, Robert K. (1973b) "The normative structure of science," in *The Sociology of Science: Theoretical and Empirical Investigations*. Ed. Norman W. Storer. Chicago: University of Chicago Press. pp. 267–78. First publ. 1942.

Merton, Robert K. (1973c) "Priorities in scientific discovery," in *The Sociology of Science: Theoretical and Empirical Investigations*. Ed. Norman W. Storer. Chicago: University of Chicago Press. pp. 286–324. First publ. 1957.

Merton, Robert K. (1973d) "Singletons and multiples in science," in *The Sociology of Science: Theoretical and Empirical Investigations*. Ed. Norman W. Storer. Chicago: University of Chicago Press. pp. 343–70. First publ. 1961.

Merton, Robert K. (1987) "Three fragments from a sociologist's notebooks: establishing the phenomenon, specified ignorance, and strategic research materials," *Annual Review of Sociology*, 13: 1–28.

Newton, Isaac (1959–77) *The Correspondence*. Ed. H.W. Turnbull, J.F. Scott, A. Rupert Hall, and Laura Tilling. 7 vols. Cambridge: Cambridge University Press.

Newton, Isaac (1980) "Account of the Book Entituled *Commercium Epistolicum*," in A. Rupert Hall, *Philosophers at War: The Quarrel between Newton and Leibniz*. Cambridge: Cambridge University Press. pp. 263–314. First publ. 1715.

Oldenburg, Henry (1965–73) *The Correspondence*. Ed. A. Rupert Hall and Marie Boas Hall. 11 vols. Madison: University of Wisconsin Press. Also London: Mansell, 1975–7.

Ortega y Gasset, José (1960) *The Revolt of the Masses*. New York: W.W. Norton. First publ. 1930.

Pollock, Sir Frederick and Maitland, Frederick William (1968) *The History of English Law before the Time of Edward I*. 2 vols. 2nd edn. Cambridge: Cambridge University Press. First publ. 1895.

Smith, Munroe (1928) *The Development of European Law*. New York: Columbia University Press.

Sprat, Thomas (1667) *History of the Royal Society of London, for the Improving of Natural Knowledge*. London.

Stigler, George J. (1965) "The nature and role of originality in scientific progress," *Essays in the History of Economics*. Chicago: University of Chicago Press. pp. 1–15. First publ. 1955.

Stimson, Dorothy (1948) *Scientists and Amateurs: A History of The Royal Society*. New York: Henry Schuman.

Tigar, Michael E. and Levy, Madeleine R. (1977) *Law and the Rise of Capitalism*. New York: Monthly Review Press.

Turner, Victor (1978) *Dramas, Fields, and Metaphors: Symbolic Action in Human Society*. Ithaca: Cornell University Press. First publ. 1974.

Turner, Victor (1982) *From Ritual to Theatre: The Human Seriousness of Play*. New York: Performing Arts Journal Publications.

Weld, Charles Richard (1858) *History of the Royal Society, with Memoirs of the Presidents, Compiled from Authentic Documents*. 2 vols. London: John W. Parker.

Westfall, Richard S. (1984) *Never at Rest: A Biography of Isaac Newton.* Cambridge: Cambridge University Press.

Woolgar, Steve (1980) "Discovery: logic and sequence in a scientific text," in Karin D. Knorr, Roger Krohn, and Richard Whitley (eds), *The Social Process of Scientific Investigation. Sociology of the Sciences*, vol. 4. Dordrecht: D. Reidel. pp. 239–68.

Zuckerman, Harrit and Robert Merton (1973) "Institutionalized patterns of evaluation in science," in Robert K. Merton, *The Sociology of Science: Theoretical and Empirical Investigations.* Ed. Norman W. Storer. Chicago: University of Chicago Press. pp. 460–96. First publ. 1961.

6

Distinguishing the Rhetorical from the Real: the Case of Psychotherapeutic Placebos

Herbert W. Simons

In the introduction to this book, I suggested that the various concepts, principles, and contending viewpoints that constitute the rhetorical tradition might profitably be brought to bear upon particular disciplines, not with a view toward resolving their problems but toward advancing consideration of the questions they confront. In so far as scholarly discourse has generally been considered outside the province of rhetoric, the stance of the rhetorical analyst is inherently ironic, often calling into question a discipline's most basic presuppositions. Thus, for example, Gross (in press) counterposed a rhetorical view of claims to the discovery of new biological species against the rational reconstructions provided by the evolutionary biologists themselves. Landau (1987) likened paleoanthropological accounts of shifts in the ape's habitat to fictive narratives – made all the more appealing because of their resemblance to children's tales. McCloskey (1985) contrasted the "official" dogma of economics – its claim to being exclusively reliant upon statistical and syllogistic proofs – with evidence of its dependence upon a wide range of argumentative forms, from appeals to intuition to "bubba" psychology. De Man (1978) provided an ironic reading of objections by philosophers to the use of rhetorical tropes, showing the tropological character of the philosophers' own writings. Gergen (1984) alleged that much of what psychologists claim to have discovered about aggression is largely embedded in ordinary language usage of the term. Weigert compared the discourse of scientific sociology to the rhetoric of a social movement, complete with "an opium for the people, as well as an identity-bestowing myth for its members" (1970: 112). Billig (1987) proposed viewing all of social psychology in rhetorical terms, extending even to claims about basic processes of cognition.

What follows is a rhetorical analysis of the uses to which the concept of psychotherapeutic placebos has been put by the mental health professions. Beyond addressing issues about psychotherapy that are of considerable importance in their own right, I shall attempt here to illustrate several broader themes that were touched upon in the book's Introduction. They include, most importantly: (1) the relationship between rhetoric and various ideologies of the real; (2) rhetoric's role as an instrument of legitimation and delegitimation; (3) the generic character of professional rhetorics; (4) the relationship between perceived legitimacy and effective rhetorical practice; and (5) the utility of recasting disciplinary issues as though they were arguments about varying conceptions of rhetoric.

No discipline is more ripe for rhetorical analysis, in my view, than the field of psychotherapy. And no task is more central than the task of rethinking psychotherapy's relationship to its so-called placebos. The various professions that equip, train, and certify psychotherapists are presently experiencing a legitimation crisis (Habermas, 1975), a crisis brought on in no small measure by the unexpected success of psychotherapeutic placebos, relative to standard treatment methods. Thus we might cast the saga of psychotherapeutic placebos as that of a failed legitimation ritual. The story begins with emulation of pharmacologists and other medical researchers in using placebo controls, a practice which, however much it invited charges of depriving patients of the help they needed, nevertheless seemed eminently justified in that it placed the comparative study of psychotherapeutic methods on a sound, scientific basis. It ends with the paradox of so much success from placebo treatments that the demarcation criteria traditionally used to separate established psychotherapies from faith healing, witch doctory, mesmerism, and the like are called into question.

For some time now medical practitioners have been testifying to the power of placebos to effect dramatic improvements in their patients' well being. More recently, researchers have asked whether most, if not all, of the beneficial influences of psychotherapy might not also be attributable to placebo effects: in particular, to the sense of renewed hope and self-efficacy born of belief in the therapy, belief in the therapist, and the conviction that someone cares. In his influential book, *Persuasion and Healing*, Jerome Frank has argued:

> Despite decades of effort it has been impossible to show convincingly that one therapeutic method is more effective than any other for the majority of psychological illnesses. This suggests that any specific healing effects of different methods would be overshadowed by therapeutically potent ingredients shared by all. (1973: 2).

Frank's observations were impressively underscored in a recent meta-analysis of the findings from some 475 empirical studies of psychotherapeutic treatment methods (Smith, Glass, and Miller, 1980). As expected, psychotherapeutic treatment groups enjoyed significantly greater success than untreated controls. However, the same could not be said for comparisons with "placebo" controls consisting of persons who had been led to believe that they were receiving an active treatment and who therefore expected to get better. Smith et al. concluded that the various approaches to psychotherapy work about equally well, and not much better than those designated as placebo treatments. They added that success across a wide spectrum of treatment methods, from behavior therapies to psychoanalysis, probably depends to a large extent on placebo-like characteristics, in particular on belief in the therapy and the therapist.

The Smith et al. study has been subjected to a range of criticisms common to meta-analytic investigations but, if anything, it appears to have understated the success of placebo groups (Prioleau, Murdock, and Brody, 1983).

To better appreciate what these findings mean, we might take a cue from Weigert (1970). He points to certain generic characteristics of all professional rhetorics. They include a rhetoric of affiliation by which the profession aligns itself with higher status groups and distances itself from lower status groups; a rhetoric of special expertise that includes claims to valid theories and distinctive methods; a rhetoric of public service that simultaneously plays down careerist motives; a rhetoric of social passage that identifies and justifies credentialing requirements; a rhetoric of self-policing that defends against "interference" from others; and a delegitimizing rhetoric of the rhetoric of outsiders, including "pseudo-professionals," "charlatans," "popularizers," and "cranks" (Simons, 1986). Each of these genres, moreover, includes predictable lines of argument (*topoi*) and stylistic characteristics. One recurring feature, for example, is that they are not labeled rhetorics at all.

These rhetorics are of course interlinked. To the extent that an academic or helping profession's claims of special expertise are undermined, its grounds for distancing itself from lower status competitors are undermined as well. Thus it is that the unanticipated success of placebo treatments has been a cause of such embarrassment for the mental health professions. Until the accumulated findings from comparative research had come in, psychotherapists could claim that placebo effects, however widespread, were only fractionally responsible for cures, just as in chemotherapy research. The experience of sizeable placebo effects in chemotherapy had not been unwelcome to psychotherapists; if anything, it showed the importance of psychological factors even in the treatment of ostensibly biological problems. But the enormous success of psychotherapeutic placebos was something else again.

What, then, is a psychotherapeutic placebo, and how is it different from "real" psychotherapy? Much can be gained, I think, by addressing these issues rhetorically. At issue fundamentally, I shall argue, are age-old controversies about relationships between form and content, manner and matter, reality and appearance, truth and effectiveness – questions about the very nature of rhetoric itself. Consider the following points.

1   The concept of a psychotherapeutic placebo derives, as we have seen, from the use of placebos in medicine. In the medical setting the placebo serves as a benign counterfeit, a form of deception or misrepresentation that trades on its metonymic resemblance to something real. The placebo, then, may be understood as a species of persuasive message in the sophistic sense of offering "mere" rhetoric, "empty" rhetoric, form without substance.

2   The prototypical placebo is of course the sugar pill, a triumph of packaging if ever there was one. The familiar tale of the patient who is "cured" by a placebo is, in Burkean terms, a representative anecdote of the power of mere rhetoric, used in place of "the real thing." In symbolizing "placeboness," the sugar pill has a special function to perform, much like the "good" birds (for example, robins, sparrows, wrens) in Eleanor Rosch's (1978) account of how we come to form simple concepts like "bird." If cognitive theorists like Rosch are correct, it is by a peculiarly nonalgorithmic, rhetorical logic that we move from a concrete exemplar to some general idea of a thing, then back again to concrete but more difficult cases (see Billig, 1987: 146–7). Always the analogy is imperfect. And as Wilkins (1984) has noted, there are interesting differences between placebos in chemotherapy research and in studies of psychotherapy. Placebos used in chemotherapy research are presumed to be inert. Not so in psychotherapy research. In chemotherapy research the nonplacebo effect is biological while the placebo effect is psychological. In psychotherapy studies both effects are psychological, and they tend to get conflated. In Derridean terms, then, there is a compounding of parasitisms (Derrida, 1978). The concept of a placebo is parasitic upon ideas of the real. The concept of a psychotherapeutic placebo is parasitic upon conceptions of placebos used in testing and administering drugs.

3   The concept of a "placebo effect" is confusing and paradoxical in that it calls attention to the very thing – the inert ingredient – that has no effect, while deflecting attention from the psychological factors in the healing context that are actually responsible for improvements in the patient's attitude or condition. Ironically, the magical notion that the pill itself may be responsible for the change survives as a remnant of

Newtonian thinking about causation that persists within the medical profession (Brody, 1977). It assumes that for any material effect there must be a material, concrete, nonsymbolic (that is, nonrhetorical) cause. The sugar pill is the only material object one can point to.

4   There is little agreement among psychotherapists themselves as to what counts as a psychotherapeutic placebo. What one labels a placebo (for example, Trexler and Karst, 1972), another labels as an exceptionally powerful method of psychotherapy (Wilkins, 1986). Some theorists have characterized all psychotherapy as placebogenic (Campbell and Rosenbaum, 1967; Bootzin and Lick, 1979). In the Smith et al. study, hearing arguments from a therapist was considered psychotherapy but getting these same arguments from a book was not. Included, in addition to bibliotherapy, as placebo treatments, were relaxation training, relaxation and suggestion, group discussion, informational meetings, reading and discussing a play, pseudo-desensitization, written information about the phobic object, and minimal contact counseling.

Presumably, Smith et al. argue, these methods qualify as placebo treatments because they have only general, nonspecific, informal effects, such as effects on client expectancies. Others argue that such terms as these are inadequate to differentiate placebo and nonplacebo treatments. Bernstein and Nietzel (1977) have observed that there may be no fundamental difference between specific and nonspecific factors in the psychotherapeutic setting. Rather, specific factors are psychological events that are understood, whereas nonspecific factors are psychological events operating from principles that are less well known. Similarly, Grünbaum (1981) insists that the commonly employed criterion of specificity has been a source of considerable confusion. Further, he suggests, any claim to the effect that a given treatment is therapeutic or a placebo is always relative to a theory of what works with respect to a particular target disorder.

5   There are fascinating parallels between rhetoric's historic relationship to its alleged alternatives (see pp. 3–4 above) and conceptions of placebo in the psychotherapeutic context – parallels, for example, between psychoanalysis and objectivist models of the real, between Rogerian therapies and ideas of the real as natural and directly expressive, and between behavior therapies and ideas of real power (that is, rewards and punishments, positive and negative reinforcements) in place of "mere" rhetoric.

Psychotherapists are not entirely oblivious to their roles as persuaders but their systems of thought tend to impose ideological blinders on the full range of rhetoric in their day-to-day practices. For example, psychoanalysts tend to be insensitive to the persuasiveness of their failure to maintain stances of analytic neutrality. Pentony observes, "The ordinary relationship with its note of friendship, tender regard, cooperation, sincerity, care, and practical reasonableness is an essential ingredient of the analysis and the nature of the outcome, but there is no way to incorporate such elements in the formulation of the analytic scheme" (1981: 88). Paradoxically, observes Pentony, therapists may be more effective the more they are able to function as "true believers" – the more, in other words, that they are able to persuade themselves that what they are offering their patients in not "mere" rhetoric.

6   Paradoxically, then, belief by psychotherapists in the superiority of their own methods *is for them a placebo of sorts*, in the sense of serving as a self-sustaining, if empirically unjustified myth.

7   So powerful and so persuasive are placebo factors that one might invert the conventional relationship between the real and the rhetorical, asserting that what has conventionally been taken to be the "real" causes of benefit from psychotherapy are mere rhetoric while belief in the therapy, belief in the therapist, and the like *are* the real causes. This, argues Grünbaum (1981) is what Frank (1973) should have claimed in putting forth a theory of healing as essentially dependent on rhetorical (that is, symbolic) factors. *Do we not have here in microcosm an example of the collapse of the distinction between the real and the rhetorical taking place throughout the human sciences?*

The general point of this extended illustration has been to exhibit the utility of rhetorical ways of thinking and communicating as applied to a set of issues in the human sciences. It should be apparent by now how varying conceptions of rhetoric map on to the placebo controversy. Yet I would be remiss if I did not carry the argument for a rhetorical perspective one step further – to a consideration of the implications of what we have been discussing for the *conduct* of psychotherapy.

The Question of Placebo Therapy

Jefferson Fish's (1973) *Placebo Therapy* begins with a series of rhetorical questions that go to the heart of the controversies we have been examining. If, as the evidence suggests, successful psychotherapy is largely dependent on such "placebo factors" as belief in the therapist, faith in the therapy, and belief that the therapist shares that faith, then shouldn't therapists be working as directly and as efficiently as possible to shape those beliefs? Why not admit that psychotherapy has much in common with faith healing and then get on with the job?

Fish would induce belief *by virtually any means necessary*. His is a form of "spiritual judo in which the therapist uses the power of the patient's own faith to force him to have a 'therapeutic conversion experience.' " The "spiritual judo" he endorses includes all manner of fabrications and misrepresentations, so long as they are perceived to be in the patient's interests.

Thus, for example, Fish and his similarly minded colleagues (O'Connell, 1983; Torrey, 1972) strategically manage the diagnostic interview. The interview may be long, the questions highly specific, the notes taken elaborate, but not because the information elicited is likely to be of great consequence to the therapist; rather, because these interview procedures can be expected to impress the patient with the therapist's interest and competence.

Similarly with the diagnosis itself. Should the presenting problem appear unmanageable – say a severe depression – Fish may assign a different label, one that inspires more hope for a cure. Always perceptions are manipulated with a view toward shaping favorable expectations. If the patient gets better, then the patient may be told that the rate of improvement is likely to accelerate. If there has been no apparent improvement, then this is perhaps a necessary plateau on the road to recovery. If there has been backsliding, that too may be rationalized on grounds that one must get sicker to get better.

Fish acknowledges that these techniques are not unlike those employed in standard psychotherapies; indeed, he is quick to cite their widespread use as evidence of the placebo-like nature of most psychotherapies. Moreover, Fish openly admits mimicking standard treatments if doing so will further the central goals of fostering faith, hope, trust, and the like. He suggests that other therapists might be more creative were they not so tied to particular theories.

In these and other respects, placebo therapy probably has most in common with other strategic therapies, and especially the various interactional "systems" therapies in the Bateson/Haley/Erickson/Watzlawick tradition. Fish is a reframer *par excellence*. Like the interactionalists, he works within the conceptual frameworks of his clients, rather than attempting to effect wholesale changes in them. And like the interactionalists, his approach is embroiled in paradox.

The paradoxes begin with the label "placebo therapy"; it is oxymoronic. The immediate objection to Fish's brand of psychotherapy is that it is dishonest, hence unethical. Here is a therapy that works more centrally than most toward reaping the rewards of a trusting therapist–patient relationship. Yet its methods of inducing trust are untrustworthy. Were Plato alive today, he might well point to placebo therapy as proof positive of the low state into which rhetoric has fallen in the West – a logical consequence of the sophistic premise, cited by Socrates in Plato's *Phaedrus*, that effectiveness is all that matters where rhetoric is concerned. It would not have been lost on Socrates that the label "placebo therapy" is ironically self-defeating.

Who among us would go to a therapist for a treatment labeled "placebo therapy"?

So goes the immediate response to rhetorics like those of placebo therapy. Its general lines of argument (called *topoi* by the Greeks) were set forth over two millennia ago by the sophists themselves. Protagoras, the father of debate, took it as an article of faith that there is always more than can be said on either side of a controversy. He would no doubt have anticipated Fish's response to the charges brought against him. So long as it is not self-aggrandizing, argues Fish, saying what is effective to a patient rather than what is known to be true is in the highest therapeutic tradition. Thus "a therapist who believes in placebo principles need never be guilty of being a con artist. He not only realizes that the placebo communication must be in his patient's best interest, but also believes that his patient's faith, not his own brilliance, is responsible for the cure. Such a therapist need not worry that he will communicate the smile of one-upmanship" (Fish, 1973: 21).

No doubt saying what is effective (but untrue) will not satisfy every reader; it does not satisfy me. At a recent presentation of the placebo paper before a group that included many psychotherapists (Simons, 1988), Karl Tom, a psychiatrist, commented that Fish's placebo therapy was much too cynical, much too deconstructive for his purposes. If Fish's sophistic perspective was representative of what rhetorical theory had to offer to psychotherapists and their patients, then perhaps the "rhetorical turn" should be replaced by the "enlivening turn," by which Tom meant a discourse of *real* rather than fabricated love, caring, and concern.

Yet perhaps we do not need a turn away from rhetoric (as if that were possible) to accomplish Tom's goals. For, within the tradition of Greco–Roman rhetorical theory, there may be the roots for an enlivened psychotherapy, one that would merge form and content, style and substance, appearance and reality. Aristotle spoke of a rhetoric that would give effectiveness to truth; Cicero of a rhetoric that would marry wisdom and eloquence, Quintilian of the orator as a good person skilled in speaking.

Perhaps too, psychotherapists can take counsel from the ancients in the art of instilling hope. Billig (1987) cites Philostratus for evidence that the ancient orators occasionally used their wisdom and eloquence for therapeutic purposes. It was Antiphon who set himself up near the marketplace in Corinth and announced "a course of sorrow-assuaging lectures" with the assurance that "there was not a grief so terrible that he could not expel it from the mind" (Billig, 1987: 53).

Thus far I have discussed the possible uses of rhetorical study in the practice of psychotherapy, but I want to end by suggesting that we also reverse the direction of our inquiry. How, we should ask, might psychotherapists add to the general stock of rhetorical knowledge and to the conversations about rhetoric taking place in other disciplines. One value of the "rhetorical turn" is that it provides a bridge across disciplines, and thus a way of enlarging and enriching the human conversation. That effect may itself be therapeutic.

References

Bernstein, D.A. and Neitzel, M.T. (1977) "Demand characteristics in behavior modification: the natural history of a 'nuisance'," in M. Herson, R.M. Eisler, and P.M. Miller (eds), *Progress in Behavior Modification*, Vol. 4. New York: Academic Press.

Billig, M. (1987) *Arguing and Thinking: A Rhetorical Approach to Social Psychology*. Cambridge: Cambridge University Press.

Bootzin, R.B. and Lick, J.R. (1979) "Expectancies in therapy research: interpretive artifact or mediating mechanism?," *Journal of Clinical and Consulting Psychology*, 47: 852–5.

Brody, H. (1977) *Placebos and the Philosophy of Medicine*. Chicago: University of Chicago Press.

Campbell, J. and Rosenbaum, C.P. (1967) "Placebo effect and symptom relief in psychotherapy," *Archives of General Psychiatry*, 16: 364–8.

De Man, P. (1978) "The epistemology of metaphor," *Critical Inquiry*, 5: 13–30.

Derrida, J. (1978) *Writing and Difference*. Tr. Alan Bass. Berkeley: University of California Press.

Fish, J.M. (1973) *Placebo Therapy*. San Francisco: Jossey-Bass.

Frank, J. (1973) *Persuasion and Healing*. New York: Schocken.

Gergen, K.J. (1984) "Aggression as discourse," in A. Mummenday (ed.), *Social Psychology of Aggression*. New York: Springer.

Gross, A. (in press) "The origin of species: evolutionary taxonomy as an example of the rhetoric of science," in H.W. Simons (ed.), *The Rhetorical Turn: Invention and Persuasion in the Conduct of Inquiry*. Chicago: University of Chicago Press.

Grünbaum, A. (1981) "The placebo concept," *Behavior Research and Therapy*, 19: 157–67.

Habermas, J. (1975) *Legitimation Crisis*. Tr. T. McCarthy. Boston: Beacon Press.

Landau, M. (1987) "Paradise lost: the theme of terrestriality in human evolution," in J. Nelson, A. Megill, and D.N. McClosky (eds), *The Rhetoric of the Human Sciences*. Madison: University of Wisconsin Press.

McCloskey, D. (1985) *The Rhetoric of Economics*. Madison: University of Wisconsin Press.

O'Connell, S. (1983) "The placebo effect in psychotherapy," *Psychotherapy Theory, Research, and Practice*, 20: 337–45.

Pentony, P. (1981) *Models of Influence in Psychotherapy*. New York: Free Press.

Prioleau, L., Murdock, M., and Brody, N. (1983) "An analysis of psychotherapy versus placebo studies," *Behavior Brain Science*, 6: 275–85.

Rosch, E. (1978) "Principles of categorization," in E. Rosch and B. Lloyd (eds), *Cognition and Categorization*. Hillside, NJ: Erlbaum.

Simons, H.W. (1986) *Persuasions: Understanding, Practice, and Analysis*. Revised edn. New York: Random House.

Simons, H.W. (1988) "The rhetoric of psychotherapeutic placebos." Paper presented at the Gordon Research Conference on Cybernetics, Oxnard, California.

Smith, M.L., Glass, G.V., and Miller, T.I. (1980) *The Benefits of Psychotherapy.* Baltimore: Johns Hopkins University Press.

Torrey, E.F. (1972). "What Western psychotherapists can learn from witch doctors," *American Journal of Orthopsychiatry*, 42: 69–76.

Trexler, L.D. and Karst, T.O. (1972) "Rational-emotive therapy, placebo, and no-treatment effects on public-speaking anxiety," *Journal of Abnormal Psychology*, 79: 60–7.

Weigert, A. (1970) "The immoral rhetoric of scientific sociology," *American Sociologist*, 5: 111–19.

Wilkins, W.W. (1984) "Psychotherapy: the powerful placebo," *Journal of Consulting and Clinical Psychology*, 52: 570–73.

Wilkins, W.W. (1986) "Rhetoric and irrelevant criteria that disguise behavior therapy efficiency: historical and contemporary notes," *Journal of Behavior Therapy and Experimental Psychiatry*, 17: 83–9.

7
Ethnography as Sermonic: The Rhetorics of Clifford Geertz and James Clifford

W. Barnett Pearce and Victoria Chen

Although rightly celebrated for his scientific accomplishments, Isaac Newton misled those who tried to understand his method when he (erroneously) declared that he did not make "hypotheses" in his analysis of data.[1] Following preachments rather than example, overzealous emulators developed what is now clearly an untenable model of scientific discourse envisioned as detached, neutral, unbiased, and objective. The scientist is supposed to produce, in one way of putting it, "knowledge untouched by human minds," and express it in discourse which resolutely refuses to "go beyond the data" and uses passive voice and third person in order to portray itself as "authorless, authoritarian, (and) objective."[2]

Exposing the pretensions of this form of discourse, the "rhetoric of inquiry" project demonstrates that even those scientists who eschew rhetoric in favor of "method" are – in the very act of eschewal – rhetors.[3] "Scientists" attempt to perform the illocutionary act[4] of "mirroring nature"[5] without the distortions of personal perspective, the various biases of language, and the subjectivity of the researcher's intentionality. However, even this discourse is constituted within a (sometimes self-denying) rhetorical community whose terministic screens, commonplaces, standards of evidence and proof, and stylistic preferences make their statements meaningful. Outside such a community, talk of operational definitions, reliability, validity, predictive utility, confidence levels, counterfactual conditionals, and the like is powerless.

However, not all scientists are positivists. Conceptually distinct genres of discourse in the sciences attempt different illocutionary acts and succeed or fail on the basis of different felicity conditions. A full-fledged rhetoric of inquiry cannot be content excoriating the obviously guilty; it should also examine the merits of what at least appear to be more laudable rhetorics.

The problem of understanding another culture has long been established as the toughest challenge for a philosophy of science.[6] Well aware of this problem, contemporary cultural anthropologists frame it as the question of what is legitimate and what is possible when representing another culture in their writings. They have become unprecedentedly self-conscious about their own work as writing, and their products as rhetorical or literary documents. Clifford Geertz advised that "if you want to understand what a science is, you should look in the first instance not at its theories or its findings, and certainly not at what its apologists say about it; you should look at what the practitioners of it do," and then noted that what anthropologists do is to write.[7] In much the same vein, James Clifford said:

> We begin, not with participant-observation or with cultural texts (suitable for interpretation), but with writing, the making of texts. No longer a marginal, or occulted, dimension, writing has emerged as central to what anthropologists do both in the field and thereafter.
>
> The essays collected . . . see culture as composed of seriously contested codes and representations; they assume that the poetic and the political are inseparable, that science is in, not above, historical and linguistic processes. They assume that academic and literary genres interpenetrate and that the writing of cultural descriptions is properly experimental and ethical. Their focus on text making and rhetoric serves to highlight the constructed, artificial nature of cultural accounts. It undermines overly transparent modes of authority, and it draws attention to the historical predicament of ethnography, the fact that it is always caught up in the invention, not the representation, of cultures.[8]

Geertz' and Clifford's descriptions make contemporary ethnography appear to have already incorporated whatever might be contributed by a rhetorical analysis. Our study of them was originally motivated by a desire to articulate and celebrate a form of scientific discourse which had successfully liberated itself from the stultifying tradition based on Newton's mistaken description of his method. As we proceeded, we discovered that there is sharp disagreement and misunderstanding about the form of this non-positivist discourse, and have come to believe that even its foremost practitioners are not aware of (or willing to confess) the rhetorical forms to which their work leads.

Self-identified with the "interpretive turn" in anthropology, Geertz is immensely popular, influential, and controversial. Clifford is perhaps the best exemplar of the "deconstructionist-semiotic turn,"[9] which produces ethnographies of ethnographies. Each provides a label for his own work: Geertz engages in "translation"; Clifford champions "interlocution." We treat these rhetorics as attempting to pull off particular illocutionary acts, and by playing the precise nature of those acts against each other in our exposition of their rhetorical form, we offer a reinterpretation of Geertz which contrasts sharply with conventional readings, which explains the extremes with which his work is criticized or praised, and which sets out a provocative model for nonpositivistic scientific discourse.

Taken as a whole, Geertz' work is a sustained sermon about the way

Western culture thinks about itself.[10] Neither *about* nor *for* the non-Western cultures who provide him his material, Geertz uses ethnography as a means of creating a language which privileges a particular way of thinking about knowledge ("local"), humankind (hermeneuts all), and cultures (semiotic, historical, and plural). Attempts to read him as depicting exotic cultures accurately, or as employing a rhetoric expressing an acceptable form of authority are profound misunderstandings of (what we believe is) his primary project: to perform an *ethical* illocutionary act by means of a locutionary act which appears to be "scientific." In this way, Geertz attempts to do for his culture as a whole what Clifford's more methodological writings attempt for the community of ethnographers.

"Translation"

Styling himself a "meanings and symbols ethnographer" and believing that meanings are "in" (not "behind") public symbols,[11] Geertz interprets the symbolic activities of natives, then translates them into a comprehensible report in the language of his own society. Interpretation occurs in a "continuing dialectical tacking between the most local of local detail and the most global of global structure in such a way as to bring them into simultaneous view."[12] Employing both "experience-near" and "experience-distant" concepts, the ethnographer is necessarily precluded from understanding a culture like a native understands it. Foreswearing "empathy" with the natives, Geertz explained, "the trick is *not* to get yourself into some inner correspondence of spirit with your informants . . . the trick is to figure out what the devil they think they are up to."[13]

Even this does not complete the ethnographer's task: it remains to write what one has figured out in ways which will make it accessible to those who have not studied the culture. Geertz is explicitly aware that his writings are literary forms. "Thick description" consists of fabricating fictions in order to render coherent accounts of exotic cultures. The process, he says, is more like what a critic does to a poem than what an astronomer does to a star, and the products are understood in the manner of grasping a proverb, catching an allusion, or seeing a joke.[14]

Thus directed away from a literal reading of his texts, we think it appropriate to ask what the devil Geertz thinks he is up to, and to employ both experience-near and experience-distant concepts. There is a common theme running through his ethnographically informed essays which focus on issues in Western culture, and their repeated articulation comprises a powerful ethical argument.

Writing in the style if not the tradition of French structuralism,

Geertz intends to be a part of the larger Western intellectual conversation, and is elated that recent turns in that conversation seem to favor anthropology. "Long one of the most homespun of disciplines, hostile to anything smacking of intellectual pretension and unnaturally proud of an outdoorsman image, anthropology has turned out, oddly enough, to have been preadapted to some of the most advanced varieties of modern opinion."[15] Geertz has produced three types of works: monographic studies of particular societies (for example, Morocco); essays on the general intellectual enterprise (for example, "Blurred genres,"[16] "Anti anti-relativism")[17] and essays which use exotica to illuminate particular Western concepts (for example, common sense, law, the self, sexuality).

> My own work, insofar as it is more than archival . . . represents an effort to edge my way into odd corners of this discussion. All the essays below are ethnographically informed (or, God knows, misinformed) reflections on general topics, the sort of matters philosophers might address from more conjectural foundations, critics from more textual ones, or historians from more inductive ones. [Their themes] are treated, one after the other, in an attempt somehow to understand how it is we understand understandings not our own.[18]

Although Geertz is transparently rhetorical, he is not rhetorically transparent. His writings have been read in a variety of ways: as an attempt "to reinvent an anthropological science with the help of textual meditations" in which "the core activity is still social description of the other;"[19] as caught in an "unresolved ambivalence" between "science" replete with the comparative descriptions of "cultures" and "the authorial mode, inscribing in language his subjects through himself;"[20] immodestly self-referential to such an extent that the "integrity" of his essays is "undone by the knowing self-consciousness that intrudes into nearly every paragraph, distracting us from the issue supposedly at hand;"[21] and insufficiently self-referential, dialogical, and situational.[22]

Such a wide array of readings does not necessarily imply a fault in the texts. Once produced, the meanings of texts pass out of the control of their producers, and illocutionary acts are "given" by their audience rather than "taken" by the actor. In this case, however, we interpret the diversity of readings as reflecting the difference between what Geertz is doing and the categories with which his readers are prepared to interpret it. The discrepancy is not helped by Geertz' rhetorical opacity.

Geertz uses many of the literary conventions of standard ethnographies, and argues that his work is unique in that it is "interpretive." Much of his "methodological" discourse revolves around his notions of "meanings and symbols." While this is not an incorrect self-description, it makes Geertz' work appear as if it should be evaluated according to conventional criteria, and under-represents the uniqueness of the illocutionary act which he is attempting.

If the metaphor is not pushed too far, it is useful to characterize Geertz as an accomplished novelist whose hard work is deliberately obscured by the grace of the finished product; and Clifford as a commentator on the problems of representation in writing.

"Interlocution"

Clifford criticizes Geertz for giving insufficient "voice" to his informants and for basing his authority on the claim that "I was there" without giving sufficient attention to the effects of his presence. Often referred to as "the voice from the campus library" by scholars distinguished for their foreign travels, Clifford's project is primarily methodological; he sets out to expose the inescapable voice of the writer in the production of ethnographies and to champion the inclusion of the informants' voices.

> James Clifford has created and occupied the role of ex officio scribe of our scribblings. Geertz, the founding figure, may pause between monographs to muse on texts, narrative, description, and interpretation. Clifford takes as his natives, as well as his informants, those anthropologists past and present whose work, self-consciously or not, has been the production of texts, the writing of ethnography. We are being observed and inscribed.[23]

Clifford's point is that ethnographers are participants in a conversation with the natives of the cultures they ostensibly represent, and that their writings should portray themselves as an interlocution rather than a narrative under the full control of the ethnographer. Like the deconstructionists, his purpose is to expose and critique the process of writing itself, and his work is best understood as a call for new ways of writing.

Using Maurice Leenhardt's ethnographic work[24] to elucidate his position, Clifford argues that the dialogical and discursive nature of any fieldwork is essential. For Leenhardt, "translation" is a process of the inventive interpretation of two cultures, not in search of the accurate version but in order to locate useful expressions. The kind of "interlocution" based on a collaborative effort must invent its own language adequate to the transmission of nuances and complex information exchanged. As a result of this negotiated vision of reality, a text is produced, and this is the textual transcription and translation *with* the natives, instead of *from* the natives *by* the ethnographer's inquisitive interview or quiet observation.[25]

Because ethnography is "actively situated *between* powerful systems of meaning," it is an intrusive or creative activity, not one of re-presenting reality. "Ethnography decodes and records, telling the grounds of collective order and diversity, inclusion and exclusion. It describes processes of innovation and structuration, and is itself part of these processes."[26] When written, the emergent, interactive, polyphonic qualities of the process should be presented in the text – although there is little agreement about just how this might be accomplished.[27]

Clifford's themes provide a useful way to display the nature of "translation" and "interlocution," and through this to get at the purposes which these rhetorical forms serve. We use the concepts of authorship, audience, and text.

Ethnographic Authorship

Geertz is clearly the authority behind his writings. He does not attempt to disguise his own role, and relies on his interpretive and translating abilities to give a good account. Repudiating Malinowski's "unsophisticated, self-serving, sentimental, and thus false" conception of rapport between the anthropologist and the informants,[28] Geertz recognized an inescapable asymmetrical relationship between ethnographer and informants. They have unshared and at times sharply contrasting backgrounds, purposes, interests, expectations, and resources. In his description and interpretation of the Balinese cockfight, Geertz clearly shows that the ethnographers' identity was highly visible among the natives, and this experience certainly mediates the description and interpretation of the cultural activity. And through the native's treatment of Geertz and his wife when the cockfight was raided by the police, we learn of the perceived high status enjoyed by American professors who want to "write a book to tell Americans about Bali."[29] Geertz' view of the relational dimension in ethnographic study implies (in agreement with Malinowski, ironically) that the mere personal experience and fieldwork, knowledge and expertise confer ethnographic authority.

Clifford, on the other hand, takes a strong position on the need to identify the native authors who are indeed the indispensable "indigenous collaborators," a term Clifford prefers over the commonly used "informants." In fact, Clifford argues that these native collaborators should be seen as "real" authors as well. Thus the original contribution to an ethnographic study always comes from the natives in the culture being explored and interpreted – Clifford plays off the etymological root of "data": "things given."

Clifford introduced Bakhtin's notion of "heteroglossia" in elucidating the polyphonic nature of ethnography. "Heteroglossia" assumes that "languages do not exclude each other, but rather intersect with each other in many different ways."[30] To extend the implication of "heteroglossia," there are always many voices speaking behind the final coherent ethnographic account produced by the anthropologist. In other words, the assembling process of any ethnographic interpretation necessitates various voices other than the ethnographer's, and these voices are frequently hidden in the final well knitted-together ethnographic account. Clifford argues for plural authorship in ethnography in light of a model which he characterizes as dialogical, discursive, and polyphonic.

Vision of the Audience

Like any writers, ethnographers create their audiences and write to them. The anticipation of the audience expresses the writer's basic assumptions about him/herself, the subject matter, and the purpose. The texts with these assumptions embedded in them then elicit responses from self-selected audiences whose characteristics – if the writing is successful – parallel the writer's intentions.

For Geertz, the audience for his ethnographies includes himself and a self-selected group of academics and general public who share his interpretive perspective and who wish to participate with Geertz in the "thick description" of culture. For Clifford, there are three audiences: the natives upon whom the ethnography is based; subsequent generations of the native culture who wish to learn about their own changing cultural tradition; and anybody else who wants to learn about the culture or other ethnographers who want to reinterpret the culture. These different visions of their audience derive from Geertz' and Clifford's conceptions of culture, their theoretical assumptions, and the way they treat ethnographic texts.

Texts

Although both Geertz and Clifford employ the notion of textualization, "texts" carry different meanings and implications for them. For Geertz, culture *is* a text which manifests itself in people's transient examples of shaped behaviors, social discourse, cultural activities, and patterns of symbols. An ethnographer's task is to "(re)construct" a reading of and to render "interpretation/thick description" (or produce a second layer of text) of the cultural texts which stand by themselves. For Clifford, the "texts" that an ethnographer needs to work with do *not* manifest themselves in the symbolic cultural events but are always produced *by* the natives as the first layer interpretation in the process of textualization.[31] Thus Geertz' notion of meaning lies *within* the symbolic cultural texts, and Clifford's *behind* the native's texts (or emerges from the dialogue on the texts).

The purpose of ethnography for Geertz is the enlargement of the universe of human discourse through a symbolic conceptualization of culture. "Thick description" requires the development of vocabulary and intellectual framework which permit "not a simple recasting of others' ways of putting things in terms of our own ways of putting them . . . but displaying the logic of their ways of putting them in the locutions of ours."[32]

Geertz treats culture as an assemblage of symbolic texts to be "read," "interpreted," and "inscribed" by ethnographers. The content of the texts includes "anything that is disengaged from its mere actuality and used to impose meaning upon existence,"[33] such as words, gestures, drawings and musical sounds. In "Thick description," Geertz maintains that behaviors can also be treated as texts to be read and interpreted within the cultural context. Geertz further argues that human thought is basically both social and public, and that its natural habitat is the house yard, the market place, and the town square.[34] Thinking, therefore, is considered a public activity which consists not of "happenings in the head," but of a traffic in what have been called significant symbols, themselves "inscriptions" of a "communal sensibility." Cultural analysis, for Geertz, is "not an experimental science in search of law but an interpretive one in search of meaning;" it proceeds by "construing social expressions on their surface enigmatical."[35]

Central to Geertz' interpretive framework lies the crucial element for any ethnographic endeavor, the participant-observation method. The ethnographer's personal experience – ever since Malinowski and Mead's colorful accounts of some exotic land – is indispensable for him/her to provide a "legitimate" and hopefully "accurate" interpretation, that is, an account from the "native's point of view" as authorized by the ethnographer. Geertz' celebrated "thick description" of the Balinese cockfight not only required his presence (which is somewhat different from active involvement), but was also "fabricated" by the ethnographer's subjective and insightful interpretation.

The notion of participant-observation implies a kind of "detached involvement" of anthropologists, and their task is to experience and interpret simultaneously. The seemingly paradoxical nature of experience and interpretation entails a continuing tacking between the "inside" and "outside" of events.[36] This means that the ethnographer not only has to grasp the significance of specific occurrences but also to step back to assess and interpret these meaning in a larger context. In other words, participant-observation in Geertz' interpretive framework is a dialectic of experience and interpretation in hermeneutic terms. The very focus on the ethnographer's personal experience in insightful interpretation thus provides the basis for thick description which is based on experiential authority.

In contrast, Clifford endorsed Maurice Leenhardt's notion of ethnographic study not as the result of decoding "textualized behavior," but as an ongoing productive and collaborative work with the natives which cannot easily be dominated by a privileged interpretation.[37] Although Leenhardt was certainly a participant with the natives in their cultural activities, his primary texts were produced in a two-staged process. First, the natives transcribed in the native language the legends, ritual discourse, etc., which comprise their cultural symbols. Second, Leenhardt then spent days, months, and years *with* the natives to translate, transcribe, and interpret the vernacular first produced by the natives. This long and arduous collaborative effort aims to produce something that both the natives and the nonnative readers can benefit from through mutual learning. In other words, the writing produced in the field study, from Clifford's viewpoint, should be accessible to reappropriation by the natives, who are often the coauthors.

Clifford believes that Leenhardt's understanding and interpretation of cultural traditions and customs is a dialectical process of questions and answers in which the ethnographer's role is to be involved in the conscious observations and reflections of the native's changing life. The ethnographer must solicit the natives' interest and awaken their thinking. Therefore, Clifford is less interested in treating culture as an object of description or texts to be read than as if it were activity "thinking itself." Instead of seeing the relationship between the ethnographer and the informants in terms of rapport or empathy (which typify Malinowski's approach), Clifford thinks that "complicity" is a better word to capture the nature of the intersubjective engagement of the ethnographer and the natives. The polyphonic nature in this negotiated vision of reality then becomes apparent in Clifford's intersubjective (as opposed to Geertz' subjective) paradigm.

According to Clifford, a crucial aspect of Leenhardt's approach to his fieldwork is the collection of a large corpus of vernacular transcriptions. By including these transcriptions, ethnography is rendered open to both scholarly reinterpretation and to reappropriation by native speakers. However, this kind of ethnographic endeavor is precisely what Geertz criticizes in his "Under the mosquito net," a commentary on Malinowski's *A Diary in the Strict Sense of the Term*.[38] For Geertz, Malinowski's "inadequately voluminous" ethnography may be detailed and comprehensive to the point of indiscriminateness. Geertz' interpretive framework emphasizes the ethnographer's careful observation, selective and creative juxtaposition of cultural phenomena, and "thick description" of the import of the cultural symbols and events. The advantage of including the transcription of any kind of social discourse in ethnography seen by Clifford is not appreciated in Geertz' practice of interpretation. In fact, one may ask if Geertz ever produced, let alone included, any detailed transcription of social discourse in his ethnographic endeavor.

In summary, the different visions of "texts" between Geertz and Clifford can be elucidated through the way they see ethnographic data. Geertz specifically states that "what we call our data are really our own constructions of other people's constructions of what they and their compatriots are up to."[39] Ethnographic texts then consist of both the first order cultural texts which can systematically be interpreted by the ethnographer to produce second order texts. Clifford, on the other hand, argues that ethnographic texts involve the ongoing "give-and-take" (negotiation of reality) between the ethnographer and natives instead of the ethnographer's own reading and coherent (re)construction of the cultural texts.

Conclusion

It is not difficult to derive ethical maxims from the writings of both Geertz and Clifford. Both dismiss the illusions of an objective representation of other cultures, for methodological and conceptual reasons. On the other hand, against the spectre of rampant relativism, they not only argue that translation/interlocution *are* possible, but that there is a moral imperative why they *should* occur. Translation and interlocution are not just methods of research; they are the antidote for particular social sins. Geertz and Clifford both envision a "devil" against which they and their audience should fight.

For Geertz, the devil to be avoided has two faces: an insufficient appreciation of the "localness" of one's own culture; and the use of a universe of discourse insufficient to account for the social semiotic of cultures other than one's own.[40] "Thick description" is better understood as a rite of passage rather than a "method" for scientific research. Performing "thick descriptions" not only signifies but creates the differences between an immature and an adult member of the improved culture which Geertz is trying to call into being.

For Clifford, intellectual imperialism is the devil to be avoided. This imperialism results from and expresses itself in two practices: (1) a one-way discourse in which ethnographers extract information about a culture but do not take those interpretations back to the natives; and (2) the tendency of ethnographers to frame their analysis within their own culture's conceptual apparatuses. The procedures of getting natives to inscribe their own texts and of citing them as co-authors are better understood as an initiation ritual, a means of inducting the natives of the culture being studied into the community of ethnographers and vice versa, than as a research or even literary "method."

Ethnography seems a curious medium in which to practice ethics. Why not write more straightforwardly about ethics? Why do Geertz and Clifford not generate a list of ethical maxims themselves rather than forcing poor scholars like us to scour them out? Why not write in the long tradition of philosophical or religious ethics rather than masquerading as social scientists?

We think there is a good reason, but preface our presentation of it with a long overdue caveat. Our analysis is, obviously, an attempt at "translation," not "interlocution." We have not negotiated the meaning of these texts with the "natives;" rather, we have attempted to do a "thick description" and comparison of them. We are not sure how either Geertz or Clifford will take to being disclosed as (or "accused of") being ethicists. If either objects, we shall have to ask Geertz how he deals with protesting native informants or Clifford how to represent the "polyphony" in a work like this.

"Translation" and "interlocution" are intended as illocutionary acts, but illocutionary acts cannot be brought off if the necessary felicity conditions do not exist. "Translation" simply cannot occur in a universe of discourse which denies the existence of any social reality other than itself; and "interlocution" is impossible in a universe of discourse which defines any difference as a "mistake" to be "corrected." If the rhetorical situation demands the creation of a universe of discourse in which a given text can be effective rather than adapting a text to the existing universe of discourse, then ethnography is an excellent method for doing ethics.

Alasdair MacIntyre has argued persuasively that the contemporary period is one of fundamental moral disorder.[41] In this situation, it is not possible to "do" ethics by argument, because the relevant parties do not share commensurate "argumentative fields" (to use Toulmin's vocabulary) or "intellectual traditions" (to use MacIntyre's) in which persuasive discourse can be framed. MacIntyre suggests the "neo-Aristotelian" concept of historically continuous traditions as the locus of both meaning and ethics which will stave off the spectre of chaotic relativism. In a similar move, we suggest, Geertz and Clifford gravitate toward ethnography because they want to create an ethical *community*, not just produce a list of moral precepts or a philosophical defense of pluralism. The *practices* of translation and interlocution, not simply the concept of them, are creative social acts, closer to a rite of passage or an initiation ritual than to philosophic treatises. Participating in these practices produces a community in which the felicity conditions for performing them are met.

Both translation and interlocution require the ethnographer to put his/her own world view "at risk." In fact, they mandate the development of vocabulary and concepts sufficiently powerful to describe social realities fundamentally different from one's own without denying those differences. The result is a rhetorical form which has these features:

1   It is explicitly self-reflexive. Geertz' talk about natives almost always comes back to deal with the perspectives, the stance, the purposes of Western culture from which come his audience.[42] Clifford's concept of how ethnography should be done explicitly focuses on the discourse in which the ethnographer is a participant. The myths of the "objective observer," or of the "mirror of nature," or of the "immaculate perception" unsullied by the mind of the observer are alien to this universe of discourse.

2   It is determinedly flexible in its logics. One of the basic "moves" in positivism was to seek a rigorous mathematical/logical scaffold. The universe of discourse in which translation and interlocution occur contains a transformed notion of rigor. Instead of the quixotic quest to be both complete and consistent, the rigor of this universe of discourse is evaluated on the basis of its capacity to portray and contrast multiple, incommensurate social realities. Both Clifford and Geertz describe culture itself as malleable, and "ethnographic assertion as . . . essentially contestable."[43]

3   It is explicitly open-minded. Neither Geertz nor Clifford attempts to say the "last word" in their description of any culture, or even of the resources used in ethnography. If "keeping the conversation going" is the objective, then "conversation stoppers" are to be avoided. When a critic shows Geertz that another reading is possible of, for example, the cultural semiotic of cockfights in Bali, Geertz should welcome this as an addition to the development of a universe of discourse in which translation is possible, not as a "refutation" of "truth-claims" offered in a universe of discourse which seeks "positive" knowledge.[44]

4   It is transparently rhetorical. Not only are the writings of Geertz and Clifford rhetorical acts, they portray themselves as expressions of particular social realities, imposing a terministic screen over the brute facts of experience and moving in ways dictated by the logic of their rules for meaning and action.

This rhetoric differs strikingly from that derived from Newton's mistake, and depends upon a set of felicity conditions quite unlike those of positivistic science. The practices of "translation" and "interlocution" should be seen as attempts to call into being communities in which the appropriate felicity conditions exist as well as to address such pre-existing communities. For this constructive act, ethnography is a particularly potent vehicle.

Notes

1 Marjorie Grene, *The Knower and the Known* (University of California Press, Berkeley, 1974).

2 Barbara Myerhoff and Jay Ruby, "Introduction," in Jay Ruby (ed.), *A Crack in the Mirror* (University of Pennsylvania Press, Philadelphia, 1982), p. 22.

3 John S. Nelson and Allan Megill, "Rhetoric of inquiry: projects and prospects," *Quarterly Journal of Speech*, 72 (1976), pp. 20–37.

4 We are using (rather than following) a line of work in the philosophy of ordinary language which examines utterances (texts) in terms of what is "done" by the speaker. An illocutionary act is defined by Austin as that "certain *force* in saying something." Searle cites as examples "stating, questioning, commanding, promising, etc." See J.L. Austin, *How to do Things with Words* (Cambridge University Press, New York, 1969), p. 24.

5 Richard Rorty, *Philosophy and the Mirror of Nature* (Princeton University Press, Princeton, 1979).

6 Peter Winch, *The Idea of a Social Science and its Relation to Philosophy* (Routledge and Kegan Paul, London, 1958).

7 Clifford Geertz, *The Interpretation of Cultures* (Basic Books, New York, 1973), p. 5.

8 James Clifford, "Introduction: partial truths," in James Clifford and George E. Marcus (eds), *Writing Culture* (University of California Press, Berkeley, 1986), p. 2.

9 Paul Rabinow, "Representations are social facts: modernity and post-modernity in anthropology," in James Clifford and George E. Marcus (eds), *Writing Culture* (University of California Press, Berkeley, 1986), p. 242.

10 This represents our reading of Geertz, of course, which in this case differs from his own account of his project. He states, "I regard my life mainly as having been devoted not to theory, methodology or 'ethics,' but to attempting to describe 'other cultures,' and to do so accurately and perceptively . . ." (personal correspondence, 16 March 1987).

11 Clifford Geertz, *Local Knowledge* (Basic Books, New York, 1983), p. 69; and *Interpretation of Cultures*.

12 Geertz, *Local Knowledge*, p. 69.

13 Ibid., p. 58.

14 Ibid., p. 70.

15 Ibid., p. 4.

16 Ibid., pp. 19–35.

17 Clifford Geertz, "Anti anti-relativism," *American Anthropologist*, 86 (1984), pp. 263–78. See also C. Geertz, *Works and Lives: The Anthropologist as Author* (Stanford University Press, Stanford, 1988).

18 Geertz, *Local Knowledge*, p. 5.

19 Rabinow, "Representations," p. 242.

20 Stephen William Foster, "Review of *Local Knowledge* by Clifford Geertz," *American Anthropologist*, 87 (1985), pp. 164–5.

21 Paul Robinson, "From suttee to baseball to cockfight," *New York Times Book Review*, 25 September 1983, pp. 11, 35.

22 Clifford, cited in Rabinow, "Representations," p. 244.

23 Rabinow, "Representations," p. 242.

24 James Clifford, *Person and Myth: Maurice Leenhardt in the Melanesian World* (University of California Press, Berkeley, 1982).

25 James Clifford, "Fieldwork, reciprocity, and the making of ethnographic texts: the example of Maurice Leenhardt," *Man*, 15 (1980), pp. 518–32.

26 Clifford, "Introduction," p. 2.
27 Rabinow, "Representations," p. 246. See also J. Clifford, *The Predicament of Culture* (Harvard University Press, Cambridge, 1988).
28 Clifford Geertz, "Under the mosquito net," *New York Review of Books*, 14 September 1967, pp. 12–13.
29 Geertz, *Interpretation of Cultures*, p. 415.
30 James Clifford, "On ethnographic authority," *Representation*, 1 (1983), pp. 118–46.
31 Clifford, *Person and Myth*, 140.
32 Geertz, *Local Knowledge*, p. 10.
33 Geertz, *Interpretation of Cultures*, p. 45.
34 Ibid., p. 360.
35 Ibid., p. 5.
36 Clifford, "On ethnographic authority," p. 127.
37 Clifford, *Person and Myth*, pp. 129–44.
38 Geertz, "Under the mosquito net," pp. 12–13.
39 Geertz, *Interpretation of Cultures*, p. 9.
40 Geertz, *Local Knowledge* and "Anti anti-relativism."
41 Alasdair MacIntyre, *After Virtue* (University of Notre Dame Press, Notre Dame, 1984).
42 Robinson finds this quality of Geertzian prose lamentable. After quoting a paragraph from *Local Knowledge*, he writes: "But surely the most striking thing about the above passage is that it so insistently calls attention to itself as a piece of writing, reminding us in virtually every phrase of the literary presence behind the text. Indeed, it tells us much more about Mr Geertz than about its putative subject. It informs us, quite gratuitously, that he is familiar with both Immanuel Kant and Wallace Stevens. At the same time, it is also eager to assure us that he is no ivory tower intellectual but a regular guy who knows the colloquial meaning of 'square' and would sooner die than be thought smug. *Local Knowledge* fairly bristles with this kind of self-referential prose. It is, in fact, one of the most immodest books I have ever read.
    "Some readers may feel that such stylistic matters are a relatively harmless affection and ought to be tolerated in view of Mr Geertz's range, inventiveness and anthropological interpretation. Its character, however, is so fierce that it eventually undermines one's confidence in the intellectual proceedings. The essays, we begin to feel, exist less as a forum for ideas than as occasions for the author to display himself. Their integrity, in effect, is undone by the knowing self-consciousness that intrudes into nearly every paragraph, distracting us from the issue supposedly at hand and insisting that we turn our attention instead to the well read yet eminently down-to-earth fellow, Clifford Geertz" (Robinson, "From suttee to baseball").
43 Geertz, *Interpretation of Cultures*, p. 29.
44 Whether he would treat such revisionists so charitably is a matter of conjecture. Geertz believes that meaning lies in the symbols of culture and can be read there with some degree of confidence. He said, "a good interpretation of anything . . . takes us into the heart of that of which it is the interpretation." Such statements justifiably lead critics into confusion about his concept of the "openness" of texts. See Geertz, *Interpretation of Cultures*, p. 18.

8

Beyond the Rhetoric of Antitheory: Towards a Revisionist Interpretation of Critical Legal Studies

Steve Fuller

Ethnographers of the knowledge-producing tribes must find the recent humanist assertions of "theory has no consequences" a puzzling practice, much like an elaborate native ritual which seems to serve no purpose other than inhibiting the tribe's reproductive capabilities. Yet a cynic amongst the ethnographers may well suspect that by disavowing any claim to either knowledge or power, these antitheoretical humanists are merely dodging fights with *real* social scientists and professional politicians, against whom they would not even make a respectable show. If the argument of this paper succeeds, the cynic will have something more than just his suspicions to go on, for I intend to argue that, contrary to its avowed aim of terminating all debates on theory, the assertion "theory has no consequences" – once properly scrutinized – radically opens the theory debates, so much as to invite the participation of the dreaded scientists, politicians, and even philosophers (on whose work theory is modeled most directly) in affairs that both theorists and antitheorists in the humanities have preferred, at least in the recent past, to keep to themselves.

The focus of this chapter will be on what is perhaps the clearest statement and defense of the "theory has no consequences" thesis: Stanley Fish's "Consequences," which originally appeared in a special issue of *Critical Inquiry* devoted to the recent antitheoretic turn in literary studies.[1] The influence of Fish's essay and related work has extended beyond his homebase in literature to include, especially, a cognate antifoundationalist movement in American legal scholarship known as Critical Legal Studies (CLS). Fish's writing serves as an ideal medium for disseminating antitheory throughout the humanities. Unlike his two main competitors, Richard Rorty and Bernstein, Fish does not presume that philosophy is the *lingua franca* of the humanities – indeed, he presumes hardly any specialized learning at all, only an intuitive sense of the interpretive process. Thus, rather than polemicizing against the Tradition to an audience of interested spectators, Fish typically makes a direct appeal to the commonsense of his audience. Consequently, it might be said that Fish reads a little *too* easily. However, this chapter aims to add some friction to Fish's smooth manner by being almost exclusively critical and diagnostic. Fish and his fellow travelers need to realize that, at this stage of the dialectic, they share enough of the deepest presuppositions of their "positivist" foes to lead the cynic to think that their antifoundationalist rage is tinged with a sense of betrayal. Moreover, the apparent finality of the "theory has no consequences" argument turns on the anti-theorists having failed to assimilate some of positivism's own attempts at self-correction. And as our closing remarks will suggest, there is yet another sense of "theory has no consequences," beyond the three discussed in the next section, that haunts the CLS debates in a particularly deep and ironic fashion.

What Exactly does "Theory has No Consequences" Mean?

Even before being exposed to Fish's often seductive arguments, we would do well to appreciate the ambiguity of the claim, "Theory has no consequences." At least three things can be meant by this claim, even if we take "theory" in its most ordinary sense (which, as a matter of fact, Fish does not).

1   *Theory cannot, by definition, have any consequences.* This is an extension of the logical thesis – normally associated with the later Wittgenstein – that the definition of a concept does not determine its range of application. At most, the definition supplies the concept's relation to other concepts in a common framework. Thus, formulating a theory (that is, a system of concepts) and specifying the contexts where it may be properly used are logically distinct activities. Indeed, the latter activity crucially relies on situated judgment calls on "hard cases" that were not anticipated in the original formulation of the theory. Thus, armed with a complete mastery of *Structuralist Poetics* but no knowledge of the history of applied structuralism, I would be liable to the same misconceptions as befell the medieval physicists who tried to reconstruct the Greek experimental tradition with only the texts of Archimedes on hand.

2   *Theory does not, in fact, have any consequences.* This is an empirical thesis that a social scientist might show about the lack of efficacy that theoretical pursuits have had on other social practices, including perhaps not only the practices that theories have been designed to influence but even the subsequent pursuit of theory itself. A vulgar Marxist materialist may find such a view attractive, as it would render intellectual discourse entirely epiphenomenal. However,

in these stark terms, the thesis flies in the face of our historical intuitions about the efficacy of certain theories, such as those offered by the figures of the French Enlightenment and, indeed, Marxists themselves. Still, the thesis may be stated more sophisticatedly to show that whenever a theory has seemed to have social impact, it has not been due to the theory *per se* but to something contingently associated with it, such as the status of the particular theorist.

3   *Theory ought not, as a matter of principle, have any consequences.* This is a normative thesis that might be formulated if theory were thought to have, or could have, the wrong sorts of social consequences. Such concerns were clearly voiced by Edmund Burke and other conservative opponents to the political impact of the French Enlightenment. Similar reservations have been recently expressed by Allan Bloom, who argues that the speculative nature of theorizing can easily turn into dangerous ideologizing once it is unleashed from the cloistered colonies of cool-headed academics into the frenzy of the public sphere.[2] Aside from preventing the gratuitous agitation of the masses, academics may want to contain the effects of theory out of a self-imposed intellectual modesty, which would both reward the efforts of data collectors, archivists, and the other "underlaborers" who supply whatever "real" content theories have, and make that content available for more direct critical scrutiny.

Needless to say, these three readings stand in a curious tension. For example, the prescription made in (3) seems to presuppose that there have been occasions in which (2) has been false, while the semantic character of (1) seems to render the claims made in either (2) or (3) beside the point. Nevertheless, all three are tightly woven into the fabric of Fish's argument, as in the following:

> This then is why theory will never succeed: it cannot help but borrow its terms and its content from that which it claims to transcend, the mutable world of practice, belief, assumptions, point of view, and so forth. And, by definition, something that cannot succeed cannot have consequences, cannot achieve the goals it has set for itself by being or claiming to be theory, the goals of guiding and/or reforming practice. Theory cannot guide practice because its rules and procedures are no more than generalizations from practice's history (and from only a small piece of that history), and theory cannot reform practice because, rather than neutralizing interest, it begins and ends in interest and raises the imperatives of interest – of some local, particular, partisan project – to the status of universals.[3]

Another way of seeing that Fish mixes the three readings of his thesis to suit his immediate dialectical purpose is to follow what he has to say about his main example of theory, Chomskyan linguistics. At first, Fish pronounces on the conceptual impossibility of Chomsky's project, but then realizing that *something* that Chomsky has done has in fact become very influential, Fish turns to debunking theory's causal role. Finally, lest the reader think that, no matter how it happened, Chomsky's success was not such a bad thing after all, Fish warns against the theory diverting attention from genuine scholarly and critical practice. Thus, the moments of Fish's dialectic pass from (1) to (2) to (3), and in so doing, he implicitly invites, respectively, the philosopher, the social scientist, and the politician to assess the merits of his claim. But all this has been said without even defining Fish's sense of "theory," to which we now turn.

Fish's Positivistic Theory of "Theory"

In locating the conceptual space occupied by theory, the key contrast that Fish has in mind is one familiar to mathematicians and computer scientists, namely, between *algorithmic* and *heuristic* procedural rules. As Fish sees it, the theorist aspires to the algorithmic in that he would like to discover rules that can function as a guide to a humanistic discipline's practice in all cases by being sufficiently explicit and neutral for any practitioner, regardless of her particular interests, to follow to the same result. A rule with heuristic status, by contrast, can guide practice only in certain cases which cannot be determined in advance of practice but only, in retrospect, once practice has in fact been successfully guided by the rule. In short, the desired distinction is between "the foolproof method" and "the rule of thumb."[4]

In the course of "Consequences," Fish smuggles additional conceptual baggage into this distinction: the foolproof method turns out to be one that, at least in principle, could be derived a priori, which is to say, prior to all practice and thus unaffected by the history of the practice it purports to govern; the rule of thumb turns out to be valid a posteriori in a rather particular way, namely, relative to the entire history of a practice and not simply to a practitioner's own experience in trying to apply the rule. These conceptual moves are properly characterized as "smuggling" because not only are they logically independent of Fish's opening moves (that is, a foolproof method need not be knowable a priori and a rule of thumb is not normally thought of as a kind of social convention), but they also ensure the success of his central argument; for Fish argues (a) that the pursuit of theory cannot succeed *because* all purported instances of theory are really generalizations from actual practice, and (b) that this failure of theory does not in the least impair the ability of practices to govern themselves locally through rules of thumb. The force of these two conclusions would not be so strong if their truth was not virtually deducible from Fish's idiosyncratic definition of the two kinds of rules. As a result, were the reader to wonder why foolproof methods could not be grounded empirically or why rules of thumb must have the force of social conventions, he would be at a loss for an answer in Fish.

Still, for all their question-begging character, Fish's tactics have precedent – indeed, in the very movement Fish claims to be opposing. For Fish's definition of "theory" as a "foolproof method" is nothing short of a positivist reduction. Before the rise of positivism in the nineteenth century, "theory" was generally used to describe privileged standpoints from which phenomena might be systematically inspected. A theory was thus typically "speculative" and "metaphysical," and the attitude of the theorist was one of contemplative detachment. It would be fair to say that this is still the ordinary sense of the word "theory."[5] However, this was precisely the sense of theory attacked by the positivists, starting even with Comte, who argued that the only way in which one could tell whether one's theory was any good was by putting it to the experimental test: "Does the theory allow the inquirer to obtain what he wishes from the phenomena?" A theory that could give a positive answer to this question on a regular basis was "theory enough" for the positivist, for it would then constitute a foolproof method for conducting one's inquiry. Like the metaphysical sense of theory, the positivist sense had to be articulated in a technical discourse. But instead of referring to subtle underlying entities which unified the array of phenomena under study in ways not always transparent to the casual observer, the positivist referred to operational procedures which any inquirer could implement and to which he could be held accountable by some larger community.

Indeed, in its more virulent twentieth century form (which followed a brush with pragmatism), a positivist like A.J. Ayer would argue that what distinguishes "scientific theory" from other forms of theory is *not* its ability to permit us a deeper understanding of reality, but its ability to permit us a more substantial control over phenomena; hence, positivist philosophy of science is typically described as *antirealist* and *instrumentalist.*[6] The implication of this view for theory in the *social* sciences, then, is clear: the better theory is the one better able to predict and control the behavior of people. Interestingly, ethical theories turn out to be crude theories of this kind, the only difference being that ethics clothes its interest in controlling behavior in the metaphysical language of "values." Fish's own remarks about "the consequences of theory" dovetail nicely with Ayer's here, since Fish believes that whatever impact theory has on humanist practice is not due to its truth directing the way to better interpretations, but to its force directing interpreters into certain desired forms of discourse. However, Fish ultimately fails to see his ties to positivism because by infusing his conception of "theory" with a priori status, he conflates the older metaphysical sense of the term, which he clearly rejects, with the newer positivistic sense, which he seems – at least in practice – to embrace.

Since Fish fails to see himself as an instance of the positivism he opposes, it is perhaps not surprising that he also misses the point of the positivist's longing for a "value-neutral" method, which Fish dismisses as patently impossible to achieve. "Value-neutrality," a term popularized by Max Weber after it had already provoked a generation of polemics among German economists at the end of the nineteenth century, was hardly ever used to characterize the activity of *constructing* a method (of, say, economic analysis) but more often to characterize the activity of *testing* or *justifying* it.[7] Already, then, this fact about the term's usage concedes the point which Fish still thinks needs to be contested, namely, that all theory construction is laden with the values of the theorist, which are determined by the local nature of his own practices.

What is open to debate, however, is whether a theory can be tested or justified in a value-neutral manner. For example, philosophically inclined practitioners of the life sciences (for example, John Eccles, Peter Medawar, Stephen J. Gould, and especially David Faust)[8] have been persuaded by Karl Popper's view that the scientific community collectively achieves value-neutrality for a theory by having the theory's tester be someone other than the person who first proposed the theory – presumably someone who does not have a stake in the theory working. Not only is this a nice myth, but it also seems to fit the sociological data, which suggest that the personalities of scientists polarize into two types, roughly the speculators and the experimentalists.[9] As long as the scientific community has a healthy mixture of these personalities, all of whom see themselves as engaged in the same inquiry, then Popper's picture appears quite workable. In any case, Fish does not address the possibility that value-neutrality is simply the mutual cancellation of individual values on the collective level.

Now the issue of whether a theory can be *justified* in a value-neutral manner is somewhat trickier to resolve, largely for terminological reasons. The logical positivists frequently spoke of "theory-neutral observation," but in so doing they were using "theory" in the metaphysical sense mentioned earlier and "observation" to describe something already placed in a technical language. For purposes of criticizing Fish, then, it would be less misleading for the reader to substitute "value-neutral theory." The motivation behind the positivists wanting such neutrality was that the two most recently heralded physical theories, relativity and quantum, were each supported by scientists of an idealist (Eddington for relativity and Bohr for quantum) and a realist (Einstein for both) bent. Yet regardless of where they stood on the idealist/realist debate, the scientists could account for the same facts from within their respective metaphysical positions. The positivists tried to generalize this insight to the idea that a theory is more justified if it can be deduced from higher-order theories, especially ones which would otherwise be mutually incompatible. Thus, the ultimately justified theory, the positivist's notorious "observation language," stands out by its ability to be deduced from all other theories and, therefore, remains justified regardless of which of those other theories end up getting rejected. And so, in practical terms, the possibility that Fish neglects here is that value-neutrality may simply be a theory's ability to be endorsed by people having otherwise conflicting values.

Towards a More Self-Critical Positivist Theory of "Theory"

At this point, it might prove instructive to increase the conceptual stakes in our critique of Fish. Instead of revealing Fish's errors by the positivist standards to which he secretly seems to aspire, we shall now turn to criticizing the standards themselves. This tactic is not as unfair as it may seem, since the positivists were among the first to realize the inadequacies of their own account of theory. Indeed, their reservations arose from further thought about the alleged value neutrality, or metaphysical indifference, of empirically testable theories.

Carnap originally set the stage when he appealed to relativistic and quantum mechanics as evidence for the "pseudo-problematic" status of philosophical (or, in Fish's sense, "theoretical") disputes, since such metaphysically divergent physicists as Bohr and Einstein could continue to add to the body of empirical knowledge while their philosophical differences remained unresolved.[10] However, if true, the truth of Carnap's claim was very much an *unintended consequence* of the many famous exchanges held between the idealist and realist physicists, since Bohr, Einstein, and others interpreted their own empirical inquiries as attempts to vindicate their respective metaphysics – an impossible task by positivist lights. Still, evidence could be found for a *deliberate* application of Carnap's thesis, and to great consequence – but in the less glamorous science of experimental psychology. Indeed, in his 1915 presidential address to the American Psychological Association, John B. Watson called for the abandonment of the entire introspectionist paradigm, on the grounds that its evidence was gathered simply by training subjects in the particular experimenter's response protocols, thereby explaining the hopelessly diverse array of data. Yet Watson quickly added that introspection's failure was behaviorism's gain, since, if nothing else, the diversity of data proved that *learning* was a robust phenomenon worthy of study in its own right, independent of the content that the subject was taught.[11] Needless to say, behaviorism was destined to become the most important antitheoretic scientific research program of the century.

After the late 1930s, when behaviorism became the academically most powerful school of psychology in the USA and the logical positivists had themselves emigrated to this country, psychology was the science to which positivists most often referred for examples about the eliminability of theory. Not surprisingly, they quickly found themselves pondering Fish-like thoughts, which Carl Hempel dubbed the Theoretician's Dilemma:

> If the terms and principles of a theory serve their purpose they are unnecessary [since they merely summarize the known data]; and if they do not serve their purpose they are surely unnecessary. But given any theory, its terms and principles either serve their purpose or they do not. Hence, the terms and principles of any theory are unnecessary.[12]

To his credit, Hempel solved the dilemma by abandoning a crucial positivist assumption. It is the assumption, rather prominent in Fish's work, that algorithms and heuristics mark a distinction *in kind*. That is, positivists generally suppose that some rules work all the time and can therefore function as proof procedures, whereas other rules are more open-ended and work only occasionally. Against this, Hempel argued that heuristics are merely *imperfectly known algorithms*. In other words, if a rule works only occasionally, it cannot be immediately inferred that the phenomena to which the rule applies are indeterminate or, in some fundamental way, escape rule-governance. Rather, it simply means that the right rule has yet to be found. Another way of making Hempel's point is that positivists act as if a theory becomes somehow less theoretical, and somehow less worthy of scientific attention, if it turns out to be *false*. This view is clearly mistaken, since a major role for theory is not merely to save but to *extend* the range of phenomena, which necessarily involves an element of risk, given that we never know in advance whether our extensions will be correct. What, then, informs these extensions of theory? According to Hempel, as well as Popper and Quine, none other than the sorts of "local" considerations that Fish seems to think vitiates the epistemic status of theory. For all its intriguing character, *there is nothing in the least self-contradictory about the possibility that certain universal truths may be discoverable only under quite particular historical circumstances.* This is a clear oversight in Fish's argument that did not equally elude the positivists.

The Universality, Abstractness, and Foolproofness of Theory

A related confusion into which Fish seems to have fallen as a result of making aprioricity essential to theory concerns the relation of *universality* to *fallibility* and *corrigibility*. Contrary to the spirit of Fish's definition, universality does not necessarily imply infallibility and incorrigibility. Admittedly, in the history of the Western tradition, several philosophers have followed Plato in believing that whatever is universal cannot be false and thus need not be changed. However, those philosophers (and it is now controversial whether even Descartes should be included among them) have also tended to think that universals are apprehended by a special mental faculty, which Plato called *nous*, whose workings are infallible in virtue of bypassing the potentially deceptive route of sensory experience. It is curious that Fish seems to think that this is still taken to be a live option among contemporary theorists in the humanities who are no doubt familiar with the conclusions of *The Critique of Pure Reason*. Moreover, both Charles Sanders Peirce and Popper are noted for having argued that as long as a universal principle is treated as a hypothesis under test, there is no contradiction in saying that it might be false and hence revisable. Isaac Levi has since gone further to separate issues of corrigibility from those of fallibility: a discipline may legitimately decide to revise a universal principle, even if it has not been shown false, simply because its interests have changed.[13]

When Fish seems to think that certain theorists believe they are possessed with "pure reason" or some other form of "intellectual intuition," he may be expressing latent skepticism about the sort of knowledge that can be gained from *abstraction*. Certainly, this would make sense of his dismissive remarks about Chomsky's project of universal linguistics. Again to cite precedent, Aristotle talked about the abstraction of a universal in two sorts of ways: on the one hand, he described it as the extraction of what is common to a set of particulars (*korismos*); on the other hand, he described it as what is left after the particularizing features of a particular are removed (*aphairesis*). Generally speaking, if a philosopher has talked about abstraction in the former way, he has tended to be sanguine about its efficacy, while if he has talked about it in the latter way, he has tended to be skeptical. Joining Fish in the list of skeptics are Ockham, Berkeley, and Bradley. All happen to believe that a conceptual distinction is legitimate only if it can be cashed out as an empirically real difference. (Even Bradley buys this line, insofar as he believes that since there are *no* empirically real differences, it follows that there are no legitimate conceptual distinctions.) With this history in mind, let us now return to Chomsky.[14]

If, as Chomsky argues, our linguistic performance is a degenerate expression of our linguistic competence, then an anti-abstractionist like Fish will demand that there be some way of empirically eliminating the degenerate elements of *our* linguistic performance – not the performance of machine simulations – so as to reveal this underlying competence. Fish claims that experiments of this kind are bound to fail because language works *only* because sentences are always situated in a context of utterance, which consists of those very elements Chomsky calls "degenerate." Fish's aversion to abstraction may, thus, be likened to the physiologist who thinks that examining dead bodies defeats the whole point of studying the human organism, which is, after all, to discover how *life* works.[15] And while both sides of this analogy have some *prima facie* plausibility, can either side, especially Fish's, hold up under stiff scrutiny?

From within Chomsky's camp, there is an instructive way of diagnosing the source of Fish's anti-abstractionism which should make us think twice about what exactly is being criticized here. Jerry Fodor distinguishes two reasons why a scientist – let us say a cognitive scientist – is interested in abstraction or "idealization." First, he might want to model the optimally rational thinker, in which case his object of study is indeed something closer to a computer simulation than a real human being. However, he might instead want to model real suboptimally rational thinkers, in which case foolproof computational methods will have to be supplemented by other rules that don't work nearly so well and, as a result, account for the numerous errors that real thinkers make.[16] Both Chomsky and Fish confuse these two interests in abstraction: Chomsky claims to be interested in modeling real speakers but his techniques suggest that he is really modeling ideal speakers; Fish catches on to this fact but mistakenly concludes that Chomsky's is the way of all abstractive projects and that, therefore, all should be rejected.

Again the error here has probably been inherited from Plato, if we understand the Platonic concept of "Form" to imply that any particular is a degenerate version of just *one* universal, or, in more Aristotelian terms, that each particular consists of one essence and many nonessential features. After all, Chomsky does not merely bracket considerations of context from his search for linguistic universals, but actually does not believe that context has much to contribute to a general understanding of language. And, certainly, Fish is reacting at least as much to this devaluation of context as *nonessential*, as to the fact that Chomsky restricts his interests in the essential features of language to whatever can be captured in a competence grammar. Both therefore err in thinking that if there are universals to be found in a given set of particulars, then there are *at most* one, when in fact a more realistic representation of the particulars may be gotten by supposing that they are governed by several universals – in the case of language, principles of *pragmatics* as well as ones of syntax and semantics.

A final set of confusions into which both theorists and antitheorists are prone to fall concerns the sense in which a method can be "foolproof." In many ways these are the subtlest confusions, and, in any case, they are the ones which most naturally lead to a discussion of the recent antitheorizing in legal studies. To get at them, we shall introduce a distinction in types of rules first raised by John Rawls in an attempt to revamp Kantian normative theory, namely, between *regulative* and *constitutive* rules.[17] A regulative rule is one drafted by a legislature and which appears as a statutory law: for example, "All wrongdoers must be punished." Notice that this rule is stated as a universal principle but does not mention which cases count as instances of the principle. The latter problem is the business of adjudication, which works by applying constitutive rules. These rules determine how and which particular cases should be constructed under the principle – say, that "John Doe is a wrongdoer" – usually on the basis of tacit criteria for which a judicial opinion provides *post facto* justification.

Among the many advantages of Rawls' distinction is that it allows us to make sense of the idea that a rule can be universally applicable without itself specifying the universe of cases to which it may be legitimately applied. To put it more succinctly, the distinction shows us that *a theory does not entail its practical applications.* This conclusion often turns out to be the point of many of the later Wittgenstein's examples of mathematical practice: namely, that my knowledge of, say, the Peano axioms and all the theorems of arithmetic – the sorts of universal principles that mathematicians study and formalize – is never sufficient to determine which arithmetic principle I am applying when I am trying to complete a particular number series. Thus, when the mathematical realist claims that there is a fact of the matter as to how the series goes, he offers small comfort to the person counting, who is interested in finding out exactly *which* fact it is.

Likewise, Fish is probably guilty of confusing Rawls' two types of rules when he claims that "foolproof methods" and "rules of thumb" are incompatible pursuits for the humanist. For even if there were a computer algorithm specifying the steps by which one correctly interprets a poem, one would still need some other rule – perhaps a rule of thumb, perhaps another algorithm – for identifying cases in which it would be relevant to apply the algorithm. In other words, knowledge of how to interpret poems still does not tell us how to recognize poems in the first place. Moreover, again *contra* Fish, Rawls' two types of rules are sufficiently independent of one another that it would be coherent for the practitioners of a humanistic discipline to agree on procedures for identifying poems without agreeing on procedures for interpreting them, or even vice versa. In the latter case, where rules exist for interpretation but *not* identification, one can imagine the discipline agreeing to "if *x* is a poem, then *x* is read in this manner . . ." and still disagree over whether a given *x* is in fact a poem. The example that seems to arise most often in the antitheory literature is E.D. Hirsch's strategy of "general hermeneutics," against which Fish inveighs.[18]

Before ending our catalogue of the conceptual problems facing the forces of antitheory in the humanities, a word should be said about a term to which Fish attaches great importance in authorizing the practices of a discipline: *convention*. In political and linguistic philosophy, conventions are contrasted with contracts and grammars, in that a convention is a practice that emerged largely without design, yet continues to be maintained in virtue of the beneficial consequences accrued by the individuals adhering to it. While Fish usually understands "convention" in this way, he also sometimes means it in the sense of "conventionalism," which is a doctrine about what confers validity or legitimacy on a theoretical statement, namely, that it follows from some explicit earlier agreement about definitions and assumptions. This second sense of convention arises especially when Fish wants to devalue the kind of legitimacy supposedly claimed for a theory by its proponents and, therefore, stresses the similarity between theories and games. However, as Hilary Putnam first observed, conventionalism's metaphysical implications are really much stronger than someone like Fish thinks, because an implicature of claiming "*p* follows by convention" is the claim, *p follows by virtue of nothing else*, which seems to commit the conventionalist to what Putnam calls "negative essentialism."[19] Thus, in terms of the sort of knowledge to which Fish must have access in order to legitimately argue that disciplinary procedures are *nothing but* game rules, he is being just as "metaphysical" as his opponent, the theorist, who believes that such procedures really represent a part of how things are.

Critical Legal Studies as Applied Antitheory

Having identified the basic conceptual problems with the antitheory movement in the humanities, let us now focus our attention on a recently vocal branch, the Critical Legal Studies movement. Articles relating to CLS have over the past decade proliferated in virtually all the major American law reviews. Among its defenders number professors in some of the most prestigious law schools, especially

Harvard and Stanford. Whenever a CLS advocate puts forth a program, it is generally negative, frequently amounting to a dissolution of the legal profession itself. The CLS advocate writes in a style that quickly moves from half-digested scholarship, through inconclusive polemics, often laced with a surreal sense of the colloquial, leaving the reader with the overall impression that the author has not yet found her distinctive ideological voice.[20] This medium, however, is part of the CLS message, which is that individuals can be "empowered" in the legal system only through "destabilizing" actions at the moments when legal institutions undergo "reproduction."[21] As we proceed to consider the antitheoretic themes in CLS, the reader should keep in mind that a concrete example of the CLS message is the defendant, especially a member of a socially disadvantaged group, realizing that there are no determinate outcomes to court cases and thereby feeling emboldened to exploit the means at his disposal to make his particular case turn out in his favor.[22]

CLS starts with the claim that the US Constitution is not sufficiently constrained by legal conventions to determine a "correct" decision for each case that comes before a judge. They support this claim on two grounds. First, they explicitly invoke a concern raised earlier, which they attribute to Wittgenstein, namely, that stating a rule is not sufficient for knowing how to apply the rule. From this CLS concludes that prior to the actual decision, there is no fact of the matter about either how the law is to be applied or even what kind of case is being judged. (This conclusion, of course, presupposes that if the relevant constitutive rule is not known, there is consequently no fact of the matter as to which rule applies, when in fact the judge's action in deciding the case could equally well be described as *discovering* the relevant rule.) Second, they point out that the Constitution stands for incompatible values that cannot be jointly maximized in every decision. For example, a tradeoff generally must be made between personal freedom and equal treatment, but there is no rule for making this tradeoff.

Despite having launched this critique of the "objectivity" of the legal system, CLS makes it clear that they do not believe that any general account of the political and economic interests of the presiding judges, such as that provided by a Marxist legal historian, is likely to be able to explain the full range of Constitutional decisions that the judges have made. One can see this as symptomatic of CLS's aversion to Fish's sense of "theory," regardless of whether its implications would support or oppose the status quo. They defend the reasonableness of this antitheoretic posture, largely by citing Clifford Geertz' anthropology and Harold Garfinkel's ethnomethodology as having demonstrated the negotiated character of local knowledge, which diminishes the likelihood that a single cause, motive, or interest would always be behind judicial decisions. Finally, CLS adds together their observations that judicial decision-making can be neither internally justified (since the available rules always underdetermine the outcome) nor externally explained on a systematic basis to conclude that all references to the "law-like" features of the legal system, such as "justice," "objectivity," and "impartiality" have purely rhetorical import, designed to weave a legitimating tale of tradition and stability around the real disjointedness of legal history.[23]

After having presented a sketch of CLS's argument, one sympathetic critic, Stanford law professor Paul Brest, wonders whether it is possible to concede CLS's major points without succumbing to the nihilistic implications its advocates have drawn. Although Brest merely offers hints here, they seem to point toward a quite reasonable move, namely, to say that terms like "justice," "objectivity," and "impartiality" do not apply principally to individual judicial actions, but to the overall long-term working of the legal system. For even if the empirical boundary between a rule-governed realm of "law" and an unregulated realm of "politics" is itself a matter of politics, which is to say, in constant fluctuation and always subject to negotiation, it may well be that having some such boundary, *regardless of how it is drawn*, is conceptually necessary for the stability of the social order.[24]

If this is Brest's argument, then it resembles the sorts of arguments that the classical empiricists gave for the a posteriori nature of metaphysical necessity. All antirealists, whether they be in the philosophy of law or the philosophy of science, refuse to have their knowledge claims authorized by anything other than brute empirical phenomena; yet they are then faced with the problem of accounting for the persistence of certain theoretical notions, whether they be "necessity," as in the case of Locke and Hume, or "justice," as in the case of CLS. The strategy most fruitfully adopted by the antirealist is to say that it is conceptually necessary to distinguish between, say, essence and accident or law and politics, if our world is to make any sense at all; but how one draws the distinction – which cases fall under which categories – is itself a matter of convention that may change over time and hence can only be determined a posteriori.[25]

However, one may want to push Brest's point further and focus on the net effect of the line between law and politics shifting over the course of legal history, which may be to make "justice," "objectivity," and "impartiality" properties of the history of judicial decision-making *taken as a whole*. Though CLS advocates would probably not endorse this conclusion, it is compatible with what we have seen their position to be. For example, if a judicial decision is "just" if its validity is guaranteed by something beyond the judge's mere making of the decision (that is, it is "objective"), and its supporting reasoning reflects an indifference to the various interests that could benefit from the decision (that is, it is "impartial"), then it clearly follows from CLS's argument – assuming its validity – that *individual* decisions are neither objective (not rule-governed) nor impartial (not independent of politics). But the story may be quite different when these cases are taken collectively.

If this collectivist gambit is successful, then a key rhetorical lesson to learn from CLS is that judicial appeals to the "justice," and "impartiality," and "objectivity" in *individual* cases are deceptive because they assume that something that is perhaps exemplified by the legal system taken as a whole need not be exemplified by any of its constituent parts. This may be small comfort to the individual who feels that a judge's decision has been "unjust" to *him*, but then an explicitly therapeutic goal of CLS is to change the individual's attitude to the legal system so that his reasonably felt frustration is channeled through an institution, no doubt political, that is more likely to reveal the true source of his frustration.[26] However, it is far from clear that the "theory has no consequences" thesis is political therapy's best friend. After illustrating the collective senses of "objectivity" and "impartiality" that we have in mind, we shall consider a reading of Fish's thesis that threatens to render the CLS project politically inert.

First, take *objectivity*. As decisions are made over the course of legal history, patterns develop as to the sorts of situations in which a judge is likely to cite a given earlier case as precedent. Needless to say, in such a situation, the judge does not make his decision merely by consulting the citation pattern of his predecessors' ruling on similar cases. Yet if an historian's horizons are wide enough, she will detect the presence of an "invisible hand" that makes the judge's decision much more predictable than anyone involved in the trial would ever imagine, especially in light of CLS's remarks about the absence of legal algorithms.[27] This suggests an emergent sense of objectivity akin to what sociologists have identified in the citation patterns in scientific journal articles: namely, that if an article continues to be cited regularly after fifteen years, then it tends to be cited for the same reason (for instance, exemplary methodology), which implies that the article has carved a definite place for itself in the body of scientific knowledge. The sociologists, admittedly, have no ready explanation for this convergence of citations, except that it does *not* involve the scientific community explicitly agreeing to assign certain epistemic roles to certain articles.[28] Perhaps something similar could be said about frequently cited precedents in the law (though the method of citation analysis is not nearly as developed to permit a ready map of the changing topography of legal knowledge).

As for *impartiality*, the situation is somewhat more straightforward. While each judge may be partial to particular interests that are determined by the context of his decision, nevertheless the collective effect of these interests waxing and waning across many contexts is to reflect an historical indifference to any given interest, which gives the legal system its globally impartial character. The principal complication here is whether our knowledge of the globally impartial character of the legal system (once we know it) compels us to do anything more than would be accomplished in the normal course of things. An answer to this question would provide greater insight into a vision of political therapy that is supposedly derivable from the "theory has no consequences" thesis.

One reading of the thesis that we have yet to entertain, one which drives the widest wedge possible between Wittgenstein and Marx, is that theory leaves the world as it found it. Theory may give us a new perspective on the world, but not a new world as such. This way of thinking is often lurking just beneath the surface of CLS debates. Consider the following set of symptoms.[29]

1   Each disputant is eager to rescue desirable bits of liberal political culture for his own side, leaving the actual dispute to turn on whether these bits ought to be called "liberal."

2   There is an explicit rejection of radical political methodologies such as Marxism ("more theory"), complemented by the "therapeutic" consolation that the supposedly ironclad character of the existing legal system is only a myth. This revelation is intended to give previously disempowered citizens the confidence to exploit the system for their own ends. Indeed, CLS is quite distinctive in emphasizing the subjective side of political action. More effort is placed on making people *feel* they have power than in ensuring that they actually *use* it.

3   Given (1) and (2), one can understand why participants in the CLS debates do not normally call for legislation specifically designed to restructure the legal system, not even to provide a compensatory mechanism (akin to affirmative action) for ensuring that disempowered citizens have access to the legal system in the future. The preferred route seems to be through informal political associations that influence the local implementation of whatever laws happen to be passed.

Considering the radical promise of CLS, its neo-liberal political therapy is rather disappointing, not to mention trendy. However, those of us who believe that theory *does have* consequences will be happy to see, in the final section, that the problem can be traced to a conceptual difficulty in all that has transpired.

Conclusion: Send in the Realists

A philosopher of science happening upon the antitheory debates would immediately be struck by the *narrowness* of the philosophical spectrum occupied by the disputants. Whereas Fish can be easily cast as a disappointed positivist, we have just seen the advocates of Critical Legal Studies turn out to be liberals in disguise. In both cases, the problem can be traced to antitheory's dialectical strategy of contesting theory as much as possible on its own terms. While the advantages of such a strategy are well known, one of them is *not* a tendency toward innovation. Consequently, it should come as no surprise that antitheory ends up as conceptually bankrupt as theory. However, had the antitheorists a position of their own, they might have fared better. The position that seems to be most missing from these debates is *realism*. Realism breaks with the presuppositions of the antitheory debates by making a clear distinction between theory and method, and hence between truth and verification. A realist, whether he be Popper in science or Dworkin in law, willingly grants the antirealist point that verification procedures regularly fail, and indeed takes that as evidence, not for the nonexistence of truth, but for truth exceeding the bounds of those procedures – thus prompting the development of ever more adequate procedures.[30]

In the case of politics, the injection of realism would be especially striking. If we recall liberalism's historical roots in the Hobbesian (and generally contractarian) idea that whatever order exists in society is due to the imposition of rules, then liberalism is fairly seen as the continuation of antirealism by political means. Thus, we should expect liberalism's dialectical antithesis to find the nonexistence or non-binding character of rules in society a liberating experience. And, certainly, this is how Critical Legal Studies would have us take this find. The problem, again, is clarifying a positive political vision that comes from all this. For example, one CLS advocate, Boston University law professor Joseph Singer, has recently identified four aims for political reform: to prevent cruelty; to alleviate misery; to democratize hierarchies; and to eliminate loneliness. However, these aims are put forward with all the vagueness of a party platform. Indeed, Singer openly admits that he has no idea how to bring about any of his reforms.[31] Antirealism does not help in moments like this. In contrast, realism may provide some comfort, since it refuses to define political reality solely in terms of the limits of legal procedure; as a result, the realist can freely enact and repeal laws to suit her own ends without fearing that political reality might revert to a state of nature in the process.

Notes

1   The special issue is W.J.T. Mitchell (ed.), *Against Theory: Literary Studies and the New Pragmatism* (University of Chicago Press, Chicago, 1985). The essay that originally sparked the antitheoretic turn was Steven Knapp and Walter Benn Michaels, "Against theory," in ibid., pp. 11–30 (appeared first in 1982). Knapp and Michaels, who cite Fish among their authorities, argued that it is illicit to infer the critic's need for a general theory of interpretation simply from the fact that critics interpret texts. More germane for purposes of this paper is Stanley Fish, "Consequences," in ibid., pp. 106–31, which encapsulates much of the argument in Stanley Fish, *Is There a Text in this Class?* (Harvard University Press, Cambridge, 1980).

2   This is Bloom's major complaint against politically active academics in the 1960s. See his *The Closing of the American Mind* (Simon and Schuster, New York, 1987).

3   Fish, "Consequences," p. 111.

4   Ibid., pp. 107–8.

5   Our source here is Raymond Williams, *Keywords* (Oxford University Press, New York, 1976), pp. 266–8.

6   The best collection of material by the logical positivists is A.J. Ayer (ed.), *Logical Positivism* (Free Press, New York, 1959).

7   Max Weber, "The meaning of 'ethical' in sociology and economics," in *The Methodology of the Social Sciences* (Free Press, New York, 1949), pp. 1–49.

8   David Faust, *The Limits of Scientific Reasoning* (University of Minnesota Press, Minneapolis, 1984).

9   Ian Mitroff, *The Subjective Side of Science* (Elsevier, Amsterdam, 1974).

10 Rudolf Carnap, *The Logical Structure of the World* (University of California Press, Berkeley, 1967), pp. 332–9.

11 Behaviorism's triumph over introspectionism is the subject of William Lyons, *The Disappearance of Introspection* (MIT Press, Cambridge, 1986).

12 Carl Hempel, *Aspects of Scientific Explanation* (Free Press, New York, 1965), p. 186.

13 Isaac Levi, *Decisions and Revisions* (Cambridge University Press, Cambridge, 1985).

14 We have drawn here on Julius Weinberg, "Abstraction in the formation of concepts," in *Dictionary of the History of Ideas* (Charles Scribner, New York, 1968), vol. 1, pp. 1–9. Fish's critique of Chomsky appears in "Consequences," pp. 108–12.

15 For a discussion of the absurdity of this argument in physiology, see Claude Bernard, *The Study of Experimental Medicine* (Dover, New York, 1964).

16 Jerry Fodor, "Three cheers for propositional attitudes," in *Representations* (MIT Press, Cambridge, 1981), pp. 100–26.

17 John Rawls, "Two concepts of rules," *Philosophical Review*, 64, (1955), pp. 3–32.

18 Fish, "Consequences," p. 107. Hirsch is also one of Knapp and Michaels' main targets in "Against theory." For a response in the same special issue, see E.D. Hirsch, "Against theory?" pp. 48–52.

19 Hilary Putnam, "The refutation of conventionalism," in *Mind, Language, and Reality* (Cambridge University Press, Cambridge, 1975), pp. 153–92.

20 For an introduction to CLS that places it among other theories of legal interpretation, see Leif Carter, *Contemporary Constitutional Lawmaking* (Pergamon Press, New York, 1985). Fish has defended CLS against more "objectivist" accounts of legal interpretation. See Stanley Fish, "Fish v. Fiss," *Stanford Law Review*, 36 (1984), p. 1325, in response to Owen Fiss, "Objectivity and interpretation," *Stanford Law Review*, 34 (1982), p. 739. In response to Fish, see Owen

Fiss, "Conventionalism," *Southern California Law Review*, 58 (1985), p. 177. For an example of some of the best deconstructive scholarship done under the CLS aegis, see Robert Gordon, "Critical legal histories," *Stanford Law Review*, 36 (1984), p. 57. For CLS' flippant side, see John Schlegel, "Notes toward an intimate, opinionated, and affectionate history of the Conference on Critical Legal Studies," *Stanford Law Review*, 36 (1984), p. 391. On the more surreal side of CLS are the frequent citations to the lyrics of current rock hits as evidence of social justice.

21 The words in scare quotes are part of the jargon of CLS' philosophical guru, Harvard law professor Roberto Unger. See his *The Critical Legal Studies Movement* (Harvard University Press, Cambridge, 1986).

22 This example is nicely fleshed out in Anna Hodgkiss, "Petitioning and the empowerment theory of practice," *Yale Law Review*, 96 (1987), p. 569.

23 This version of the CLS argument is drawn largely from James Boyle, "The politics of reason," *University of Pennsylvania Law Review*, 133 (1985), p. 685.

24 Paul Brest, "Interpretation and interest," *Stanford Law Review*, 34 (1984), p. 765.

25 A good modern account of the metaphysical strategy of classical empiricism may be found in Stephen Schwartz, "Introduction," in *Naming, Necessity, and Natural Kinds* (Cornell University Press, Ithaca, 1977). For an analogous line of argument pursued with respect to the law/politics distinction, see Roberto Unger, *Knowledge and Politics* (Free Press, New York, 1975).

26 This is the main thesis of Roberto Unger, *Passion: An Essay on Personality* (Free Press, New York, 1984), which, so the Appendix suggests, has had considerable impact on American psychiatrists.

27 This is noted in John Stick, "Can nihilism be pragmatic?" *Harvard Law Review*, 100 (1986), p. 332.

28 A synopsis of the science citation literature may be found in Marc De Mey, *The Cognitive Paradigm* (D. Reidel, Dordrecht, 1982), pp. 111-31.

29 The CLS debate on which this is mainly based involved Joseph Singer (Boston University Law) and John Stick (Tulane University Law). See Singer, "The player and the cards: nihilism and legal theory," *Yale Law Journal*, 94, (1984), p. 1; and Stick, "Can nihilism be pragmatic?" The subjectivism of CLS is especially highlighted in Boyle, "The politics of reason."

30 For more, see Jarrett Leplin (ed.), *Scientific Realism* (University of California Press, Berkeley, 1984); Steve Fuller, "Playing without a full deck: the cognitive limits of legal theory," *Yale Law Journal*, 97 (1988), p. 549.

31 Singer, "The player and the cards," p. 67.

9
Limits of Consumption: an Ironic Revision of Televisual Experience

Jenny L. Nelson

This chapter focuses on some of the discursive strategies used by mass communication theorists to conceptualize the relationship between television, its audiences, and the world. Specific attention is given to deconstructing certain rhetorical devices and figures of speech which function as implicit strategies of argumentation (logic) in traditional and contemporary theories of mass media experience. Using Hayden White's (1978) model of tropic discourse, I chart the growth from the naive (or metaphorical) apprehensions of televisual "consumption," through its critical (or metonymical) deconstructions, and finally to the self-reflective (or ironic) apprehensions of it.

Televisual communication is an ambiguous phenomenon – what John Hartley (1984) calls a "dirty category" – and the discourse surrounding and constituting television research attests to this. A rhetorical analysis of TV audience research recognizes that such research contains not only a certain amount of information and explanation of what this information "means," but also a more or less overt message about the attitude the reader should assume before *both* the data reported *and* their formal interpretation. In this case, my concern with the rhetoric of audience research takes two directions: (1) the way the TV audience is constituted tropically in mass communication research which involves an implicit separation between "them" (naive TV viewers) and "us" (critical researchers); and (2) the ways in which these tropes function in discourse itself, that is, how we, as an academic audience, are tacitly encouraged to "see" the TV audience within a limited and nonreflexive framework.

Insofar as media studies is a discourse in search of an object (Caughie, 1984), its initial project requires that it create a coherent subject. One way of accomplishing this is to circumscribe televisual experience within certain boundaries, and the resulting categories must somehow be named in order to be recognized by others. These names, then, precede and guide any analysis. Yet, naming is neither an arbitrary nor a completely determined activity. To name a situation or experience is a "process by which all discourse constitutes the object which it pretends to describe realistically" (White, 1978: 2). The act of naming, then, can "increase the intensity of adherence to certain values" while appearing to be "apparently uncontroversial and without practical consequence" (Perelman and Olbrechts-Tyteca, 1969: 49). The strength of a taken-for-granted term like "consumer" lies precisely in its metaphoricity – its ability to designate a cluster of attributes or semiotic values (signified) attached to a signifier. It is the ambiguous dynamics of "consumer," a word used both as a narrowly economic and broadly cultural concept, which neither traditional nor contemporary media theorists have fully understood. These views present, in Cartesian fashion, a set of arguments about TV which are divorced from questions about experience. The consequence is that, despite the value of many of the specific arguments offered, this persistent negative version of "consumption" as a passive process is ultimately one-sided and enfeebled.

My purpose is to explore and expose the limits of consumption. By this I mean to suggest that the term "consumption" as a signifier function has thus far been confined to a restricted range of signified functions: those associated with passivity and given negative value. I propose to expand these semantic limitations by freeing the signifier (consumption) from its present signifieds (its meanings) or, on the other hand, by expanding the range of signifieds to which the signifier "consumption" might correspond. Drawing upon "philosophers of everyday life" (Baudrillard, Certeau, and Lefebvre), I argue that "consumption" *can* be an appropriate term to describe televisual experience, but only when considered in its full phenomenological (reflexive) sense, as bodily practice. The title of this chapter, "limits of consumption," also entails the thesis that consumption is not limitless, that is, that when one engages in televisual experience, one does not devour with total abandon. Rather, one invariably displays one's tastes by exercising preconscious and conscious choice and judgment within an established order of things. This is to some extent socially determined, but it is also personally synergistic.

A Metaphorical (Naive) View of Consumption

"Consumption" is one of the most widely and least critically used terms to describe televisual experience. It is employed by functionalist researchers and their critics alike, so that while debates regarding the status/function of the viewer appear quite heated, there is nevertheless a tacit agreement regarding the word, "consumer," even though its meanings and referents may vary. For instance, Elliot (1974: 254) distinguishes between active and passive audience behavior. Unlike the "passive activities" of viewing/listening to TV, "active consumption" refers to the purposive achievement of certain goals or the gratification of certain needs external to televisual experience itself. This presupposes that the "active consumer" *uses* "information" learned from television to solve problems encountered in "the real world." Consumption therefore entails both a positive (active, external, visible) and a negative (passive, internal, invisible) valence.

From an industry standpoint, these valences are reversed. Within this particular sign system, "active viewing" refers to a condition in which viewers sustain a continuing interest in the television message, a message whose form and content encourages viewers to consume (buy) advertised products and consume (buy into) televised images. From a Marxist standpoint, these images reproduce the values, assumptions, and attitudes essential to the continuation of capitalist social relations. "Passive viewing," from an industry standpoint, refers to a condition in which viewers are less committed to a TV program, and leave the room to "gratify" external needs, for example, to perform household tasks (Haldi, 1981: 94). This corresponds to Rosengren's (1974) methodological distinction between "consumption relations" (those that occur while watching TV) and "outside relations" (those that occur in "real life"). In either case, the focus is generally on content, information, and the causal relations between mass media consumption and real-world behavior.

Within this framework, television is considered only as a means to an end, rather than as an experience of value in and of itself. This view has perpetuated research that takes as unproblematic the actual experience of the viewer. What is of "objective" value here is the viewer's *visible* behavior *after* watching a television program – usually chosen by the researcher and for certain purposes not revealed to the research participant. Other epistemological and methodological dilemmas arise as well. Since televisual experience is not considered, not even as a variable in an experimental design, positivist research is content to naively "reproduce" viewing conditions in artificial laboratory settings, isolated from all the contextual features that are integral to televisual experience. Here, researchers naively assume similarities between two environments that are, in fact, very different. To name but a few of these differences, television is most often viewed in the comfort of the home, is structured around and into the person's daily (objective) schedule and her/his shifting (subjective) moods, and is watched very differently according to whether the person is alone or with others (Nelson, 1985). Seen in this light, laboratory conditions are so far removed from the material conditions in which television viewing actually occurs, that whatever "results" are produced can hardly be considered relevant to reality as it is lived by human beings. Several ethnographic studies of television viewing have been conducted in order to correct such positivist limitations, for example, by observing natural settings during TV viewing, but these studies still depend primarily on recording the *visible behavior* of viewing subjects (Nelson, 1986). Again, a metaphorical similarity is posited that is untenable, namely, that only visible behavior is "real."

Media theorists also characterize television as a temporal quasi-subject, for example, as a "consumer of time" ranking only behind sleep and work (Comstock, 1980). Television's profits derive not from the direct sale of goods and services, but from the containment and sale of time. TV appropriates the "free time" of persons in order to produce economic value. The assumption here is that one's time might be better spent engaged in more concrete and materially productive activities. Leisure – the consumption of unproductive time – is no longer one's free and personal choice to "waste free time" (time not spent in labor), but an obligatory social activity demanded by the system.

Consumption is both a digestive and economic industrial metaphor. Mass culture is "fabricated by technicians hired by businessmen; its audiences are passive consumers limited to the choice between buying and not buying [viewing and not viewing]" (MacDonald, 1957: 60). Consumers are provided with an illusion of freedom which mystifies the fact that their choices are already made for them. As such, consumers operate within a predefined, preferred order of things. Williams (1976: 69) notes the significance in the decline of the word, "customer," which implies some degree of regular and continuing relationship to a supplier, whereas "consumer" indicates the more abstract figure in a more abstract market. Consumption, therefore, is now primarily related to signs and not to material objects *per se* (Lefebvre, 1971; Lowe, 1982). Not only are we confined to "choose" among advertised products whose essential difference is in packaging and advertising, and which therefore promote semiotic rather than material values (status versus use), but we are also limited in our choice of TV programs. There are a limited number of channels from which to choose, a standard repertoire of genres (sitcoms, soaps, ads, and such), all with their own rhetorical formats within the ideology of advanced capitalism.

The digestive metaphor-system entails a similar thesis: that the consumer is "fed" on symbols of happiness and despair (publicity images) which substitute for everyday life experiences. Von Eckartsberg (1967) sees the TV director's role as *premasticator radicalis* and *distributor maximus* of our "image food." The digestive metaphor bears an interesting relation to the popularity of pre-packaged, pre-cooked TV dinners and to the observation that television viewing is most often accompanied by eating activities (Bechtel et al., 1972). The viewer-as-consumer exercises and subsequently shows his/her taste.

Anders (1957) develops a sustained digestive metaphor in his discussion of mass media consumption. He argues that TV has replaced the communal dining table with a "negative family table." Rather than providing a centripetal common center, it provides a common avenue of escape.

The reduction of experience to a single language (television's sign system) produces what MacDonald (1957) refers to as "homogenized" culture. MacDonald fears the destruction of values resulting from the indiscriminate juxtaposition of unrelated elements. By making everything equivalent, the code of television serves to normalize everything within its scope. The entire sign system is the source of viewer passivity insofar as it predefines the viewers' responses and channels them within a preferred set of meanings. Selective judgment is not possible; the viewer is overwhelmed by details and facts and is unable to make sense or find a unifying thread with which to connect these discrete items. The viewer is caught in a free, manifest play of signifiers that disguises and displays that they refer to nothing but themselves (Baudrillard, 1981). Rather than actively producing meanings grounded in experience, people become abstract consumers of abstract meaning, which implies the using up of a finished product. According to Arendt:

> The entertainment industry is confronted with gargantuan appetites, and since its wares disappear in consumption, it must constantly offer new commodities. In this predicament, those who produce for the mass media ransack the entire range of past and present culture in hopes of finding suitable material. This material, however, cannot be offered as it is; it must be prepared and altered in order to become entertainment. (1971: 98)

Thus, the essential, immortal nature of cultural objects is obliterated when "life seizes upon them and consumes them for its pleasure, for entertainment" (1971: 100). It is the disappearance of "true culture" and "original meaning" that Arendt fears. "If we understand by culture what it originally meant (the Roman *culture* – derived from *colere*, to take care of and preserve and cultivate), then we can say without any exaggeration that a society obsessed with consumption cannot at the same time be cultured or produce culture" (1971: 100). In Arendt's analysis, modern society, through its need for mass entertainment, uses up cultural objects, leaving us without material to grasp and truly move us.

The "need" for mass entertainment is often likened to the compulsive behavior of a drug addict. "Narcotization" is a term used to describe a negative effect or "dysfunction" of the mass media in which television functions as an opiate for the masses, inducing apathy and political inertia. Increased media exposure to information concerning social issues leads to decreased action and involvement. From the "hypodermic needle" theory of the 1950s to Marie Winn's metaphorical title in *The Plug-in Drug* (1977), the central suggestion is that media induce a drug-like stupor in the audience. Lazarsfeld and Merton (1948) suggest that "increasing dosages of mass communications may be inadvertently transforming the energies of men [sic] from active participation into passive knowledge." Herbert Marcuse questions the quality of that knowledge, calling it "a state of anaesthesia from which all detrimental ideas tend to be excluded" (1964: 91–5). The manipulated consciousness of the modern person means almost total ignorance of world affairs. In effect, the consumer suffers from cultural and political "malnutrition" by ingesting the irrelevant and/or contradictory information produced by "TV dinners."

Arendt's view of consumption is limited by an elitist tradition which distinguishes between cultured and uncultured people or practices. Those who hold to the "narcotized" metaphor make a similar distinction between those who are politically and socially "active" (through accepted channels of "proper conduct for the true citizen") and those who are not. The distinction itself and the evaluation associated with it are not analyzed.

A Metonymic View of Consumption

Cultural studies, developing in Britain in the late 1970s, and gaining recent popularity in the USA, has been directly influenced by the struggle to dis-cover such assumptions, and to criticize the tendency to perpetuate class differences and other inequalities. Cultural studies attempts to recover the cultures of hitherto neglected groups (such as, women and blacks), and is itself at the margins of traditional academic disciplines (a condition similar to that of rhetoric in the human sciences). Cultural theorists use semiotics as a tool with which to study television as a text-producing sign system. Fiske and Hartley's seminal work, *Reading Television* (1978), provided a new way to look at TV. It accomplished this by introducing a metaphor that rescued televisual experience from the pathological domain of disease and addiction, and delivered it into a domain an academician could appreciate: watching TV is like reading a book! TV's shift to academic respectability was not altogether surprising, and probably inevitable, although the way in which this shift took place was exceedingly clever. For years, television was seen as the primary force contributing to the decline in children's reading scores and to the increase in violent crime. From Fiske and Hartley, we learn that physical violence on TV is a metaphor of cultural/ideological violence. The shift to a rhetoric of the text contributed greatly to the academic community's understanding of television. Yet, an implicit distinction continues to be made between passive consumption – wherein viewers accept uncritically the latent (metaphorical) structure of televisual discourse as a literal reality – and active "reading," whereby viewers understand how implicit value assumptions are encoded into the rhetoric of the televisual text, and how this code both differs from and confirms real social (class) relations. From this point of view, "active consumption" (reading) requires an understanding of television's discursive strategies as well as an understanding of its relation to the real, objective social world.

Yet, television need not be consumed solely for its content (informational or symbolic) in order to serve expressive purposes. For instance, it "says" something even in its silent status as a household object in relation to other household objects. As an object of consumption, the TV set functions as proof of cultural membership and assumes meaning (significance) not in symbolic relation with the subject nor in operational relation to the world, but by its difference from other objects according to a hierarchical code of significations (Baudrillard, 1981: 64). A large console color set is not the same as a black and white portable. Similarly, a TV set in the bedroom is not a TV set in the kitchen is not a TV set in the living room. Television's status as object is rarely considered by media theorists, even though it may induce a great number of ambiguous cultural behaviors in image reception.

Seeing television as a literal household object reveals the degree to which these digestive and economic metaphors share a model of "communication" based on an epistemological and methodological separation between televisual representation and the "real." It is argued that "real life" is neither structurally as orderly, nor substantially as exciting as television programs suggest. Or that television consumes cultural objects that have "real" meaning, or swallows up forms that allow "real" communication, or blocks us from "real" experience, or prevents us from recognizing that we are not experiencing the real. In any case, the question usually revolves around the ways in which television affects "real" perception and behavior or, more recently, how televisual discourse constructs and situates the viewer (Davies, 1984). This digital logic generally affords more weight to the televisual text as the primary reference point for signification. Although it is recognized that the audience has some degree of interpretive freedom, this "freedom of decoding" is ultimately directed by, and subordinate to, the televisual text (Eco, 1979; Himmelstein, 1984: 281). These studies deal with how the structure of the text leads the audience to perceive, think, feel, believe, understand, or act in an arguably predictable way. The research community claims the importance of the audience by naming them as "producers of meaning," while continuing to deconstruct only TV's narrative code and drawing inferences about the audience from television's structures and/or modes of address. Each of these models characterizes televisual experience as deleteriously affecting the capacity for deepened and extended experience by transforming us and/or the cultural material we share. In effect, these researchers have decided to establish TV's modes of address as the sign-vehicle (simulation) of the audience's modes of use. The audience becomes the equivalent of a word (a sign exchanged by researchers) and is thus spoken for rather than allowed to speak. The actual persons who use TV are construed as a fairly unproblematic or universal entity. Or rather, the viewer's role in the process is of little consequence (s/he cannot speak) and hence, of little value. The audience is presupposed and their codes or tactics of consumption ignored.

Perhaps even more problematic than the metaphor of consumption are terms that have become so integrated into the discourse of contemporary television research that it becomes difficult to even speak of televisual experience without using them. For instance, "viewer," "consumer," and "audience" indicate not a particular person or group of persons, but *the class of all possible persons engaged in television*. An abstract, timeless, and collective concept is meant to function metonymically as a material, historical, and embodied subject. In converse relation, an embodied subject is meant to function as part of this collective concept. Nielsen families are the most obvious illustration, broken down, objectified, and gathered as they are into demographic attributes. This rhetorical transformation corresponds to Eco's (1979) notion of the "ideal reader" which refers not to any actual living person but to a constructed textual category.

An Ironic View of Consumption

Taking the digestive metaphor to its logical extreme, to consume is to embody. The phenomenological concept of embodiment entails the twin modes of expression and perception. The etymology of "consumption" suggests a double valence which renders the person as both subject and object, consumer and consumed. To eat, use up, devour or absorb suggests that the significance of consumption lies not in *what* is consumed, but in the bodily *act* of "using up" or "digesting" something. "You are what you eat" implies that consumers become, through the very process of consumption, one of the producers contributing to their own transformation. In other words, production and consumption coincide. Unlike the "pure" production of the televisual system, which defines a space (a language, *langage*) and composes an order of places (a code, *langue*), procedures of consumption (speaking, *parole*) maintain their difference within the space of the other. This ironic view of consumption recognizes that choice is limited, and that a person does what s/he can within those boundaries. Certeau introduces a rich heuristic metaphor in his consideration of everyday life as "the subtle art of renting," that is, how we make someone else's permanent property into a suitable temporary living space for ourselves. As a social tactic of persons (rather than a strategy of institutions), consumption has no proper or permanent locus to which it might withdraw in order to reflect upon the situation as a whole. Instead, the dialectics of tactics depends upon timing and the chances of an occasion.

As such, taste is no longer limited to simple possession of objects. Rather, taste entails a more subtle semiology of their organization and social usage (Bourdieu, 1984). The everyday practices of consumers refer to an art of re-use, ways of using the dominant order of signification by establishing within it a degree of plurality; an art of being in-between. It is the human being who functions as a medium of communication (Certeau, 1984: 30ff.). Consumption is a scattered and hidden poeisis in that it does not manifest itself through originating its own visible products, but rather through its ways of using products/ signs imposed by a dominant economic and cultural order. As the dimension of generalized sign exchange (Baudrillard, 1981), the consuming of signs results in the production of excess: waste, refuse, and garbage, that is, an excess of meaning. As such, consuming TV's meanings is simultaneously a re-production and transformation of those meanings. This view has important repercussions for the research community. For example, how do we reconcile the apparently contradictory aims of those researchers who perform arduous rhetorical analyses of "electronic preachers" and those viewers who watch such programs as a form of "comedy relief"?

In order to better illustrate the ironic view of consumption, let us take a brief look at some of the actual tactics of televisual viewers. The following styles of viewing, which contribute to, but are not necessarily dependent upon semantic properties, have emerged from interviews I have conducted concerning televisual experience (Nelson, 1985). For instance, there is the *scan mode* (also referred to as "channel hopping" or "zapping"), in which the viewer gains control of montage by switching channels every five minutes or so. This particular style of (literal) remote control is, in a sense, made possible by recent technological developments and so functions within an existing order of things. There is also a *silent mode*, wherein the sound is turned off in favor of music or conversation; an *invisible mode*, in which the set is on all the time as background noise, but rarely or sporadically attended to. Closely related to this is a *stable mode*, whereby a person stays tuned to a particular channel for the duration of viewing time. The stable mode, it might be added, is becoming an increasingly problematic category with the advent of remote control. A person need not "wait out" an uninteresting program, or even an uninteresting segment of a program. Finally, there is a *choice mode*, in which the person selects particular programs on time and for their duration, then consciously chooses another program or turns the set off. Within these broader styles of consumption, there exist even more subtle ways of engaging television. The interviews I have conducted reveal that persons are, at the very least, preconsciously aware of their own perceptual distinctions, and this awareness is manifest in the very words they use to describe how they experience television. "Watching" is not "seeing" is not "looking" is not "listening." Each entails varying degrees of tension and focus in attention.

These different styles of consumption, though rarely attended to by audience researchers, point to an oblique and latent signification. The contextual, circumstantial, and intentional selections which permeate everyday practice are necessary conditions for relationship, the essential basis of communication (Eco, 1976). Televisual styling, therefore, points to the reciprocal nature of the viewed/viewer relationship. The latter (*parole*) is the personal and creative use of the former (*langue*). By repositioning and recontextualizing television (and the persons who consume it), by extending and subverting existing codes (rather than the "pure" expression of creative drives), these televisual stylists open up the world of televisual experience to new and covertly oppositional meanings.

Television audience research, thus far dependent on the bifurcation of TV/audience, TV/experience, and researcher/researched, might find it instructive to make a move to ironic (self-reflexive and self-critical) discourse (White, 1978). Instead of simple lateral movements from one domain to the other (metonymic and synecdochic discourse), the subject is dispersed into various enunciative modalities. Television and viewing, like TV and reality, are modalities of a single discursive system: that of televisual experience. Here, "televisual experience" suggests that viewers-as-subjects no longer perceive television-as-object, but rather they reckon with a complex system of signifiers and a network of intentionalities that they themselves have helped to construct. "Televisual experience," like "consumption," neither designates an object nor describes a content. Rather, it is an acknowledgment of *relation*, that is, that both viewer and viewed are using an embodied perspective to determine how a particular experience is constituted. "Televisual experience" only tells us something about the how of vision (and experience) and the treatment of what this perceptual experience considers. Here, "perception" should not be reduced to mere eyesight. For phenomenologists, the senses do not exist as autonomous entities. As Merleau-Ponty (1979) observes, "To see is as a matter of principle to see farther than one sees, to reach a latent existence. The invisible is the outline and depth of the visible . . ., the opening of a dimension of the visible." The televisual, then, can be understood as perceptual space, that is, as a complex form of discursive behavior with delimiting and projecting capacities. Televisual experience is, literally and metaphorically, an extension of vision into experience and, reflexively, an extension of experience into vision. One does not pass from one "side" (television) to another (experience), but rather remains within the dimension of discourse.

References

Anders, G. (1957) "The phantom world of TV," in B. Rosenberg and D.M. White (eds), *Mass Culture: The Popular Arts in America*. New York: Free Press. pp. 356–67.

Arendt, H. (1971) "Society and culture," in B. Rosenberg and D.M. White (eds), *Mass Culture Revisited*. New York: Van Nostrand Reinhold. pp. 86–102.

Baudrillard, J. (1981) *For a Critique of the Political Economy of the Sign*. Tr. C. Levin. St. Louis: Telos Press.

Bechtel, R.B., Achelpohl, C., and Akers, R. (1972), "Correlates between observed behavior and questionnaire responses on television viewing," in E.A. Rubinstein, G.A. Comstock, and J.P. Murray (eds), *Television and Social Behavior*. Washington DC: Government Printing Office. pp. 274–344.

Bourdieu, P. (1984) *Distinction: Social Critique of the Judgment of Taste*. Tr. R. Nice. Cambridge: Harvard University Press. First publ. 1979.

Caughie, J. (1984) "Television criticism: a discourse in search of an object," *Screen*, 25 (4–5): 109–20.

Certeau, M. de (1984) *The Practice of Everyday Life*. Tr. S.F. Randall. Berkeley: University of California Press.

Comstock, G. (1980) "Television and its viewers: what social science sees," in G.C. Wilhoit (ed.), *Mass Communication Review Yearbook*, vol. 1. Beverly Hills: Sage. pp. 491–507.

Davies, J. (1984) "Television modes of address as a semiotic system," *RS/SI*, 4 (3/4): 338–55.

Eco, U. (1976) *A Theory of Semiotics*. Bloomington: Indiana University Press.

Eco, U. (1979) *The Role of the Reader: Explorations in the Semiotics of Texts*. Bloomington: Indiana University Press.

Elliot, P. (1974) "Uses and gratifications research: a critique and a sociological alternative," in J. Blumler and E. Katz (eds), *The Uses of Mass Communication*. Beverly Hills: Sage. pp. 249–68.

Fiske, J. and Hartley, J. (1978) *Reading Television*. London: Methuen.

Haldi, J.A. (1981) "Network affiliate programming," in S.T. Eastman, S.W. Head, and L. Klein (eds). *Broadcast Programming: Strategies for Winning Television and Radio Audiences*. Belmont, CA: Wadsworth. pp. 89–106.

Hartley, J. (1984) "Encouraging signs: television and the power of dirt, speech, and scandalous categories," in W.D. Rowland, Jr. and B. Watkins (eds), *Interpreting Television: Current Research Perspectives*. Beverly Hills: Sage. pp. 119–41.

Himmelstein, H. (1984) *Television Myth and the American Mind*. New York: Praeger.

Lazarsfeld, P.F. and Merton, R.K. (1948) "Mass communication, popular taste and organized social action," in L. Bryson (ed.), *The Communication of Ideas*. New York: Institute for Religious and Social Studies. Reprinted in W. Schramm (ed.), *Mass Communications* (Urbana: University of Illinois Press, 1960).

Lefebvre, H. (1971) *Everyday Life in the Modern World*. Tr. S. Rabinovitch. New York: Harper and Row.

Lowe, D.M. (1982) *The History of Bourgeois Perception*. Chicago: University of Chicago Press.

Lyotard, J. (1984) *The Postmodern Condition: A Report on Knowledge*. Tr. G. Bennington and B. Massumi. Minneapolis: University of Minnesota Press.

MacDonald, D. (1957) "A theory of mass culture," in B. Rosenberg and D.M. White (eds), *Mass Culture: The Popular Arts in America*. New York: Free Press. pp. 59–73.

Marcuse, Herbert (1964) *One Dimensional Man*. Boston: Beacon Press.

Merleau-Ponty, M. (1979) *Phenomenology of Perception*. Tr. C. Smith; tr. rev. F. Williams. London: Routledge and Kegan Paul. First publ. 1946.

Morley, D. (1980) *The Nationwide Audience: Structure and Decoding*. London: British Film Institute.

Nelson, J.L. (1985) "The other side of signification: a semiotic phenomenology of televisual experience." Paper presented to the Iowa TV Symposium and Conference on Television Criticism. Iowa City, Iowa.

Nelson, J.L. (1986) "The linguistic turn in television research." Paper presented to the annual meeting of the Speech Communication Association. Chicago, Illinois.

Perelman, C. and Olbrechts-Tyteca, I. (1969) *The New Rhetoric: A Treatise on Argumentation*. Notre Dame: University of Notre Dame Press.

Rosengren, K.E. (1974) "Uses and gratifications: a paradigm outlined," in J.G. Blumler and E. Katz (eds), *The Uses of Mass Communication*. Beverly Hills: Sage. pp. 269–86.

Von Eckartsberg, R. (1967) "Automation, leisure, and the organization of consciousness: the television experience from a phenomenological perspective," *Humanitas*, 3: 67–91.

White, H.V. (1978) *Tropics of Discourse: Essays in Cultural Criticism*. Baltimore: Johns Hopkins University Press.

Williams, R. (1976) *Keywords: A Vocabulary of Culture and Society*. New York: Oxford University Press.

Winn, M. (1977) *The Plug-in Drug*. New York: Viking.

10

The Value of Theory in the Academic Market Place: The Reception of *Structuralist Poetics*

Linda Brodkey

Think of theory as an acquired taste. A taste for the poststructural theories of the human sciences would then, like other tastes in, say, food or film or clothing, be acquired in response to and be contingent on the social and political arrangements that define scholarly practice for a given group. Inasmuch as the "rhetoric" of poststructuralism is resistance, a common rhetorical strategy is to name and oppose a hegemonic discursive practice by exploring possibilities that are suggested by, but not well-accounted for, in the theory and/or methods warranting its dominance. This would mean that post-structuralism is *literally* constructed from the material discourse of structuralism. Jacques Derrida's concept of "supplementarity," for example, deconstructs the widely accepted structural notion of the linguistic arbitrariness of binary oppositions, by arguing that because the ordering of terms in such pairs as "man/woman" is hierarchical rather than arbitrary, the positive definition of "man" is achieved by suppressing and thereby negating "woman" (Derrida, 1974). The order of these signs is not then a material artifact of an arbitrary linguistic relationship, but is instead a material production – in language – of the political oppression of women.

Supplementarity produces, and might even be said to reproduce, a portion of Derrida's larger argument that linguistics as well as language is socially constructed. Yet reading or receiving his text on supplementarity is materially different from writing or producing or even reproducing it. In particular, production anticipates (think of revisions) but does not literally predict the unevenness of reception (think of readers' reports and book reviews). That is, production does not directly address the variable readings that characterize, say, the scholarly reception of a book or article. It is this variability in readers' assessments of worth that makes reception a matter of rhetoric, rather than simply a problem in reading comprehension or literary interpreta-tion, if by rhetoric is meant the study of the complex process of deter-mining how the value as well as the meaning of spoken or written texts are constituted in a social circuit of writers, publishers, and readers.

Such a rhetorical examination of the discursive practices that materially constitute a discourse – on science, medicine, law, education, literature – would assume that those who speak a discourse do so within the historical and social constraints of time and place. If a rhetoric represents and articulates a socially constructed reality, then Pierre Bourdieu's *Distinction* (1984), a study of how taste is determined by class interests, also suggests that the rhetoric of any social group asserts what is valuable in its articulation of the meaningful.

> A cultural product – an avant-garde picture, a political manifesto, a newspaper – is a constituted taste, a taste which has been raised from the vague semi-existence of half-formulated or unformulated experience, implicit or even unconscious desire, to the full reality of the finished product, by a process of objectification which, in present circumstances, is almost always the work of professionals. It is consequently charged with the legitimizing, reinforcing capacity which objectification always possesses, especially when, as is the case now, the logic of structural homologies assigns it to the prestigious group so that it functions as an authority which authorizes and reinforces dispositions by giving them a collectively recognized expression. (Bourdieu, 1984: 231)

For Bourdieu, taste is a cultural product constructed by professionals in their spoken and written expression, in which the objectification of taste is of course legitimated by the discourse of science. A rhetoric of that discourse would be a systematic study of the scientific/objective representation and articulation of taste.

A rhetoric of discourse privileges evaluation over interpretation and is conspicuously at variance with those literary theories of reception that define reading as a process in which readers make texts meaningful. Although explanations vary according to whether a theory attempts to describe the activity of reading in psychological, social, or aesthetic terms, reader response theories all presume that what readers *do* is interpret texts. Hence, whether they are seen as extracting, constructing, or deconstructing meaning, readers are portrayed as "animating" inert texts by interpreting them.

Among reader response critics, Stanley Fish has offered the most promising, because it is the most social, literary theory for a rhetoric of reception. Meaning is determined socially in his view because readers always read as members of interpretive communities: "meanings are the property neither of fixed and stable texts nor of free and independent readers but of interpretive communities that are responsible for both the shape of readers' activities and for the texts those activities produce" (Fish, 1980: 322). Fish posits the theoretical construct of an interpretive community to explain variation in literary reception as a function of a reader's adherence to a particular set of interpretive principles or strategies – aesthetics or structuralism or psychoanalysis. While members of different interpretive communities may disagree about what constitutes a just interpretation, they would not disagree, as Fish sees it, that "interpretation is the only game in town" (1980: 355). And, since most literary critics do interpret literature, interpretive communities provide a theoretical ground from which to explain variation in interpretive practice.

Yet, as Mary Louise Pratt has pointed out, by refusing even to consider actual readers, Fish has avoided the full implications of a socially constituted theory of reading, in which "what people actually do, the interpretations they produce, are attached to everything outside themselves, to the whole of their social and material world" (Pratt, 1982/3: 222). Pratt is saying, in other words, that were Fish to study actual readers and their readings, he would have to explain that the social and material world not only constitutes their interpretations, but valorizes the readings of some communities and within a given community privileges the interpretations of some members over those of others. A theory that describes variability in reading practices as if these individual and social differences were inconsequential to a theoretical, analytical, and practical understanding of readers and reading is not a social construction theory. Fish has instead used social construction theory to naturalize a dominant literary practice.

When communities of actual readers are studied, as they are in Janice Radway's *Reading the Romance*, interpretation fails to describe the activities that define reading for the women, whose activities range from reading for information about the world, to reading to validate one's own world view, to reading to signal one's temporary unavailability to family members (Radway, 1984a). Although she used Fish's notion of interpretive community to organize data collected in her interviews of the Smithton romance readers, Radway later describes her extended analysis of their reading as "a structural explanation of the social facts that led not only to the behavior [reading] itself but their construction of it as well" (1984b: 65). Radway turned to literature on patriarchy, gender, and family because interpretation only partially explained how this group of white, married, middle-class women talked about what they were doing as readers. Moreover, her ethnographic reconstruction of the reading practices of one particular group of romance readers, and her incidental deconstruction of reading as interpretation, suggests that even in the case of literary critics, who obviously do read to interpret, interpretation may not be the *only* game in town.

To summarize: a rhetoric of reception assumes that readers assign value as well as meaning to texts, and that the value of a published text is constituted and reconstituted and even deconstituted in a circuit of readings. A writer who submits a manuscript for publication has evaluated it, an editor who decides to publish a manuscript has had it evaluated by others, and a reader who reviews a book performs yet another evaluation, as does one who cites it or recommends it to friends or requires students to read it, and so on. Each of these more or less explicit acts of judgment is performed interdependently, that is, within a complex social and historical matrix that identifies the meaningful with the valuable. An interpretive community is then like all communities an evaluative community whose members not only share the means for interpreting texts, but also the criteria for evaluating them.

Describing and Analyzing Variable Reception

In the field of literary studies, the uneven reception of Jonathan Culler's *Structuralist Poetics: Structuralism, Linguistics, and the Study of Literature* can be read as an early episode in the chronicle of the emerging taste for theory among literary critics. Published in England by Routledge and Kegan Paul in 1975 and reprinted in America by Cornell University Press, later in the same year, the book is introduced by Culler as an attempt to shift the attention of Anglo-American literary critics from literary interpretation to theory of interpretation: "Rather than a criticism which discovers or assigns meanings, it would be a poetics which strives to define the conditions of meaning" (1975: vii). His structuralist poetics openly derives from Noam Chomsky's theory of linguistics, for Culler posits the notion of literary competence as an analogue of grammatical competence and argues that the ability to interpret literary texts like the ability to comprehend the sentences of a language is a matter of having "internalized the 'grammar' of literature" (1975: 14). His is one of the first of many attempts in the 1970s to persuade critics to reorganize literary studies and among the first Anglo-American poststructural works, if not the first, to be widely reviewed in American as well as European academic journals.

There is a striking resemblance between the extensive reviewing of *Structural Poetics* – in at least fourteen American academic journals between 1975 and 1979 – and the first phase of literary canon formation that Richard Ohmann writes about, a process in the 1960s and 1970s that begins with a "nearly closed circle of marketing and consumption, the simultaneous exploitation and creation of taste, familiar to anyone who has examined market place culture under monopoly capitalism" (1983: 202). The fourteen reviews of *Structuralist Poetics* could also be said to have created and perhaps to have sustained a taste for a specific object – literary structuralism – along with an academic market for other examples of the genre – literary theory. The book won the James Russell Lowell award in 1976, the annual prize awarded by the Modern Language Association to the "best book" of literary criticism published in the previous year (the books are nominated by publishers or members and voted on by members of the committee). So it seems likely that the early reviews in the American as well as European journals created the possibility of its canonization along with an academic market for *Structuralist Poetics*.

The first phase of canonization, in which a few novels are selected to be talked about, is followed by a second stage, during which fewer still receive what Ohmann calls "the right kind of attention" (1983: 206) to sustain success in the market place. Among other things, he mentions their inclusion in courses on contemporary literature. In this second stage, the English professoriat joins the corporate network of writers, publishers, and reviewers who select and value the stories these novels tell. That *Structuralist Poetics* is in print more than ten years after its publication and has sold in excess of 23,000 copies in paperback is further evidence from the market place that the book is a serious contender for academic canonization.[1] At least it is reasonable to presume that a new generation of consumers, students, is buying the book.

The taste in contemporary American novels is constituted in Ohmann's view in a procedure dominated by principles of market economy: "a small group of book buyers formed a screen through which novels passed on their way to commercial success; a handful of agents and editors picked the novels that would compete for the notice of those buyers; and a tight network of advertisers and reviewers, organized around the *New York Times Book Review*, selected a few to be recognized as compelling, important, 'talked about'" (1983: 204). While a taste for theory is not developed outside the market place, it is in the first instance a taste constituted in language. Hence, the valuing of theory is radically contingent on economy, but the academic economy is materially based in language. If discourse and the valuing of discourse are at the base of the academic economy, then theory is a cultural product – an article, a book, a proposal, a lecture – whose market value is contingent on its reception by academics in reviews, articles, books, lectures.

The difference between the two approaches to cultural production and cultural value is the difference between a classical Marxist analysis in which discourse is in the superstructure, and a material analysis in which discourse is in the base along with the economic relations that are driving cultural production (Coward and Ellis, 1977). Ohmann's economic analysis of literary canonization is appropriate to the extent that trade publishing is organized from marketing principles alone. But to the extent that academics are a group, their social organization is decidely discursive – publications, lectures, memoranda. Academic labor uses discourse to produce research proposals, articles, books, reviews, and lectures, which are in turn used as currency when bartering for tenure and promotion. The market value of any of these academic objects depends, however, on the received institutional value of its discourse, and the institutional value of a discursive practice – a scientific or literary theory, a quantitative or qualitative research method – is contingent on the political circumstances governing scholarly practices at a given historical moment.

As Barbara Herrnstein Smith so eloquently states: "value is radically contingent, being neither an inherent property of objects nor an arbitrary projection of subjects but, rather, the product of the dynamics of an economic system" (1983: 11). Primarily concerned with the economic processes that converge on literary canonization, Smith argues that all objects of value in a culture rely on standardizing "the particular contingencies that govern the preferences of the group and discounting . . . all other contingencies" (1983: 18). Unlike the notion of interpretive community, which neither acknowledges nor accounts for cultural hegemony, radical contingency presumes that to value something (a particular reading practice) is, necessarily, to devalue something else (other ways of reading). In other words, during any historical period a number of reception theories are in play – usually one dominant theory and several emergent ones.

Smith's argument for contingency makes it clear, however, that one cannot choose among them on the basis of validity, because what one values "is a matter not of its 'truth-value' but of how well it performs various desired/able functions for the various people who at any time may be involved with it" (1983: 22). Since a book written by an academic for other academics and published by an academic press is by definition academic, the criteria for valuing and devaluing a book, or even portions of a book, in reviews are not then academic but the extraordinary ones having to do with contingent desires.

In his study of taste, Pierre Bourdieu argues that the newspaper reviews of Françoise Dorin's parody of avant-garde theatre, *Le Tournant*, are contingent on the class interests of their respective readerships. So, while most of the reviews identified the same criteria – "technical skill, *joie de vivre*, clarity, ease, lightness, optimism as opposed to tedium, gloom, obscurity, pretentiousness, heaviness, and pessimism" (Bourdieu, 1984: 235) – the value was adjusted by each reviewer to match the class interests of a newspaper readership. Thus, the very "technical skill" praised by a reviewer "representing" a constituency identified with Dorin's anti-avant-garde play would be used by a reviewer who "represents" a readership of avant-garde readers to demean her work. In Bourdieu's analysis, all the gradations of value represented in the various newspaper reviews reproduce and are reproduced in the class concerns or ideologies of their respective readerships.

Analyzing Variability in the Reception of *Structuralist Poetics*

Following Bourdieu, variation in the value assigned to *Structuralist Poetics* in the reviews is analyzable to the extent that reviewers deal with the same criteria. The values assigned to these shared criteria would then vary according to contingencies that form not the class distinctions that Bourdieu argues govern taste in France, but the ideological distinctions that distinguish one interpretive community or school of literary criticism from another. Although the contingencies that concern individual scholars will be ideologies, similarities between what Fish calls interpretive community and Bourdieu calls class are analogic.

A map of the variation among reviewers in the valuing of shared criteria would provide an analytical starting point for exploring contingencies either stated or suggested by their preferences. Yet the poststructural theories that arise out of the human sciences have considerably altered our relationship to the empirical world. On the one hand, reviews of Culler's book exist and can be taken as data; on the other hand, data do not speak for themselves and must be organized if they are to be informative. Interpretive or analytical practices like any socially grounded discursive practice are constituted at the outset by the theories and methods that govern the selection and organization of data as information. Simply put, social construction theory implicates scholarship inasmuch as it obviates even the possibility of a disinterested analysis or interpretation of data.

In this instance, the interested analysis of data begins by establishing shared criteria across reviews and noting variation in the valuing of those criteria. The values ascribed to these criteria are understood as *pointing* to possible contingent interests of interpretive communities, rather than literally representing or reproducing their contingent interests – as in Bourdieu's analysis by class. Even in the absence of reliable data regarding the socioeconomic status of the reviewers and the readership of the journals, however, the high regard that theory now enjoys in literary studies suggests that variation in the reception of *Structuralist Poetics* may well have been producing a social hierarchy of interpretive communities, that is, may have been establishing the academic status or prestige of the reviewers and their constituencies as well as delineating their taste for poststructural theory.

Fourteen reviews of the Cornell edition of *Structuralist Poetics* that appeared in American academic journals between 1975 and 1979 are listed in the *Book Review Index: A Master Cumulation, 1965–84* and/or *An Index to Book Reviews in the Humanities* (1975, 1976, 1977, 1978). Table 1 describes the "universe" of journals in which the reviews appeared according to institutional affiliation, subject matter, circulation, audience, estimated number of reviews per issue, and estimated average length of reviews. These data were compiled from descriptions in the *MLA Directory of Periodicals* (1974–9, 1984–5) and *Magazines for Libraries* (*c.* 1978).

The table displays the range as well as the quantity of journal interest in the book, which was reviewed for readers of practical criticism, literary theory, comparative literature, and philology. And it is this range that gives special point to a study of *Structural Poetics* as a cultural product whose variable reception would illustrate how distinct readerships within the academy might represent their interest and distinguish themselves in relation to one another in their judgment of a book's value.

The fourteen reviews in this study can be readily categorized into three discernible types: Type I – review essays of a set of books (3); Type II – comparison reviews of two books (3); and Type III – reviews of a single book (8). One way that review editors of popular journals, such as the *New York Times Book Review* typically exercise judgment is "by specifying the length of the review and thereby suggesting to the reviewer the importance one attaches to the work" (Coser et al. 1982: 322). The longer the review, they argue, the more important the editor believes the book to be. Since Coser et al. deal exclusively with reviews of a single book, their rule of length only applies in this instance to Type III reviews. Table 2 describes the eight Type III reviews by journal, reviewer, estimated average length of reviews and length of the review of *Structuralist Poetics*.

Judging by length, it certainly looks as if *Structuralist Poetics* was frequently identified by journal editors as a book worth reading. Six of the eight Type III reviews equalled or exceeded the word or page limit, and in two cases – *Boundary 2* and the *Yale Review* – the reviews are far longer than usual. Of the two that do not equal the journal's word limit, the review in *Comparative Literature* (1093) tends toward the lower figure (800) and the review in *Philological Quarterly* (1354), toward the upper limit (1500). To the extent that the rule of length indicates the importance journal editors ascribe to the books publishers send out for review, it seems more than likely that editors believed *Structuralist Poetics* to be an important book. Whether reviewers' verbal judgments of its value agree with their editors' judgments, measured by length, is of course another matter best addressed by analyzing the contents of reviews.

The topics evaluated across reviews, irrespective of type or number

Table 1 *Analysis of journal reviews of Jonathan Culler's Structuralist Poetics*

Journal	Institutional affiliation	Subject matter	Circulation	Audience	Estimated number of reviews per issue	Estimated average length of reviews
Boundary 2	SUNY, Binghamton Dept of English	Twentieth century literary criticism and theory	1,000	Academic	2	8–14 pages
Centrum	University of Minnesota	Theory of language and literature	500	Academic		
CLIO	Indiana University Purdue University	History and philosophy of literature	500	Academic	7–9	2–3 pages
Comparative Literature	University of Oregon American Comparative Literature Association	Literary theory and history	3,500	Academic	5–9	800–1500 words
Contemporary Literature	University of Wisconsin	None	2,000	Academic		1500 words
Georgia Review	University of Georgia	Literary criticism	2,094	Academic General	4–6	1500–3000 words
Hudson Review	Hudson Review, Inc.	Literary and cultural criticism	3,500	Academic General	5	2000 words
Journal of Aesthetics and Art Criticism	Temple University American Society for Aesthetics	Philosophy and theory of art	3,000	Academic	17–19	1700 words
Modern Philology	University of Chicago	English and American literature	1,970	Academic	5	1200
Partisan Review	Boston University	Literary, intellectual and political essays	10,000	Academic General	7	3–6 pages

Table 1 *continued*

Journal	Institutional affiliation	Subject matter	Circulation	Audience	Estimated number of reviews per issue	Estimated average length of reviews
Philological Quarterly	University of Iowa	Classical and modern languages	2,250	Academic	2	1500 words
Sewanee Review	University of the South	Literary criticism	3,800	Academic General	11	900 words
Style	Northern Illinois University	Style in English literature	800	Academic	7–9	1000
Yale Review	Yale University	Domestic affairs, literary criticism	6,500	Academic General	7–9	5–17 pages

Table 2   *Type III reviews*

Journal	Reviewer	Estimated average length of reviews	Length of review of *Structuralist Poetics*
Boundary 2	Paul Bové	8–14 pages	22 pages
CLIO	F.W. Galen	1000 words	1285 words
Comparative Literature	Edward Wasiolek	800–1500 words	1093 words
Contemporary Literature	Gary W. Davis	1500 words	1616 words
Journal of Aesthetics and Art Criticism	George McFadden	1200 words	1607 words
Philological Quarterly	Michael Ryan	1500 words	1324 words
Style	Gerald Bruns	1000 words	1285 words
Yale Review	W.K. Wimsatt	5–7 pages	11 pages

or length, constitute Bourdieu's shared criteria of evaluation. Yet the practice of embedding evaluation in interpretation is so widespread in the academic reviews of *Structural Poetics* that establishing common topics and coding them for value is a material enactment of post-structural indeterminancy. For instance, since Culler presents literary competence as the keystone of his poetics, I assumed that all reviewers would evaluate its worth. While it was discussed directly or indirectly in twelve of the reviews, literary competence was not even alluded to in two of the three review essays. At such times, one is forcibly reminded of the intertextual basis of "present absence," for only those who had already read the book would have found literary competence conspicuously present by its absence. The criteria listed in Table 3 are the four topics most frequently mentioned and evaluated across reviews: structuralism, Culler on structuralism, literary competence, Culler on literary competence. The table lists the reviews by type, reviewer, and journal and displays the results of a binary coding of each reviewer's evaluation of the four topics and the book.

That reviewers' evaluations of the four topics and the book is not readily translated into the either/or language of binary coding is evident in the number of times I used the combinations, +/- or -/+, which indicate a tendency toward either positive or negative evaluation. Yet these coded ambiguities do make it possible to see the extent to which the practice of embedding evaluation in interpretive statements distinguishes this set of academic reviews from the newspaper reviews in Bourdieu's study.

The principle of coding for positive and negative value is fairly easy to apply when judgments are more or less explicit. For instance, I judged the following assertion by Edward Wasiolek to be positive with respect to *Culler on Structuralism*: "Jonathan Culler has written a much better book, and despite the ostensibly specialized nature of the book, one gains a deeper and more complex understanding of structuralism from it than one does from Scholes' book" (Wasiolek, 1977: 354). I found the following assertion by Marvin Mudrick to be negative with respect to both *Structuralism* and *Culler on Structuralism*:

> A decade ago Barthes published a structuralist study of fashion called *Système de la Mode*, and Jonathan Culler, self (if you'll pardon the expression) appointed Anglo-American protégé and epigone of these operators, reverently summarizes its argument, which to anybody who has never in his life looked at a fashion ad in *The New Yorker* or anywhere else comes as a surprise. . . . In other words the writer of fashion ads, whose personal presence in the ads is so obvious that his efforts to conceal it have to be noticed even by a structuralist, proves to be a structuralist himself who treats his texts exactly as Barthes treats his, as for example Barthes treats *Sarrasine* with stupefying charm in *S/Z*. . . . (Mudrick, 1977/8: 588)

Table 3 *Reviewers' evaluations of Culler's treatment of specific topics and of the book as a whole*

Type	Reviewer	Journal	Structuralism	Culler on structuralism	Literacy competence	Culler on literary criticism	Book as a whole
I	Frances Ferguson	*Partisan Review*	+/-	-/+	+	-	+/-
I	David H. Hirsch	*Sewanee Review*	-	-	0	0	-
I	Marvin Mudrick	*Hudson Review*	-	-	0	0	-
II	Daniel L. Greenblatt	*Centrum*	+/-	+	+	+	+
II	Paul R. Olson	*Georgia Review*	+/-	-/+	+	-	+/-
III	John Paul Russo	*Modern Philology*	-/+	+/-	0	+	+/-
III	Paul Bové	*Boundary 2*	-/+	-	-	-	+
III	Gerald Bruns	*Style*	-/+	+	+	+	+
III	Gary W. Davis	*Contemporary Literature*	-/+	+	+	+	+
III	F.W. Galen	*CLIO*	+/-	+	+	-	+/-
III	George McFadden	*Journal of Aesthetics and Art Criticism*	+/-	+	+/-	+/-	+/-
III	Michael Ryan	*Philological Quarterly*	+	-	-	-	-
III	Edward Wasiolek	*Comparative Literature*	+	+/-	+	+/-	+/-
III	W.K. Wimsatt	*Yale Review*	-	-/+	-	-	-/+

In asserting Culler to be a *self*-appointed protégé and *epigone* of *operators*, who *reverently* summarizes Barthes' arguments for structuralism, Mudrick is effectively arguing that Structuralism attracts followers rather than scholars. I see no way around the implication that Jonathan Culler is the victim of the *stupefying charm* of Roland Barthes, the charismatic leader of a cult called Structuralism.

I found many claims, however, considerably more difficult to code. After much deliberation, for instance, I finally decided that the following assertion by F.W. Galen is more positive than negative with respect to *Culler on Structuralism*:

> But at the same time, anxious as he is, to avoid "premature foreclosure – that unseemly rush from word to world," Culler, like other "structuralists," remains confined in what is principally the realm of syntactics. Although his concept of the "ideal reader" representing the normative notion of acceptability points in the right direction, it does not go far enough; for a full–fledged literary pragmatics must ultimately situate the institution of literature within a larger socio–cultural structure (the structure of structures). (1976: 373)

In Galen's view, the structural practice of syntactics has attenuated Culler's thesis. Yet even as he asserts Culler's shortcomings as a structuralist, Galen affirms his contribution to structuralism, the ideal reader. On balance, and a very fine balance it is, I decided that placing Culler in the company of other structuralists (in tandem with praise for "the normative notion of acceptability") tips the scales toward a positive evaluation of *Culler on Structuralism*.

Based on the following kinds of assertions in W.K. Wimsatt's review, I coded his evaluation of *Culler on Structuralism* as veering toward negative:

> Even *man* disappears under the pressure of structural analysis. Says Levi-Strauss, the goal of the human sciences is to dissolve man. Man, as Michel Foucault cheerfully observes, is only a recent invention. Culler recites these opinions with some caution. "There is, of course, no question of denying the existence of individuals." (1975: 78)

Or consider Wimsatt's last words on *Structuralist Poetics*:

> Chapter 11, "Conclusion: structuralism and the qualities of literature," is a short and difficult essay – on pleasure, for example, on boredom, on ecstasy – about which I am content to say no more. (1975: 87)

In the first example, I reasoned that the unmitigated absurdity of the structural project as Wimsatt understands it (even man disappears) undermines the value of Culler's "caution." Wimsatt would have found Culler's caution more admirable, I suspect, had he realized along with Wimsatt that such claims as Foucault's (man is only a recent invention) are not simply the hyperboles of poststructural rhetoric, but among its most dangerous assertions. Wimsatt's refusal to say more about Chapter 11, having already said that it is short and difficult, implies, or at least leaves a reader room to infer, that Culler's chapter simply does not justify the time and effort it would take to evaluate it or, for that matter, read it.

The frequent positive–negative and negative–positive combinations that characterize my attempt to code the value of shared criteria across reviews call attention not so much to my inability – to comprehend sentences or even to interpret their meaning (though these possibilities can't be ruled out) – as to a tendency among reviewers to ambiguate evaluative statements. In poststructural terms, the combinations are *traces* of indeterminancy and suggest that ambiguity is a widely applied principle in the reviewing of this book. Consider that in seven of the fourteen reviews, I was unable to decide whether the book itself was positively or negatively reviewed (and each combinatory evaluation is literally arguable, that is, plausible at best), that I found eleven of the reviews indeterminant with respect to at least one of the shared criteria, and that indeterminancy is *the evaluative practice* – in nine of the fourteen reviews – when the topic is *Structuralism.*

Structuralism and the Taste for Theory

In Barbara Smith's essay on contingent values referred to earlier, she argues that the exclusive focus on interpretive criticism has been costly, since "the fact that literary evaluation is not merely an aspect of formal academic criticism but a complex set of social and cultural activities central to the very nature of literature has been obscured, and an entire domain that is properly the object of theoretical, historical, and empirical investigation has been lost to serious inquiry" (1983: 6). These reviews of Culler's book suggest that more than the social and cultural activities related to *literary* production and reception are obscured. Even when the putative task is to evaluate a text, judgments of value are often masked by interpretation. That this set contains as many indeterminant as determinant reviews of *Structuralist Poetics* also raises the possibility that academic book reviews are not meant to function as a consumer's guide to academic prose, for the part they play in the academic economy seems to be more in the nature of the ostensive gesture of advertising rather than, or in addition to, a report on a particular product from a consumer's or reader's perspective. No matter what is said in the reviews of the product, *Structuralist Poetics*, determinant and indeterminant reviews alike gesture, as do advertisements, toward a genre. In much the same way that an advertisement for *Tide* is an advertisement for detergent as well as for a brand name product, these reviews invariably create an interest among American academics in the genre of theory.

The major economic phenomenon is the discursive creation of a market for theory. What Culler and others in literary studies have been producing is theory. Whereas their predecessors, the New Critics, can be said to have organized literary studies according to a *method*, close reading, the New New Critics have reorganized the field as the study of *theories*. In addition to the aesthetic considerations first introduced in *Structuralist Poetics* and to the Derridian and Lacanian psychoanalytic concerns later introduced by Culler and others interested in deconstruction simply as theory, Afro-Americanists, feminists, and Marxists have extended or adapted literary deconstruction to include the political concerns of their respective social construction theories, and their respective constituencies, namely, people of color, women, and the working classes.

This burgeoning and uneven preference for theory over method is itself a social change of some magnitude, suggesting that even if academic reviews did not say "Read this book!" or "Don't read this book!", they effectively said "Read theory!" The utter complexity of the social and political arrangements in literary studies, in which method had reigned supreme for some forty years, is evident in the seven reviews that do not determine the value of the book, and the problem is patently manifest in the nine times that the topic of *Structuralism* is undetermined. Consider that while five reviews determined its value, two positively and three negatively, that of the *nine* that did not, five tend toward a positive and four toward a negative evaluation.

The two positive and three negative reviews can be said to represent the manifest interests of two well-known constituencies or interpretive communities – the formalists in comparative literature and the New Critics in English and American literature. Hence, the positive value that Michael Ryan and Edward Wasiolek attach to *Structuralism* could be said to represent the contingent interests of the formalists in comparative literature, the first American literary critics to read and adopt French structural theory. And the negative value that David Hirsch, Marvin Mudrick, and W.K. Wimsatt attach to *Structuralism* is also consistent with the known interest of the New Critics in method – interpretation – and their distrust of theory. In other words, those who can articulate their ideologies – formalism and explication – can also determine the value of the book in relation to their interests.

As for the others, the nine who express uncertainty about *Structuralism* are arguably between ideologies and therefore susceptible to ideological change. What I have in mind is best described as "structures of feeling," a term that Raymond Williams introduces in

Marxism and Literature to explain what others might call a practical or social consciousness arising out of lived experience. Structures of feeling refer to the social experience of individuals *that is not generated by institutions* and is at variance with and therefore goes unrepresented by current ideologies. Williams argues that "structures of feeling can be defined as social experiences *in solution*, as distinct from other social semantic formations which have been precipitated and are more evidently and more immediately available" (1977: 133–4; emphasis his). If we take *Structuralism* to be an exemplar of theory, then it's possible to read a +/– as veering toward structuralism *and* theory and to read a –/+ as veering toward theory *but not* structuralism. This would mean that literary structuralism is being variably received, but that reviewer interest in theory in this group is invariable.

I am suggesting that what is being displayed in the indeterminant valuing is the transformation of structures of feeling (the experiences of those who were writing about literature were not adequately articulated by the method of close reading that served the New Critics) into a taste for theory. What is articulated is not simply a taste for theory, but a desire for what theory promises. Theories offer precisely what methods cannot, namely, the possibility of asking rather than answering questions. Think of the human sciences as generating theories and think of these theories as rhetorics of possibility that deal not with the mathematical probabilities that ground quantitative argumentation, but with speculative and persuasive claims that deal with the arguably possible rather than the demonstrably probable (Brodkey, 1987a, 1987b; Kinneavy, 1971). That theories abound in literary studies suggests that this generation is not one but several constituencies whose interests are not articulated by a single theory because their questions, their tensions, are not the same. In other words, the possibilities of the human sciences are rendered differently across literary studies because the structures of feelings that bond the scholars attracted to theory have since been articulated as several rather than one set of questions about literature. Simply, feminists do not have precisely the same questions about reading literature that new historians do. And the possibilities offered by theories of the human sciences in the social sciences show there to be an even greater range of variation in structures of feelings across the academy.

Conclusion

The indeterminate reception of *Structuralist Poetics* raises interesting questions about the reception of interdisciplinary research across the academy. In his book, Culler publicly announced a refusal to respect the disciplinary boundary the New Critics had carefully drawn around literary criticism in the late 1940s. Specifically, he introduced foreign imports into a market that had long been protected from European literary structuralism and structural linguistic theory as he understood it to be practiced by the Anglo-American generative linguists. The New Critics rejected these imports out of hand, other formalists closely inspected them and found them wanting, but still others were sufficiently intrigued by the possibilities to sustain a market for theory. As it turned out, literary competence did not catch on. But theory did. And theory now functions as a *lingua franca* for those who are more inclined to see English departments as their administrative than intellectual homelands.

Many of the uncertainties that contributed to making theory a *lingua franca* in literary studies have also penetrated the borders of other disciplines, particularly those sciences and social sciences most uneasy about the vestiges of positivism that threaten to diminish the value of empirical research (in anthropology, see for example, Brodkey, 1987a, 1987b; Clifford and Marcus, 1986). To the extent that social psychologists (for example, Gergen, 1985; Wexler, 1983) and feminist sociologists (for example, Vance, 1984) and feminist scientists (for example, Longino and Doell, 1983) are able to carry on a conversation with one another, they "speak" social construction theory. And to the extent that they are not able to talk with those of their colleagues who "speak" only methodology, they too must experience the boundaries of their respective departments as administrative conveniences that reflect the history of another generation's academic struggle for disciplinary status and autonomy, but that more often than not frustrate their desire to read and write and publish interdisciplinary research.

What bears watching, then, is the reception of the many varieties of theory across the academy. For a theory not only defines the work of those who speak it, but revalues all academic work in the course of re-mapping the borders of interdisciplinary scholarship. In the unevenness of reception reside those contingencies that construct a community of scholars whose taste for theory, in this, an era of theories, varies according to its ability to positively define *their* interests and *their* work. Variation in reception is then a map of how the members of a community deal with the critique and the desire for change expressed in the publications of those whose interests have been deemed marginal by previous academic cartographies.

Notes

I wish to thank several people who generously contributed to this essay: Michael Boyd, Michelle Fine, Tamar Katriel, Herb Simons, and Frank Sullivan.
1   This is the figure that Bernhard Kendler, an editor at Cornell University Press, quoted in our phone conversation on 31 May 1986.

References

Bourdieu, Pierre (1984) *Distinction: A Social Critique of the Judgement of Taste.* Cambridge: Harvard University Press.

Bové, Paul (1976) "The poetics of coercion: an interpretation of literary competence," *Boundary 2,* 8 (Fall): 263–84.

Brodkey, Linda (1987a) *Academic Writing as Social Practice.* Philadelphia: Temple University Press.

Brodkey, Linda (1987b) "Writing ethnographic narratives," *Written Communication,* 4 (Jan.): 25–50.

Bruns, Gerald L. (1976) "Review," *Style,* 10 (Summer): 264–7.

Clifford, James and Marcus, George E. (eds) (1986) *Writing Culture: The Poetics of Ethnography.* Berkeley: University of California Press.

Coser, Lewis A., Kadushin, Charles and Powell, Walter W. (1982) *Books: The Culture and Commerce of Publishing.* New York: Basic Books.

Coward, Rosalind and Ellis, John (1977) *Language and Materialism: Developments in Semiology and the Theory of the Subject.* Boston: Routledge and Kegan Paul.

Culler, Jonathan (1975) *Structuralist Poetics: Structuralism, Linguistics, and the Study of Literature.* Ithaca: Cornell University Press.

Culler, Jonathan (1981) *The Pursuit of Signs: Semiotics, Literature, Deconstruction.* Ithaca: Cornell University Press.

Culler, Jonathan (1983) *On Deconstruction: Theory and Criticism after Structuralism.* Ithaca: Cornell University Press.

Davis, Gary W. (1977) "Review," *Contemporary Literature,* 18 (2): 241–6.

Derrida, Jacques (1974) *Of Grammatology.* Baltimore: Johns Hopkins University Press.

Ferguson, Frances (1977) "Structuralist ambassadors," *Partisan Review,* 44 (3): 475–80.

Fish, Stanley (1980) *Is There a Text in this Class? The Authority of Interpretive Communities.* Cambridge: Harvard University Press.

Galen, F.W. (1976) "Literary theory," *CLIO,* 5 (3): 371–4.

Gergen, Kenneth J. (1985) "The social construction movement in modern psychology," *American Psychologist,* 40 (Mar.): 266–75.

Greenblatt, Daniel (1974) "Structuralism and literary studies," *Centrum,* 2 (Fall): 73–83.

Hirsch, David H. (1977) "Deep metaphors and shallow structures," *Sewanee Review* (Winter): 153–66.

Kinneavy, James L. (1971) *A Theory of Discourse: The Aims of Discourse.* New York. W.W. Norton.

Longino, Helen and Doell, Ruth (1983) "Body, bias, and behavior: a comparative analysis of reasoning in two areas of biological science," *Signs: Journal of Women in Culture and Society,* 9: 206–27.

McFadden, George (1976) "Review," *Journal of Aesthetics and Art Criticism.* 352–3.

Mudrick, Marvin (1977/8) "Adorable ideas and absent plenitudes," *Hudson Review,* 30 (Winter): 387–95.

Ohmann, Richard (1983) "The shaping of the canon: US fiction, 1960–75," *Critical Inquiry,* 10 (1): 199–223.

Olson, Paul R. (1976) "Review," *Georgia Review,* 30 (2): 467–79.

Pratt, Mary Louise (1982/3) "Interpretive strategies/strategic interpretations: on Anglo-American reader response criticism," *Boundary 2,* 11 (Fall/Winter): 201–31.

Radway, Janice (1984a) *Reading the Romance: Women, Patriarchy, and Popular Literature.* Chapel Hill: University of North Carolina Press.

Radway, Janice (1984b) "Interpretive communities and variable literacies: the functions of romance reading," *Daedalus,* 113 (3): 49–73.

Russo, John Paul (1979) "Review," *Modern Philology*, (May): 444–8.
Ryan, Michael (1976) "Review," *Philological Quarterly*, (Spring): 294–6.
Smith, Barbara Herrnstein (1983) "Contingencies of value," *Critical Inquiry*, 10 (1): 1–36.
Vance, Carole S. (ed.) (1984) *Pleasure and Danger: Exploring Female Sexuality*. Boston: Routledge and Kegan Paul.
Wasiolek, Edward (1977) "Review," *Comparative Literature*, 29 (Fall): 353–5.
Wexler, Philip (1983) *Critical Social Psychology*. Boston: Routledge and Kegan Paul.
Williams, Raymond (1977) *Marxism and Literature*. Oxford: Oxford University Press.
Wimsatt, W.K. (1975) "Review," *The Yale Review*, 65 (Oct.): 77–87.

11

The Meta-Communicative Role of Epigraphs in Scientific Text Construction

Tamar Katriel and Robert E. Sanders

Where wilt thou lead me? Speak, I'll go no further.

(*Hamlet*, Act I, Scene V)

It is definitive of scientific writing that the text is formed in such a way as to cohere a progression of statements from data to generalization, or from problem to solution, or from theory to prediction to methodological protocol and finally to data. This norm of textual coherence is central to the characterization of a text as being scientific, as well as to the assessment of its adequacy.

With this norm in mind, it struck us as an anomaly that epigraphs would ever appear in scientific texts. Epigraphs do not contribute to achieving textual coherence of the kind that is normative for scientific writing (rather, as we will illustrate, they often do the reverse). Their inclusion thus transgresses that norm, both when the epigraph functions to enrich and complicate the way the text will be read (the prototypical case in our analysis), and also when the epigraph is entirely cosmetic – to entertain the reader, or to show off the author's erudition, before getting to the business at hand in the main text.

Commensurate with Grice's Cooperative Principle, our point of departure is that when an author takes the trouble to produce a textual element, like an epigraph, then readers will presume that he or she means something by it. Therefore, we take as given that the insertion of an epigraph between the title and the main text insinuates that the writer had something to communicate apart and separate from the scientific concerns of the main text. To identify what this is, we have examined a variety of cases, and found in them regularities of content and form that are strongly indicative of their function.

Our account thus sheds light on epigraphs as textual devices, devices that are unexpectedly useful for intensifying and complicating the way a text is read. In addition, perhaps more importantly, our account reveals that in writing scientific texts, authors sometimes cannot achieve their purposes just by achieving a coherent progression of statements. In addition they sometimes have to shape readers' expectations about the text and about the author him or herself – to establish an authorial voice.

The Function of Epigraphs

Epigraphs are devices of text construction that are not obligatory or even expected. One cannot meaningfully speak of the omission of an epigraph in the same way that one could remark upon the omission of a title. As their etymology indicates, epigraphs are "textual fringes."

However, a close inspection of this device indicates that it has a distinctive meta-communicative role, mediating between the writer, the text, and the reader.[1] Epigraphs have a riddling quality. They are supposed to be relevant to the main text, yet taken literally, they are not. This creates a puzzle where the question is not, "What does the epigraph mean?," but instead the question is, "What is it doing here?" The solution at minimum requires the reader to infer the author's reason for heading the text with that quotation, an inferential problem that often engenders a circular reading back-and-forth between the epigraph and the main text, in opposition to the assumption of linearity in text processing. Epigraphs thus involve the reader consciously and more intensely in the formation of expectations, and construal of authorial intentions.

Epigraphs also give presence and shape to the authorial voice in the main text.[2] In so doing, epigraphs tease the text-as-formation out of its fixed self-contained existence by playing with the fundamental dialectic that underlies all texts, the tension between language use as a subjective process and language structures as objective cultural products.

That epigraphs have a specific function (rather than being merely ornamental) is apparent from the fact that authors are constrained, not free, in the selection and placement of epigraphs. Breaches of these constraints result in anomalies. The constraints on epigraphs vary somewhat betwen genres of writing, especially between poetry and scholarly writing.[3] In this chapter, we offer an account of epigraphs in scientific writing. We will proceed by specifying the principal constraints on epigraphs in this genre, and show from an examination of the consequences of breaching those constraints that epigraphs have the function we described above, as well as how they achieve this.

Our inspection of epigraphs in scientific texts indicates that they are constrained in such a way that they *implicate* the attitudes, purposes, expectations, and so on, the author has. Epigraphs are thus a type of indicating device,[4] because of their general discursive function of indicating differential attitudes of the author relative to aspects of his or her text. What is of particular importance about these indicating devices is that, unlike titles and explanatory footnotes, they enable authors to avoid explicitly stating their (personal, non-scientific) meta-textual purpose, beliefs, and attitudes.[5] Epigraphs thus circumvent the need to add orienting statements to the main text that could interfere with the authorial position and topical progression that will achieve coherently the author's scientific purpose. Moreover, by implicating rather than stating such orientations, authors avoid being officially accountable for those attitudes, purposes, or expectations, and thus they protect themselves from being discredited for them, or dragged into a (tangential) debate about them.

The Constraints

The particular constraints involved are evident from regularities we found in most epigraphs in scientific texts, as summarized below. While some authors have breached these constraints, most typically the first one, those that did so made the device trivial or defective in the ways the analysis below predicts.

   1   The content of epigraphs is relevant to the content or issues presented in the main text, but the relevance of the epigraph is indirect and the basis of it in each case has to be surmised. *This constraint is essential. The other three constraints presuppose this one and have the effect of strengthening it; the other constraints are hollow if this one is breached.*

   2   Epigraphs are positioned "out of text," prior to and detached from the body of the text or a clearly demarcated textual sub-unit (for example, a book chapter). This detachment of epigraphs from the main text is often amplified in scholarly works by the convention of placing the citation of its source with the epigraph, and not among the footnotes or the reference list used for citations in the main text; in addition, the citation of the epigraph's source rarely has either the completeness or the style of citations in the main text.

   3   Epigraphs are discursively segregated from the main text by the following means:

(a) Epigraphs are quotations from someone else's work (or at least are statements not identifiable as one's own) unaccompanied by comment or explanation; self-quotation, or embedding the quoted material in additional writing of one's own, is avoided.

(b) Epigraphs are from a genre, time, and/or cultural milieu sharply different from the main text (for example, poetry is a common source of epigraphs for scholarly prose). However, there are more likely to be exceptions to this than to the previous three regularities, indicating that the constraint involved is weaker and the consequences of breaching it less serious.

To illustrate these respective constraints on epigraphs, and examine the consequences of breaching them, we will focus on a single example. The epigraph we use for this purpose is from a physics text by J.M. Ziman,[6] which he wrote to make accessible to advanced students and researchers the mathematics of theoretical physics, particularly quantum mechanics. This epigraph heads Chapter 7, "The algebra of symmetry." The mathematical property of symmetry results in considerable simplification in the analysis of physical phenomena, or as Ziman puts it, "In his search for material systems that might be capable of mathematical analysis, the theoretical physicist devotes particular attention to those which, by nature or design, exhibit symmetry."[7] This is Ziman's epigraph for that chapter:

> *Thomas Nunn*, Breeches-Maker, No. 29 Wigmore Street, Cavendish Square, has invented a System on a Mathematical Principle, by which Difficulties are solved, and Errors corrected; its usefulness for Ease and Neatness in fitting is incomparable, and is the only perfect Rule for that Work ever discovered. Several hundreds (Noblemen, Gentlemen, and Others) who have had Proof of its Utility, allow it to excel all they ever made Trial of.

(Advt. 1815)

The First Constraint: Indirect Relevance

In terms of its literal content, the advertisement of a nineteenth century tailor that Ziman quoted – even a mathematical tailor – is not relevant to a text for physicists on the algebra of symmetry. In search of a solution to the riddle this poses, a reader who is knowledgeable of the importance that physicists attach to the criterion of symmetry, or becomes aware of it as he/she reads the chapter, is likely to be struck by the *parallel* between the tailor's claims and the theoretical physicist's – both profess to have found a "mathematical rule" powerful enough to resolve all difficulties and correct errors.

But this parallel does not hold up unless we either take the tailor's conviction as seriously as we normally would the physicist's, or if we regard the physicist's beliefs (as having the potential to be) as fallible and ingenuous as the tailor's. Since Ziman's main text is not about tailoring, we have to suppose that he did not intend to implicate an elevated opinion of his mathematical tailor. In that case, he must have intended the epigraph to implicate reservations, or just irreverence, towards the physicist's belief in the power of the "rule" of symmetry.[8]

Thus, Ziman's epigraph for Chapter 7 implicates his ironical view of claims for the power of this particular mathematical "rule" by showing, as many epigraphs do, that similar claims have been made (and in this case, discredited) before. Because this ironical view is not professed "on the record" by Ziman – rather, it is a view that *the reader* is led to take note of because of the epigraph – Ziman avoids seeming inconsistent by going on to treat the topic seriously and positively in his main text.

The logic of the first constraint on epigraphs, then, is that by being relevant in a particular, discoverable way, but not directly so, epigraphs will foster attributions to the author for which he/she will not be strictly accountable. This is the key to their utility as devices of text construction.

The inferential process described above that the reader has to engage in to solve the puzzle of an epigraph's relevance to the main text is precisely the inferential process that Grice describes. Grice postulates that interpreters take it as true before the fact that any utterance a speaker (or author) makes is intended to be a meaningful contribution to the unfolding discourse. Accordingly, when utterances do not make a meaningful contribution on a literal reading, interpreters will attribute purposes, beliefs or attitudes to the speaker or author in light of which the utterance does make a contribution after all. Thus, we can posit that readers take as true before the fact that authors intend epigraphs to make a contribution, to be relevant, and that if this is not borne out on a literal reading of epigraph and text, attributions of the author's purpose, belief or attitude will be made that explain that epigraph's selection and placement.

Given the regularities we have observed, and a Gricean account of the reason for them, we can expect epigraphs to be anomalous in either of two circumstances. The first is when their content is directly, literally, relevant to the content of the main text; the second is when the connection between the epigraph's content and the main text is so obscure that an authorial intention that makes the epigraph relevant cannot reasonably be construed.

First, let us examine the consequences of using as an epigraph for Ziman's seventh chapter quotations whose content is directly, literally, relevant. First, Ziman might have used a directly relevant quote that made a positive statement about the importance of the algebra of symmetry in theoretical physics. Such an epigraph would function at most as a kind of chapter summary or abstract, but with the added weight of showing an intellectual precedent for the chapter. At the same time, its redundancy would prevent any inferences about Ziman's purpose, beliefs, or attitudes distinct from those warranted by the main text, thus trivializing the device, and perhaps puzzling readers about the need to establish a precedent "out of text" that could be simply addressed within the chapter.

Alternatively, suppose that Ziman had used a quote that directly expressed the kind of reservations that he implicated by using the tailor's ad:

In the last analysis, it's a practical mistake as well as naive to be so preoccupied with whether the system described by a physical theory exhibits symmetry, that we end up downplaying or ignoring other indices – both formal and empirical ones – of that description's adequacy.

(John Doe, *Nova*, 1983)

Unlike the tailor's ad, John Doe's comment could be included in the main text because its content is directly relevant. If it were part of the main text Ziman would be obligated to comment on it. Therefore, if this quote were placed *above and apart* from the main text and not discussed further, no reason for placing it there could reasonably be inferred. This is because it would be equally possible to attribute to Ziman his agreement with Doe's remark (but then why would he go on to treat the topic in a serious and positive way?) – or to attribute to Ziman his disagreement with Doe (but then why quote Doe, particularly apart from the main text, without going on to rebut his position?).

It would also be anomalous, obviously, if an epigraph's relevance to the main text were so obscure that readers were generally prevented from solving the riddle. In that case, no purpose, belief or attitude could be attributed to the author because of the epigraph, and instead there would be puzzlement about his or her purpose. This would be the result if Ziman had, for example, headed his chapter on the algebra of symmetry with a quotation from the present essay:

Epigraphs are devices of text construction that are found in a variety of genres. These devices are not obligatory or even expected. . . . As their etymology indicates, epigraphs are "textual fringes."

The Second Constraint: Place the Epigraph apart from the Main Text

The logic of this second constraint has two aspects. First, epigraphs have "scope," in the sense that the implicatures they foster are about a defined portion of the main text. Ziman's quotation of the tailor's advertisement implicates a point of view about the topic of his seventh chapter, not about some sub-part of the text or any larger portion of the book. There is no obvious alternative way to specify the scope of an epigraph except to set it apart from and directly above the demarcated portion of the main text to which it is intended to be relevant.

Second, the purpose, beliefs, or attitudes implicated by an epigraph depends partly on what theme or quality in the main text the epigraph is (surmised to be) relevant to. Embedding the quotation used for an epigraph within the main text will make it relevant (if at all) to constituents of its immediate textual neighborhood, and obscure its relevance to more general features of the main text. At minimum, moving an epigraph down into the text would make it incoherent (insofar as it has no local relevance), or at least alter what it implicates. The severity of the effect of such a move is a matter of degree, however, depending on the content of the epigraph and the main text respectively. Thus, it would be an unqualified anomaly if the tailor's ad appeared anywhere within the main text of Ziman's seventh chapter:

> It is proper, therefore, that the fundamental algebraic theory of symmetry – the theory of *groups* – should play a major part in advanced quantum theory. "*Thomas Nunn*, Breeches-Maker, No. 29 Wigmore Street, Cavendish Square, has invented a System on a mathematical principle, by which Difficulties are solved, and Errors corrected . . ." It is argued, indeed, that this algebra [of symmetry] is truly fundamental, providing a primitive connection between such universally acknowledged principles as the isotropy of empty space and the observable quantized parameters of the elementary particles.

On the other hand, relevance to the immediate textual environment could be accomplished, particularly with a small addition to the present text, if a quotation from Samuel Johnson that Ziman used as the epigraph for his "Preface" appeared at a certain place in his main text:

> But in the past half century, quantum mechanics has soared to such rarefied heights that most research workers in physics can no longer comprehend the published theory of their own discipline. Surely it is unhealthy to put all the observing into the hand of "experimenters" and leave all the thinking to those arrogant and plausible experts, the "theoreticians" [who seem to have the attitude that Samuel Johnson neatly captured: "Sir, I have found you an argument: I am not obliged to find you an understanding"].

Of course, once a quotation is embedded in the main text so that its relevance there is direct, the first constraint on epigraphs is breached and the utility of the device lost. The consequence in this example is that instead of implicating it, Ziman would be on record as attributing to theoretical physicists indifference, even disdain, towards the problem he is describing.

The Third Constraint: Discursively Segregate the Epigraph from the Text

The first part of this constraint – to quote others rather than oneself – is related to the first constraint in the sense that if the author's own writing is used as an epigraph, he/she will then be "on the record" and be accountable for the purpose, beliefs, or attitudes either stated or implicated by the epigraph. However, if such self-quotation is indirectly relevant, then even if the basis of its relevance is construed, it will be puzzling why the author was so indirect when the point of self-quotation is precisely that it puts one on record. Suppose, for example, that Ziman had used the following self-quotation as the epigraph for his chapter on the algebra of symmetry:

> It is remarkable how often I manage to find comprehensive mathematical principles to solve problems and correct my errors in everything, down to routine household chores. I am convinced that I will soon discover a single principle that will get me through every job from fixing the plumbing to replacing rotted door sills.

> (J.M. Ziman)

This seems about as silly as the tailor's advertisement and thus on one level could implicate the same ironical view of the power that the criterion of symmetry is thought to have. However, because Ziman has authored this material – and not someone else who is unequivocally subject to ridicule – it is just as possible that he is sincere as that he is mocking, and that he intended to project unqualified reverence for the rule of mathematics. Thus, instead of orienting the reader, this self-quotation focuses attention on Ziman rather than the text, and raises questions about what his views are and why he did not express them directly.

The second part of this constraint – to draw quotations from sources dissimilar to the main text – also relates to the first constraint in that the more an epigraph is a quotation from a genre, period, or cultural milieu markedly different from the main text's, the less will it be directly relevant. But the distinctive effect of this constraint is that the more an epigraph emphasizes that ideas relevant to the main text (even if indirectly so) have been expressed before, and in highly dissimilar contexts, the more an inevitability and universality becomes attached to the purpose, belief, or attitude they implicate. As noted in the initial statement of this constraint, however, the consequences for breaching it are not as severe as for the first three. Adhering to this constraint is helpful for ensuring that the epigraph is not directly relevant to the main text, but it is not essential. Adhering to this constraint is also helpful for ensuring that what the epigraph implicates has the appearance of universality and inevitability, but it is not essential for this purpose either.

Shaping the Reader's Response

Within this set of constraints, epigraphs can be artfully employed by an author to frame his or her text in an attempt to shape readers' response to it. Consider, for example, Dell Hymes' use of epigraphs in his book

Foundations of Sociolinguistics.[9] Hymes' book was written in an intellectual climate that overwhelmingly equated linguistic science with Chomskyan formalizations, and attached relatively little importance to empirical study of the uses of language as social practices. His book therefore had a dual purpose – to explicate the goals and methods of his "ethnographic approach" to sociolinguistics, and at the same time to dislodge from centre stage the Chomskyan view of what counts in linguistics as science.

The problem Hymes faced in this was that readers would tend to assume that he wanted to dislodge the Chomskyan program entirely, whereas his purpose was to integrate it with his own; and readers would also assume that to challenge the Chomskyan program, Hymes' program would have to be as technically elegant and self-contained, whereas it was not.

Hymes' book is divided into three sections, and he headed each with an epigraph that orients readers away from those anticipated misexpectations. He regarded the three as forming a progression paralleling his development of the main text (Hymes, personal communication). The first section, titled "Toward ethnographies of communication," describes the research goals and methods he advocated. In brief, he proposed amassing as much observational data as possible about the components of speech events and their interrelation in different social contexts in different communities, and seeking generalizations from those data about the way the roles of speaking are realized from one culture to the next. This is the epigraph for that section:

> To make a start
> out of particulars
> and make them general, rolling
> up the sum, by defective means – '
>
> (William Carlos Williams,
> *Paterson: Book I*)

The force of Williams' poetry in this instance, and the value of the quotation for Hymes' purpose, is the simplicity with which Williams mentions "defective means" for arriving at generalizations. This simple mention suggests that such fallibility is natural and human and it serves to implicate Hymes' acceptance of, and forewarns the reader about, the uncertainties and tentativeness to be expected in the program he describes.

The epigraph for Hymes' second section, where he directly tackles the thinking that puts Chomskyan linguistics at the center, implicates his intention to engage the Chomskyan position dialectically, not competitively:

> Cooperating in this competition
> Until our naming
> Gives voice correctly,
> And how things are
> And how we say things are
> Are one.

(Kenneth Burke,
Dialectician's Prayer)

In his third section, Hymes sketches the problems linguists can tackle in a new order which balances the Chomskyan program and his own. This is the epigraph for that final section:

> But General Forms have their vitality in Particulars, & every Particular is a Man. . . .
>
> "For Empire is no more, and now the Lion & Wolf shall cease"

(William Blake, *Jerusalem*, ch. 4, sec. 91;
America: A Prophecy)

At times, however, for particular readers an epigraph misfires. Although through their indirectness they insulate the author from official responsibility for what they implicate, it appears that authors are held directly accountable for the selection of the epigraph itself. For example, Katriel used the following quotation from T.S. Eliot's *Four Quartets* for her book on the ethnography of Israeli "straight talk":[10]

> We shall not cease from exploration
> And the end of all our exploring
> Will be to arrive where we started
> And know the place for the first time.

However, an Israeli reader of German origin took offence at this use of T.S. Eliot's poetry, not because of the authorial attitude it implicated, but on the grounds that Eliot was such a notorious anti-Semite that his writing had been banned by the pre-war Zionist youth movement she had belonged to. This reader held Katriel accountable for the anomaly of using an anti-Semite's writing, no matter how helpful to orient readers, as the epigraph for a book by an Israeli author about an aspect of Israeli culture. In addition to the potential for being judged in that way as distasteful and offensive, the selection of quotations for epigraphs (and thus the author who selected them) can be judged as pretentious, or erudite, or unimaginative, or witty, or heavy-handed, and so forth. This accounts for the fact that writers practice great care and invest emotional energy in the selection of epigraphs.

Conclusions

Epigraphs problematize the notion of textual coherence as well as the textual mechanisms through which it is usually achieved and displayed. They tend to be derived from the expressive repertoires of 'distant' times, of 'distant' places, different genres, other disciplines, sometimes even different languages. As a result, they establish an indirectly conveyed order of textual relevancy that the reader is invited to fathom, one that bridges over the aforementioned 'distance' between the epigraph and the text.

In the use of an epigraph, the author sets himself or herself apart from the main text, indicating that he/she is not exhausted by it, that there is more to say, emphases to add or reservations to voice. This resonance that epigraphs create between the main text and the author's intellectual and personal agenda give them the force of devices for the author's presentation of self,[11] something that authors are otherwise unable to do without jeopardizing the coherence of the main text, particularly in scientific texts.

Traditional scientific writing necessarily has to be self-contained and highly monologic, an effect achieved through the deliberate suppression of the polyphonic potential that attends any complexly structured discursive domain.[12] By prefacing his or her text with an epigraph, the author "complicates" the text by consciously introducing an element of multivocality into his or her writing without the direct intrusion into the main text of the authorial voice this creates. The author also broadens the scope of the text by anchoring it in a wider context of relevance in a way that is somewhat reminiscent of, yet different from, the way authors use acknowledgments in scientific texts.[13]

The force of epigraphs in scientific contexts, then, is that they make it possible to achieve otherwise conflicting goals of text construction. On the one hand, scientific texts must display data, reasons, and conclusions, without relying on the introduction of personal or communal factors that might predispose readers to accept at face value the scientific content of the main text and its coherence, or even blind readers to defects of data, reasoning, or conclusion.

The use of epigraphs in scientific prose predates more recent, more direct and more adventuresome modes of introducing an elaborate rhetoric of authorial voice into scientific writing through the various devices of what Bakhtin calls "polyphony."[14] Charting the uses of such devices in different genres of writing, which find their grounding in different modes and rhetorics of inquiry, will help us improve our comprehension of the interplay of authorial voice and text construction.

Notes

1　Employing Goffman's 'deconstruction' of the notion of the speaker, we might say that in the use of epigraphs, as in the use of citations, the writer assumes the *animator* role, which involves the actual production of the speech sounds/ graphemes; the *principal* role, which involves the discursive construction of identity and a commitment to what the words say; but not the *author-role*, which involves the encoding of the message. Compare Erving Goffman, *Forms of Talk* (University of Pennsylvania Press, Philadelphia, 1981).

2　Raymond Williams, "Structures of feeling," in *Marxism and Literature* (Oxford University Press, Oxford, 1977).

3　A preliminary look at the use of epigraphs in poetry suggests that it differs considerably from their use in academic prose. In poetry, epigraphs seem to constrain the understandings of an intrinsically open-ended text, whereas in the case of academic prose they 'open up' a text presented as fixed and self-contained. For a discussion of academic prose as a textual genre, see Linda Brodkey, *Academic Writing as a Social Practice* (Temple University Press, Philadelphia, 1987).

4　Tamar Katriel and Marcelo Dascal, "What do indicating devices indicate?," *Philosophy and Rhetoric*, 17 (1984), pp. 1–15.

5　The differences in the inter-textual relations that obtain in these devices of text construction can be described as follows. Titles are forward-looking but relatively self-contained, so that they carry information about the subsequent text in and of themselves. Footnotes are backward-looking and serve as addendums to the text without which they cannot be understood. Epigraphs are forward-looking but not self-contained, and engender a circular reading between epigraph and text that promotes new understandings of both.

6　J.M. Ziman, *Elements of Advanced Quantum Theory* (Cambridge University Press, Cambridge, 1969).

7　Ibid., p. 213.

8　It happens that Ziman's authorial attitude does not have to be inferred from this epigraph alone. He provided epigraphs for all of his chapters which, in addition to setting the stage for each chapter, collectively implicate his objection to viewing the mathematics of theoretical physics with excessive reverence. For example he quotes Samuel Johnson – "Sir, I have found you an argument: I am not obliged to find you an understanding" – above his "Preface," in which he states that his purpose is to "demystify" the mathematical formalisms of quantum theory. The epigraph for Ziman's third chapter on "Perturbation theory," about the recursive nature of the mathematical development of perturbation theory is this: "It were a dark and stormy night; and t'rain came down in loomps. Cap'n said 'Tell us tale', and tale it ran as follows: 'It were a dark and stormy night; and t'rain . . .' "

9　Dell Hymes, *Foundations of Sociolinguistics: An Ethnographic Approach* (University of Pennsylvania Press, Philadelphia, 1974).

10　Tamar Katriel, *Talking Straight: 'Dugri' Speech in Israeli Sabra Culture* (Cambridge University Press, Cambridge, 1986).

11　Erving Goffman, *Presentation of Self in Everyday Life.* (Doubleday, New York, 1959).

12　M. Bakhtin, *The Dialogic Imagination* (University of Texas Press, Austin, 1981).

13　E. Ben-Ari, "On acknowledgments in ethnographies," *Journal of Anthropological Research*, 43 (1987) pp. 63–84.

14　J. Clifford and G. Marcus, *Writing Culture: The Poetics and Politics of Ethnography* (University of California Press, Berkeley, 1986).

PART III

PROBLEMATICS OF RHETORICAL ANALYSIS

12
Objectivity, Disagreement, and the Rhetoric of Inquiry

William M. Keith and Richard A. Cherwitz

What is the problem with the recent interest in having all forms of human inquiry be rhetorical, in having a rhetoric of whatever is currently interesting?[1] There seem to be a lot of benefits in being able to explain the obvious role of communication and persuasion in practically all of the sciences and arts. Yet we think that a problem arises, in the form of a vicious skepticism. We call it "vicious" in opposition to an ordinary, or moderate skepticism, which is not problematic. Skepticism becomes vicious when it threatens to overwhelm the very enterprise which produces it; and skepticism stemming from the "hermeneutic" or "anti-epistemic" views seems to do just this.[2] An example of a vicious skepticism would be one which casts doubt on the possibility of interpreting written language, yet does so in written form. Similarly, a thoroughgoing relativism obviates the possibility of its own acceptance as a true theory, and therefore represents a vicious skepticism. What we propose to show in this essay is that a vicious skepticism threatens newfound "rhetorics of inquiry"; but such skepticism can be avoided, while still preserving the vast majority of important insights issuing from a rhetorical approach to inquiry.

The skepticism to which we object can be identified with two separate but related issues. These issues are the nature of *disagreement* and the place of *objectivity* in inquiry. Our response to the problem of skepticism will be to claim that the "anti-epistemic" elements which have become associated with rhetoric are in fact neither necessary to, nor consistent with, the requirements of a rhetorical perspective on inquiry.

Roots of Skepticism

In this section we try to show how a faithful representation of seemingly sensible arguments for a rhetorical theory of inquiry leads to a vicious skepticism. Since this brand of skepticism, *ex hypothesi*, renders itself incoherent, it is antithetical to the purpose of a rhetoric of inquiry. Most of the arguments for rhetorical theories of inquiry given here are not ones we endorse, but ones our thesis obligates us to take account of. Accordingly, we shall attempt to reconstruct the line of reasoning that has brought rhetorical scholars to their current views.

The mainstay of discussions leading to conclusions of relativism or skepticism is the seemingly infinite disagreements which inquirers are heir to. There are several levels of disagreement potentially problematic for traditional, "positivistic" views of the objectivity of scientific inquiry. One level is that of the *expert inquirer*, the scientist. It is a commonplace that in almost any field there are disagreements that even the experts in the field seem unable to address. But this level is not much of a problem, since it is exactly the type of disagreement that the traditional scientific methodologies are designed to solve. A second level is disagreement over *theory*. Even within a single research tradition, different theories may validate different theses, and so researchers are forced to choose among theories, a choice for which no decision procedure exists in their methodology. But still a third level, identified by Thomas Kuhn, arises when disagreements over theory-choice become disagreements over *how theories are to be chosen*. Kuhn has identified this general level of disagreement as ranging over what he calls "paradigms" (Kuhn, 1972: ch. 5).

The problem arises when a basic assumption of traditional research is pitted against the picture of disagreement just drawn. The Baconian scientific tradition assumed that there should be an obvious way to solve every empirical disagreement. But, as Kuhn has noted, the very possibility of empirical disagreement is rooted in theoretical or paradigmatic agreement. So the resolution of empirical questions requires agreement on nonempirical matters. Not only does this undermine confidence in the success of empiricist science; it also raises troubling questions about the legitimation of the entire enterprise.

Kuhn himself claims to give no answers on the question of legitimation, although a skeptical response is often attributed to him (1970: 263). But other scholars have been quick to fill the breach. In particular, problems of legitimation of the scientific enterprise have been attractive to rhetorical and communication theorists, for rhetoric seems to hold a solution to the regress problem inherent in the picture of disagreement we have drawn.[3] For example, there is seemingly a vicious regress built into the conventional (that is, nonrhetorical) picture of disagreement resolution. Suppose there is some level of disagreement *M*: any resolution of disagreements on level M will require agreement on some level N, which contains substantive theses which insure the resolution of any and all disagreements in M. But suppose there is no agreement on level N; then the disputant will have to attempt to find agreement on level N + 1, and so on. This regress seems vicious because there is no principled way of telling when it will stop. It is now considered naive to think that any construal of "the facts" can be such that no disagreement is possible, thus preventing the generation of the regress. So there does not seem to be a possibility of knowledge at all. And this is exactly the conclusion on which many rhetorical theorists have predicated their work.

Since it is unsettling to think that the entire cognitive enterprise cannot get off the ground, some of those who accept the above argument have developed a variety of skepticism, which eliminates this regress by undermining one of the assumptions required to generate it.[4] This is the assumption that objectivity is a transcendental precondition of disagreement, that without some notion of objectivity, no sense can be made of disagreement. Perhaps, adherents say, the problem lies not in the regress itself, but in the assumption that such disagreements are meaningful. What the regress demonstrates is that there really is no objectivity, no "fact of the matter" about these disputes. If there were a fact of the matter, an objective reality independent of all inquirers, then why (ask rhetoricians in the spirit of the Sophists, (1) do the disagreements persist, and (2) does there seem to be no principled way to resolve such disagreements?

Many answers have presented themselves to these questions, and, at least with respect to communication and rhetorical theory, all are predicated on the rejection of "objectivity." The argument generally made is similar to the one given above. It is a well-known staple of persuasion theory that there are many different ways to see the world. A great deal of persuasion revolves around getting the persuadee to see the world ("the facts") as the persuader does, for whatever reason. Now, if there were really an objective reality, how could it be that there are so many conflicting views of it, and that reasons for deciding on one view rather than another seem so often to turn on a point of personal or political interest rather than epistemic principle?

There can be little doubt either that this is the vicious skepticism detailed in the first section, or that these are, at least informally, the major arguments given. We wish to emphasize that our view holds this to be a legitimate line of reasoning, and we fully agree with many of the rhetorical insights that serve as premises for these arguments. But we also hold that the conclusions drawn from these premises are mistaken, and that their force can be preserved without recourse to a vicious skepticism. In the next section we will focus on conclusions which we think can legitimately be drawn from the difficulties surrounding "disagreement" and "objectivity."

The Nature of Disagreement

Our main task has been to show that a total rejection of objectivity leads to a vicious skepticism/relativism, and this skepticism/relativism is inconsistent with the concept of disagreement, which is in turn required to make sense of inquiry. This is a complicated argument, and we will tackle it in three main parts. This section will attempt to show that admitting the presence of disagreement, even in more radical varieties, does not entail a rejection of objectivity. In the following section, we will try to show that in fact objectivity, at least in some version, is required to make sense of the disagreement of inquirers. In the final section of the essay we will try to show that our version of objectivity preserves the role of rhetoric, without entailing any of the unpleasant consequences so justly criticized in the past.

There are two possible sources of ignorance, analogous to levels of stasis, about whether or not some proposition p, which is the object of inquiry, is true:

1   Not knowing what p means, exactly (that is, not knowing under what conditions p would be true).
2   Not knowing whether the conditions that would make p true actually obtain.

Since these are sources of ignorance, they are just as surely sources of disagreement. Our task is to show that, in each case, persistent disagreement is consistent with the objectivity or the objects of inquiry.

Addressing the second case first, let us make a couple of initial arguments which will lead to a more general proof. These two arguments are intended to show that there are intuitively good reasons for thinking disagreement to be consistent with objectivity. Both demonstrate how a lack of conflict may underlie a real disagreement.

The first argument concerns perceptual qualities, for example, shape. Suppose Jones and Smith are in complete agreement on the meaning of the predicates "oval" and "round." Also suppose that there is a flat metal object, a coin, lying on a table, and that Jones and Smith are in disagreement as to whether it is oval or round. Jones claims that his vision is clear and unobstructed, and he sees an oval coin. Smith also claims to have adequate viewing conditions, and yet claims to see a round coin. So it seems as though two normal observers cannot agree on a quality of an object, its shape. Are we to despair of the objectivity of the two predicates? Of course not. The solution of this chestnut is obvious: the observers are standing at different angles to the coin, and so it appears differently to each of them. But if each stood at the other's perspective, there would be agreement on "the shape from this angle," and further investigation would reveal that we call round anything which looks round when viewed straight on (Cherwitz and Hikins, 1983: 249–66; 1986; McGilvary, 1956).

Certainly all cases of disagreement are not so simple as this, but an important moral is clear: hesitate in denying objectivity until it has been established that no other difference accounts for the disagreement. Of course it is difficult to establish the "no other difference" condition, since it is hard to tell when all the possibilities have been exhausted. But that merely indicates that presumption lies on the side of objectivity.

A second argument (really a parable) demonstrates a similar point. The familiar tale of the blind men and the elephant is as follows:

> Five blind men stumble upon an elephant and try to compare the characteristics of what they have found. The first, holding the tail, claims that the creature is thin and limp, like a snake. The second, holding a leg, claims that the beast is thick and heavy, like a tree trunk. A third grabs the trunk, claiming that the animal is strong and supple, like a great lizard. The fourth holds a tusk, and proclaims the creature to be hard and curved. The last takes the ear, and says that the animal is broad and flexible, like a palm tree. (Rescher and Brandom, 1979: 166)

The moral of the parable is this: establishing that there are equally contradictory propositions involves not only adducing the evidence but establishing that the propositions are truly contradictory, that is, could not possibly all be true together. This is difficult enough that one should be slow in denying objectivity. Kuhn has noted that the search for the "crucial experiment" which will disqualify one proposition while confirming another is a difficult one.[5]

The general argument here is that for most objects of inquiry, the "empirical" disagreement that inclines one to revoke objectivity is difficult to find. There is always the possibility that there really is no disagreement about the facts, and in fact this possibility is more palatable than the denial of objectivity. If there is no disagreement about the facts, then where do disagreements arise? The first source of ignorance, cited above, is the most likely source: disagreement over the *meaning* of the terms of the dispute. This is similar to the *quid sit* of classical stasis, and leads to issues which have been much discussed in recent philosophy.

Consider Jones and Smith again. This time they are presented with a dog, and they agree completely on all of its perceptual features. But they disagree about whether or not the dog is an Airedale. Examining the dog's parentage will not help since the parents are mixed breeds, and it is possible that one or another breed ran true in this animal. The disagreement is over the meaning of the "Airedale" as applied to dogs. Jones claims that the characteristics of the dog are sufficient to confirm it simply as an Airedale, while Smith claims that there are too many anomalous characteristics for it to be so identified. What consequences does this type of disagreement have for the objective "fact of the matter" as to whether or not the dog is an "Airedale?"

Clearly we are in murkier waters than with the cases discussed above. It is not clear, in terms of objectivity, what is at stake. Is it the objectivity of:

(a) the concept of "Airedale?"
(b) the application of the concept of "Airedale?"
(c) an actual property of the dog, "Airedalehood?"

Clearly, we cannot even discuss (c) until (a) and (b) have been settled, for the terms of (c) are ambiguous between the two concepts of "Airedalehood" (Smith's and Jones') that are at issue. Kuhn is credited with the view that this is exactly the right way to characterize disagreements over *theory*: they are disagreements about the meanings of the terms shared by competing theories. And while in some cases an appeal to "the facts" may settle such a question of meaning, in the long run it cannot, since the disagreement may be complete enough that there are no "neutral" (agreed-upon) terms available in which to cast claims about "the facts."

Let us make the disagreement in the example more precise. Say that Jones and Smith together agree about the set of characteristics C which jointly constitute Airedalehood, with one exception: Jones claims C is sufficient to confer Airedalehood, while Smith claims that C and the dog lack one important quality c, without which no dog is an Airedale. Now the disagreement is this: must a dog have c in order to be an Airedale? Is c a necessary condition of Airedalehood? From here there are several ways to proceed, but it is important to notice that on only one account can we answer this type of question in advance: on a strictly subjectivist account, any term means what one wants it to mean, and so Jones and Smith are both "right."

In essence, we can now distinguish two questions:

Is the connection between language and the world (reference) an objective matter?

Is there an objective construal of claims about the meanings of words?

These questions must be distinguished both on the basis of prior research and the fact that they might be answered independently. Beginning with an influential paper by Hilary Putnam, many philosophers have answered "yes" to the first question, affirming that for certain terms, such as "water," that function as the names of natural kinds, there is a fact of the matter about how they refer and to what they can refer (Putnam, 1970). A great deal of energy has been expended in the past ten years in discovering how objective the connection is between names (or name-like nouns and noun phrases) and their objects (Schwartz, 1977).

For now the important question is the second one (taking for granted that "Airedale" is not a natural kind term, which it probably isn't). What is a disagreement over meaning like? What are its implications for objectivity? We hold that there is a commonplace argument which purports to show that these questions are of the utmost importance for a theory of inquiry. The argument is this:

P1: If we are never able to agree on meaning, then we are never in a position to assess objectivity.

P2: Only rhetoric can produce agreement about meaning (*ex hypothesi*, nothing objective can).

C1: Only rhetoric can put us in a position to assess objectivity.

An equally important argument follows immediately from this:

P3: Only rhetoric can put us in a position to assess objectivity, so objectivity depends on rhetoric.

P4: If objectivity depends on rhetoric, it is not objectivity at all.

C2: There is no coherent concept of objectivity.

Our claim is that the truth of C1 does not entail the truth of C2, which means that we must show P4 to be false, which the next two sections will accomplish in two stages, by first showing that rhetoric requires *some* notion of objectivity, and then showing that there is a sense of objectivity consistent with a role for rhetoric in inquiry which does not run afoul of the charges of absolutism, foundationalism, and so forth, that plague current and traditional notions of objectivity.

Objectivity, Rhetoric, and Inquiry

In this section we wish to establish the claim that a sense of objectivity can in fact be derived from certain very general requirements one might place on the concepts of "language," "meaning," and "communication." In the final section we shall argue that this sense of objectivity is exactly adequate to the needs of a rhetorical theory of inquiry.

In the last section, we concluded that the kind of disagreement most troubling to objectivity was disagreement over meaning. Disagreement over meaning does not in principle seem to have the resolution procedures that disagreement over "the facts" does. Let us look for a moment at the relationship between language and meaning to see why rhetorical scholars should be inclined to agree with this.

The stock-in-trade of rhetoric has always been the manipulation of language. From ancient times, rhetoricians have tried to probe the possibilities and the flexibilities inherent within language. Playing fast and loose with language has always incurred the wrath of those, mainly analytically inclined philosophers, who believe that language can be no looser than the structure of the world. A current generation of rhetorical scholars, in response to questions about whether or not it makes sense to talk about "the structure of the world," has asked how it is that language is so very malleable, and can be turned to so many purposes. The answer usually given, as we argued above, is that language simply *determines* or *constitutes*, rather than represents, the way the world is.[6]

Intuitively plausible as this account of the malleability of language might seem, it encounters real problems in explaining itself. What we claim is that there is no consistent way for such a view to give an account of language and communication which does not simply undermine its own rejection of objectivity. The general conditions which make it possible for language to be a means of communication require a minimal, and essential, form of objectivity.

Consider what, at minimum, is required for communication to take place: communicators (at least two); a language (or code or set of symbols or whatever) which is shared by the communicators. It is hard to imagine how communication could be described without at least these elements. We hold that anything so described would simply not be communication, in the sense of communication invoked by saying, "People communicate with/through language." But what commitments does this minimal view presuppose? Surely the most important commitment is that at least two items have some kind of objective status: the people communicating and the language they use. Why must such a commitment be made?

Suppose that one was willing to deny objective status to the other person in a communicative situation. Then that person would be constituted by one's own language habits, and thus the situation would amount to talking to oneself. This, of course, would not constitute "communication" – at least in the most generally understood sense of the term. Similarly, suppose that one was willing to deny the objectivity of the language that is used as the means of communication. Then it would be difficult (or impossible) to explain how it is that the communication happens. This is Humpty Dumpty's problem: if language means just what one wants it to mean, then it is very difficult for anyone else to understand the language.[7] Since it is clearly the case that the vast majority of the time we understand each other well enough to get along, there must be something objective about language that permits it to be a medium of exchange.

The historical locus of this argument can be found in Wittgenstein's *Investigations*. In section 242 he claims: "If language is to be a means of communication there must be agreement not only in definitions but also . . . in judgments" (Wittgenstein, 1953). This is a variant of the argument just given. Suppose that the putative communicators are discussing the color of a table. In order for them to be communicating about the color of the table it must be the case that in general they can reach agreement about colors. If they could never systematically distinguish, say "red" from "green," then they cannot be said to be sharing that part of the language that includes "red" and "green." In other words, there must be some quality of tables (and other things) independent of the communicators which provides for the agreement in their judgments. There must be, in a minimal sense of the term, something "objective" or else there would be no reason why the judgments of the communicators do in fact agree. This is not, it should be noted, a blanket endorsement of the pernicious view that either people always *do* agree about everything or *should* agree about everything.

Having thus shown that facts of language and communication entail an objective status for language and its users, it makes little sense to deny an equivalent objective status to the objects of inquiry, whether they be the "brute facts" of scientific inquiry, or the seemingly more ephemeral phenomena attached to (say) philological research. This follows clearly from a premise which is usually used to refute objectivity: that language actually constitutes or creates the objects of inquiry. If it does, then those objects (which are not limited to physical entities) must have exactly the same objective status as the language and the inquirers that constituted them. Denying this premise merely asserts the objectivity of objects of inquiry. It also follows that all types of inquiry have an equivalent degree of objectivity; mathematics and physics have no special status.

In short, not only do rhetorical views of language and communication not defeat objectivity, they actually entail it. While one may offer independent grounds for asserting a strong objectivity, the fact that these grounds fail does not mean that the only resort is to a viciously skeptical position based on the ability of rhetoric to manipulate language and concepts. Disagreement itself can be objective, which is just the argument made previously: there is nothing inconsistent in holding that real disagreement is possible and that the objects of disagreement are objective. In the final section we will attempt to explain how disagreement operates under such a notion of objectivity, and thus how rhetoric's role in inquiry is preserved by objectivity.

Rhetorical Functions of Inquiry

A major intellectual motivation for exploring the rhetorical nature of inquiry is a perceived failure on the part of objective/absolutist/ foundationalist theories to explain inquiry. Perhaps, some authors have reasoned, if "objective reality" fails, a door is opened for rhetoric.[8] There is a widespread perception that only the denial of the objectivity of inquiry can provide a basis for saying that inquiry is essentially rhetorical. It is this latter assumption that we wish to take up in this section. What, exactly, is the role of rhetoric in objectively based inquiry? How is disagreement possible, and how may it be resolved? While we cannot hope to completely answer these questions here, we expect to indicate what answers to them would be like, consistent with our view.

First, though, some caveats must be observed. Many discussions of issues surrounding rhetorical inquiry and epistemology founder on account of the similarity of the many available positions, and it is of utmost importance to distinguish the view offered here from others that employ similar terminology. In particular, there are four controversies about which we reach no conclusion: our view is consistent with both sides of these controversies, and hence one's position on them ought to have no impact on the acceptability of our view. The controversies we have in mind surround terms such as: "positivism," "absolutism," "foundationalism," and "incorrigibilism." In each of these areas, there is debate over objectivity; and it seems as though a resolution of each depends on an account of objectivity. But we have not provided one that is strong enough to do so: objectivity, on our analysis, regulates inquiry without *necessarily* forcing us to make substantial epistemic claims about "knowing what is really out there." All we have shown is that an extreme relativism or subjectivism of inquiry is untenable. It still remains to be shown whether or not there is a justifiable notion of objectivity available strong enough to show foundationalism (or one of the other positions) to be true. This means that, even though we have argued for the kind of objectivity which is essential to a role for rhetoric in inquiry, there are still epistemic questions left over, like bones for philosophers to gnaw.

Given, then, the minimal (yet essential) role that objectivity plays in our account of inquiry, how do we describe the role of rhetoric in inquiry? What function does rhetoric serve in the process of inquiring about the truth of propositions? As an initial effort, we will delineate six functions of rhetoric in inquiry: the differentiative, inferential, preservative, abductive, managerial, and socially ameliorative.

The *differentiative* function of rhetoric consists in the ability of language users to develop alternative schemes for naming and describing reality.[9] There are always different possibilities available for doing so which are objectively consistent. For example, consider different ways of describing a table:

This table is a work of art.
This table is in my den.
This table was my Grandmother's.
This table is of a fine-grained wood.

Each of these propositions might be part of, or the result of a different inquiry, and there is no need to choose among them the "real" description of the table: the table is all these things and more. The point is that the terms of no particular inquiry limit what can be truly said of the table, and exploring these linguistic possibilities is the function of rhetoric. Rhetoric here represents a particular way of *using* language: not merely creative, but *instrumental* (with respect to inquiry).

The *inferential* function of rhetoric consists in systematic linkage of ideas by an audience into relationships such as entailment, logical validity, enthymematic validity, causation. While this may seem to be merely a general cognitive activity, rhetoric is engaged in the specific case where there is a dispute and some inferential relationship is called upon to resolve the dispute. For example, if Jones is unsure about a telephone number and Smith looks it up in the telephone directory and gives it to Jones, Jones will accept it without significant doubts. Why? There are easily explained properties of rhetoric which compress so trivial a sequence of reasoning. This not only facilitates inquiry, but rhetoric in this sense is fundamental to inquiry because it embodies the principles of reasoning accepted by a community of scientists. These principles of reasoning are themselves part of the objective fabric of inquiry. Whether or not some specific set of principles is the "right" one is not a question about the rhetoric which embodies the principles; it is a question to be answered by a specific epistemology (which may itself be a "rhetorical epistemology").

The *preservative* function of rhetoric is essential to inquiry. Without the memories and argumentative skills of a community of inquirers, there would be no way for a disputed thesis to survive. If one accepts that the truth of a thesis has any relevance to whether or not in the long run it will be accepted, then it is essential that there be some way of preserving or maintaining a thesis until evidential conditions are right for epistemic appraisal. If there were no arguers to hold an unpopular or unproven point of view, then a change in data or theory could not eventually validate the truth of the (currently) unpopular point of view.

The *abductive* function of rhetoric lies in its creative ability: the ability to generate and manipulate the hypotheses to be tested by inquiry. The concept of abduction derives from Peirce, and is essentially the same as the traditional rhetorical concept of invention Rescher, 1978: ch. 3). At the beginning of inquiry, we don't know what is true, but wish to find out. Thus there must be some way of manipulating the possibilities consistent with what we already know, in order to generate the hypotheses to be tested. Rhetoric is creative in the sense that it creates possibilities, not truth or reality.

A fifth function of rhetoric in inquiry is the *managerial* function (Campbell, 1963). Since inquiry is by nature a social or collective activity – the lone researcher is only made possible by the community of which he is a part – there must be some way of managing or coordinating the activities of the various inquirers. Suppose a group of people are researching a single question, of whatever type; they must constantly communicate in order to make sure they are in agreement about the question and methods, to insure that there is no duplication of effort, and to coordinate disparate facets of the research process. On the level of a community of scholars, there must be communication (and thus rhetoric) in order to share and compare the findings made by various researchers. Since scientists or other inquirers rarely come to blows in their discussions, they must have some systematic way – amounting to a rhetoric – of managing such interactions.

The final function of rhetoric in inquiry is somewhat subtle. Rhetoric in inquiry is *socially ameliorative* to the extent that rhetoric is used to enforce the limits of inquiry. Even with epistemologies which admit of certainty, we rarely attain it. This raises a natural problem about the fruits of inquiry: How are we to take them? What should be done with them? It is a function of rhetoric to encourage intellectual tolerance and social cohesion among both inquirers and the general public. We need to acknowledge the ambiguity forced on us by the defeasible results of most inquiry, and work towards a general tolerance of dissenting points of view. This does not mean that *any* view can be legitimated through enough rhetoric, just that a knowledge of rhetoric can expose the persuader who would convince people his/hers is the only truth. Rhetorical critics can remind us that, with respect to the results of their inquiry, scientists, like politicians and other traditionally recognized rhetors, are in a position where they must engage in persuasion.

Conclusion and Implications

The view presented in this chapter amounts to relinquishing the scheme/content distinction, as Davidson (1973) and Rorty (1979) have urged. Davidson argues that a distinction between the content of experience and the scheme which organizes that experience is incoherent, because it offends the concept of communication. If there is something inexpressible in some language different from ours, then it is impossible to say what that something is; in short, it must remain merely an abstract possibility that it exists. Yet if, *ex hypothesi*, no examples are forthcoming, then there is no reason to worry that the conceptual scheme represented by this foreign language is so different from ours as to be completely unintelligible. Thus a problem with incommensurable schemes or languages cannot arise, since the distinction between schemes and content has been rendered nugatory.

It is crucial to realize that renouncing this distinction virtually emasculates certain kinds of "rhetorical" critiques of science or inquiry. For these critiques depend on the assumption (explicit in Johnstone's work) that, if knowledge is nothing more than the effective application of this or that scheme, then knowledge is merely rhetoric, merely a way of speaking. And, claims this line of reasoning, if science or inquiry pretend to more than merely rhetoric, then they must be unmasked as rhetoric. By this method, Simons has recently suggested, rhetoric might become the center or foundation of all inquiry, in the sense that the knowledge resulting from inquiry is just a form of rhetoric (Johnstone, 1978; Simons, 1985).

Our approach shows several difficulties with this suggestion:

1 It has been based to some extent on Rorty's anti-epistemological view, but is in direct contradiction to the view in *Philosophy and the Mirror of Nature*, since there Rorty holds that if epistemology is not to be the foundation, then nothing can replace it, not even rhetoric (Rorty, 1979, ch. 7).

2 It is premised on a rejection of objectivity, which in turn is based on implications drawn from the scheme/content distinction. But we have shown that there is a coherent view of objectivity which does not require the introduction of a scheme/content distinction. And without this distinction, rhetoric cannot assume a central place as the regulator of schemes, as the discipline which unmasks. Instead, rhetoric allows, in a transcendental sense, the process of inquiry to occur. It is not the same as the process of inquiry, but it is essential to and cannot be separated from inquiry.

3 By making rhetoric *the* center of intellectual activity, one risks that this is merely a rhetoric of rhetoric, too weak to justify even its own existence. This is the unpleasant possibility we began with, that the skepticism required for such of view of rhetoric might be vicious.

Another way to understand our conclusion is to consider the difference between two questions about science/inquiry:

1   How does science/inquiry work?
2   Why does science/inquiry work?

What we have tried to show is that we can answer question (1), while remaining neutral on question (2). We have given arguments for a concept of objectivity which is strong enough to explain the prominent role of rhetoric in assessing (1), but leaves open for further argument the traditional epistemic disputes of (2): foundationalism/coherentism, realism/idealism, fallibilism/incorrigibilism, etc. We sidestep the issue of whether or not one might wish to incorporate rhetoric in an answer to (2), not only because one author holds (2) irrelevant and the other that rhetoric provides a positive answer to realism, but because these really are separate issues. While (1) and (2) are relevant to each other, they are in principle independent. We may agree about (1) and yet consistently give different answers to (2).

Hence, it is ironic that so many rhetoricians have relied on a skeptical answer to (2) as the only hope for the legitimation of rhetoric as a feature of inquiry. If our arguments are correct, this endorsement of skepticism may be misguided. All that is really needed is a way of deflecting (2) while still giving a sense to (1). The notion of objectivity we have defended here does just this: it preserves science/inquiry in a familiar role, but leaves a place for rhetoric by emphasizing the elastic nature of objectivity. Thus the irrelevance of the unmasking gambit: rhetoricians should instead work hand-in-hand with methodologists and researchers in the social and physical sciences to enrich our understanding of those sciences through an appreciation of rhetoric.

Notes

1   Most of the material relevant to the rhetoric of inquiry, as opposed to epistemology, may be found in the documentation on the 1985 Iowa Symposium on Rhetoric and the Human Sciences. See especially Lyne, 1985; Simons, 1985; Nelson and Megill, 1986. We will refer to the general view of these authors and those that sympathize with them as "the Iowa Symposium school;" while any given "member" of this "school" may not hold exactly the view we attribute to the school, we feel that some of the observations made below are generally true of the school as whole.
2   Derrida is representative of the hermeneutic position and the anti-epistemic position is represented by Rorty, 1979; 1982.
3   See the Iowa Symposium school, especially Nelson and Megill, 1986.
4   Out of the Iowa Symposium school, Simons has especially emphasized this; see Simons (1985: 53).
5   See his response to Popper in "Logic of discovery or psychology of research?" in Lakatos and Musgrave, 1970.
6   While this a popular position among rhetoricians, the most notable adherent is Barry Brummett, 1976. For a recent discussion of the constitutive vs. instrumental/representational views of language, see John Stewart, 1986.

7   See Lewis Carroll: " 'When I use a word,' Humpty Dumpty said, in rather a scornful tone, 'it means just what I choose it to mean – neither more nor less' " (1960: 269).
8   This seems to be a generally held position among rhetorical theorists; see Scott, 1967. This view is also represented by Brummett, 1976, and some of the Iowa Symposium school.
9   This function of rhetoric, along with the next two, have been borrowed from Cherwitz and Hikins (1986: ch. 5), where the inferential function is referred to as the "associative function."

References

Brummett, Barry (1976) "Some implications of 'process or intersubjectivity': postmodern rhetoric," *Philosophy and Rhetoric*, 9 (1976): 21–51.
Campbell, George (1963) *The Philosophy of Rhetoric*. Ed. Lloyd F. Bitzer. Carbondale: Southern Illinois University Press.
Carroll, Lewis (1960) *Through the Looking Glass*. With notes by Martin Gardner. New York: Bramhall House.
Cherwitz, Richard A., and Hikins, James W. (1983) "Rhetorical perspectivism," *Quarterly Journal of Speech*, 69: 249–66.
Cherwitz, Richard A., and Hikins, James W. (1986) *Communication and Knowledge: An Investigation in Rhetorical Epistemology*. Columbia: University of South Carolina Press.
Davidson, Donald (1973) "On the very idea of a conceptual scheme," *Proceedings of the American Philosophical Association*: 1–21.
Johnstone, Henry W. Jr (1978) *Validity and Rhetoric in Philosophical Argument*. University Park, PA: Dialogue Press of Man and World.
Kuhn, Thomas S. (1970) "Reflections on my critics," in Imre Lakatos and Alan Musgrave (eds), *Criticism and the Growth of Knowledge*. Cambridge: Cambridge University Press.
Kuhn, Thomas S. (1972) *Structure of Scientific Revolutions*. Chicago: University of Chicago Press.
Lakatos, I. and Musgrave, A. (eds) (1970) *Criticism and the Growth of Knowledge*. Cambridge: Cambridge University Press.
Lyne, John (1985) "Rhetorics of inquiry," *Quarterly Journal of Speech*, 71: 65–73.
McGilvary, E.B. (1956) *Toward a Perspective Realism*. Ed. Albert G. Rampsberger. LaSalle, IL: Open Court.
Nelson, John S. and Megill, Allan (1986) "Rhetoric of inquiry: projects and prospects," *Quarterly Journal of Speech*, 72: 20–37.
Putnam, Hilary (1970) "Is semantics possible?" in H.E. Kiefer and M.K. Munitz (eds), *Language, Belief, Metaphysics*. Albany: State University of New York Press.
Rescher, Nicholas (1978) *Peirce's Philosophy of Science*. Notre Dame: University of Notre Dame Press.
Rescher, Nicholas and Brandom, Robert (1979) *The Logic of Inconsistency*. Oxford: Basil Blackwell.
Rorty, Richard (1979) *Philosophy and the Mirror of Nature*. Princeton: Princeton University Press.
Rorty, Richard (1982) *Consequences of Pragmatism: Essays 1972–80*. Minneapolis: University of Minnesota Press.

Schwartz, Stephen P. (ed.) (1977) *Naming, Necessity and Natural Kinds.* Ithaca: Cornell University Press.

Scott, Robert L. (1967) "On viewing rhetoric as epistemic," *Central States Speech Journal,* 18: 9–17.

Simons, Herbert W. (1985) "Chronicle and critique of a conference," *Quarterly Journal of Speech,* 71: 52–64.

Stewart, John (1986) "Speech and human being: a complement to semiotics," *Quarterly Journal of Speech,* 72: 55–73.

Wittgenstein, Ludwig (1953) *Philosophical Investigations.* New York: Macmillan.

13

The Rhetoric of Inquiry and the Professional Scholar

Robert Hariman

A meditation in the manner of Willmoore Kendall, the only member of the Yale faculty whose tenure rights were bought out by the University:

1   Why do the academic costumes worn at the ceremonial occasions emphasizing the traditions of university culture distinguish the graduates not according to the studies of the medieval *trivium* or *quadrivium* but instead according to those ancient university studies of nursing, forestry, agriculture, business and commerce, journalism, pharmacy, physical education, social work, and public administration?

2   Why did those architects of the modern university, men such as Charles William Eliot and Noah Porter, why did those men belong to or lead or sponsor such organizations as the American Social Hygiene Association and such movements as the American temperance movement? And why is a university degree required if one is to be allowed to have any authority in a hospital, an asylum, a prison, a court of law, a church, a school, a military service, a public service agency, any governmental office, or the mass media?

3   Why is it the case that the many academicians who now admire the work of such continental writers as Foucault, Barthes, and Derrida, that is, the work of a group of writers known for their powerful criticisms of bourgeois culture, why do these academicians not apply that critique to the premier incorporation of bourgeois culture – that is, university culture?

4   Why do those who are pursuing knowledge not encounter tragic knowledge, or otherwise confront the penalties of knowledge, and why do they declare themselves free of sentiment and patriotism and religious conviction, and who are they writing for anyway?

5   Why is it the case that Harvard once had a chair in oratory, a chair occupied at one time by John Quincy Adams, and yet today does not have a chair in oratory, or a department in oratory, or a program in oratory?

6   What is a discipline, as in: the discipline of speech?

7   What is a field, as in: the field of antebellum Southern oratory?
8   Why, if rhetoric provided a bridge between two disciplines, would that bridge not be used?

Knowledge and Power

So far the rhetoric of inquiry has had it too easy. No doubt there has been many a heroic moment as each of us has found our way out of the gulag of positivism, but as the many arguments against scientific philosophy accumulate one begins to wonder if we are amidst nothing more than a logomachy – a battle of words – and if perhaps the practices sustaining the social and political apparatus of modernism remained unscathed. But a rhetoric of inquiry, of all perspectives, should include the caution that a change in words need not entail a change in deeds. A shift from a philosophy of science to a rhetoric of the human sciences can change our understanding of how knowledge is produced and used without motivating us to change more than our understanding. Philosophers grown tired of distinguishing between description and explanation may come to enjoy parsing metaphor and metonymy, but a shift from championing logic to championing practical reasoning is not automatically a challenge to put one's thinking at risk.[1]

This polemical essay offers a critique of the premier ideology of our university culture: the professional ethic. My basic idea is that the professionalism now ascendent in university culture is the dominant power shaping our thought and our conduct, and that this power has become more a repressive than a productive power. This broad claim can be divided into several more specific assertions. (1) Understanding American intellectual discourse requires a critique of professionalism – and particularly of its administrative structure, known as the academic disciplines – as the dominant apparatus of power shaping our rules for determining truthfulness and probity. (2) If rhetorical studies are read into a disciplinary scheme they are read poorly; if they are read sympathetically they subvert the disciplinary reading. (3) Stronger rhetorical scholarship, and especially scholarship in the rhetoric of inquiry, requires a reform of university culture away from the disciplinary schemes and other conventions of professionalism.

I cannot discuss fully each of these claims here; I hope to show that these matters are important concerns for a comprehensive rhetoric of inquiry for the human sciences. In addition I shall follow the current fashion by drawing upon a continental perspective for my analysis. In doing so I also want to advance a fourth claim relevant to the project. (4) If the continental texts now influential in the humanities, texts by Foucault, Barthes, Derrida, and others, are read into a disciplinary scheme they are read poorly; if they are read sympathetically they subvert the disciplinary reading. In this chapter I shall rely upon Foucault's vocabulary of power to describe the system of mental administration called professionalism, giving special though brief attention to the significance of this system for development of the rhetoric of inquiry.

Together these claims can serve two general purposes of the rhetoric of inquiry: first, identifying how knowledge is determined by its manner of production; second, identifying how rhetoric exceeds the account of it included in the milieu of contemporary epistemology. Like other work in the rhetoric of inquiry, I shall assume that a writer's discourse discloses a social situation, and that understanding the truth claims of a discourse requires analysis of its communicative conventions, and that this analysis in particular requires attention to textual strategies for unobtrusively composing textual authority. My specific point of departure is to direct our attention to the institutional pressures upon the academic writer. For the writer is not the sole author of the work, which also is the product of inventional patterns provided by (and sustaining) the writer's dominant social organization. Academic discourse is made by the academic institution, and discovering the relationship between the rhetorical and epistemological dimensions of such discourse should include a critique of its institutional invention.

My argument is frankly derivative of other scholarship: the critique of professionalism has recently been voiced at the margins of many disciplines, yet it has not been identified theoretically as more than a minor area of American studies. Frankly, this critique belongs under the rubric of a rhetoric of inquiry, where it can join a larger analysis of the problematic of knowledge and power and can supply the institutional analysis often missing in current rhetorical criticism. Nor should writers in the rhetoric of inquiry be hesitant to appropriate work begun elsewhere, or otherwise bend the conventions of scholarly writing toward more public forms of writing such as the editorial or essay. As Paulo Valesio has observed, "in rhetoric more than in any other of the language sciences the metalanguage is closely interwoven with the ambiguities and conflicting connotations of the object language."[2] These impurities (impieties) are often the traces of other genres or other audiences and they offer the academic writer opportunities for thinking anew. In sum, the rhetoric of inquiry can itself be aggressively rhetorical – which means more than recognizing that one's own text is as fabricated as any other. The full-blown rhetorical perspective replaces disinterestedness with advocacy, balances specialization with generality, and confronts expertise with an assertion of voice. It is, then, less a change in philosophical doctrine and more a change in style.

University Culture

The standard definition of a profession is a community of skilled workers characterized by a distinct body of knowledge, a code of ethics, and peer review.[3] Professionalism includes these elements as well as the beliefs that entrance to the profession should be determined by certification rather than privilege, that advancement should be determined by merit rather than privilege or seniority, that competence should be valued more than sociability or loyalty, that professional work is hampered by supervision, that the profession should serve the public interest, and that the professional possesses more self-control than the layman.[4] Academic professionalism includes all of these beliefs as well as a set of conventions governing the specific activities of academic work. These conventions include the academic ranks, academic disciplines, tenure, special languages, the elite forums of the journals, conferences, and conventions, and the rules of decorum – especially the rules of "disinterestedness" and of political neutrality. Each of these elements occasionally receives some criticism: as the apolitical rule did in the 1960s, or as the use of special languages does periodically. These criticisms have themselves become conventional, co-opted into the system.

This university culture does have a history, albeit one usually told in terms of the individual disciplines or particular institutions. Several larger accounts are available, however, and all the writers tell much the same story:[5] the American university of the first half of the nineteenth century had declined considerably from its colonial precursor. The curriculum consisted entirely of recitations, those primarily in Latin, Greek, math, and theology. The students devoted most of their time to brawling. The faculty were exploited if young, underpaid regardless of rank, and often lived in fear of their students (sometimes with good reason). The facilities were atrocious. The schools were controlled by the remnants of the colonial aristocracy and were seen as the means to produce docile Unitarian ministers and to refine those boys too weak or too wild to enter business immediately. In short, the American university was in great need of reform. In the second half of the century the reform came.

The Victorian era in America was the scene of a revolution in class structure.[6] As real wealth increased yearly the middle class came to produce and control more and more of that wealth. The transition from an agrarian to an industrial society and the rise of entreprenurial commerce are familiar themes in American history, and each transformation was the means and the effect of the ascendency of the middle class to power. As this expanding class looked to break the established aristocratic monopolies (for example, in the law) and to secure the means for its own advancement and security, it quickly seized upon the university as its leading institution.[7] The universities, now led by men epitomizing middle-class origins, conduct, and values, responded. During a period of strong growth and stronger competition all of the fundamental customs of contemporary university culture were established, from grading to the elective system to the academic ranks to the disciplines to the idea of academic administration. Harvard during the presidency of Charles William Eliot provides the most ready example: the school grew during his forty-year term from 60 to 600 faculty and introduced or adopted each of the customs mentioned.

The key to this transformation of American society, the rhetorical innovation capable of redefining American culture, was the invention of the professions. "Every subject was made into a natural 'science,' from calisthenics to the architecture of the home to religious worship. What strikes the historian is the totality of the mid-Victorian impulse to contain the life experiences of the individual from birth to death by isolating them as science."[8] This reliance upon science combined with an obsession for social control to remake all of American life in a few decades. From *Sanitary News* to the *Ladies Home Journal* to *Scientific American*, all of the new house organs of the middle class persuaded their readership to become professionals so that they could continue their assault upon those privileges withheld by the aristocrats above them while protecting their newly won gains from the immigrant hordes pouring in below. The second half of the century saw the formation of the professional baseball leagues, the first national associations of law, librarianship, and social work, the first university schools of architecture, pharmacy, school teaching, veterinary medicine, and accounting, the first school of business, the first women's colleges and "domestic sciences," and hundreds of other professional societies.[9] The radical specialization occurring during this period included separate societies for ophthalmology, neurology, dermatology, gynecology, laryngology, surgery, orthopedics, chemistry, chemical engineering, electrical engineering, forestry, ornithology, geology, statistics, mathematics, physics, history, church history, political science, folklore, and on and on.[10] As Bledstein summarizes, "The Gilded Age was also a guilded age, developed around the novel uses of space and protective boundaries to regulate the social experience of the individual."[11]

The Role of Professionalism

To review: I am assuming that most American intellectual discourse today is written and read within the context of university culture; university culture was formed in the latter half of the nineteenth century and incarnates and perpetuates the dominant practices of that time; the dominant practices of that time were the practices of professionalism. The next step in evaluating these practices is to ask how they cohere and what their effects are. To do this, I shall use Michel Foucault's discussion of knowledge and power to re-describe professionalism's rationale that it serves society by producing knowledge in a community of peers. In place of this rationale I elaborate three claims about the role of professionalism in the determination of knowledge: first, knowledge is a product of a specific system of social control; second, knowledge is defined by its spatialization; third, disciplinary knowledge consigns rhetoric to the status of a subjugated knowledge.

My first claim is an application of Foucault's concept of disciplinary power to university culture. My point is that the current organization of learning according to the disciplines (of psychology, sociology, and such) is produced by the mechanism of power Foucault calls the disciplinary system. Foucault's concept of disciplinary power may be his signal contribution to understanding modern society. By turning from the language of sovereignty and the "model of Leviathan in the study of power" (that is, from undue emphasis upon the State), and by looking less at political doctrine and more at "the production of effective instruments for the formation and accumulation of knowledge – methods of observation, techniques of registration, procedures for investigation and research, apparatuses of control,"[12] we can discover this system of power which is "one of the great inventions of bourgeois society."[13] The disciplinary system consists of all of the means by which people's time, labor, and conduct are directed towards approved activities of production and consumption without the use of force. Foucault's research has been directed at key institutions of control such as the asylum, prison, and hospital, but his subject is no less than the entire set of rules, rationales, and practices that comprise the full range of our ordinary activities. Foucault would ask why we treat mental illness in hospitals and treat mental retardation in schools, and why we allow chapels in public hospitals but not in public schools, and why we require both hospitals and schools to be well lighted and allow neither to require loyalty oaths, and he would ask how these various rules cohere into a pattern of conditioning allowing "the minimum expenditure [of power] for the maximum return."[14] And he would ask why every position of control in the disciplinary system requires a university degree, and why the university is defined as "an institution that grants degrees."

The disciplinary system in America developed through the construction of the modern university.[15] The key observation here is that expertise is the fundamental instrument in the disciplinary system.[16]

Disciplinary power is the exercise of the authority coming from expertise. Knowledge in the disciplinary system becomes that which is established by certification and grounded in "methods of observation, techniques of registration, procedures for investigation and research," in other words, expertise. Foucault argues that the extension of expertise to the social realm has transformed our traditional problems of power, freedom, knowledge, salvation, and so forth. The extent of this change is revealed in the technologies of coercion: where once a criminal was put in chains (subjected to the sovereign's use of force) now he is put under observation (subjected to the expert's use of definition). As an ad for a psychotropic drug in the *American Journal of Psychiatry* claims, "Compliance has come of age." As the one institution acknowledged to produce knowledge and certify expertise, the university becomes the central institution in the disciplinary system and the disciplinary schema its central mechanism.[17]

What is expertise? It is disciplined behavior, behavior marked by strict conformity to procedure rather than by Yankee tinkering. It is disciplined knowledge, acquired by careful attention to a carefully delimited space. It is knowledge made to order, that is, knowledge that can be reproduced by reference to its set of specifications, just as one could reproduce a manufactured object. It is a code of discipline, shaping the student to become someone capable of powerful emotional control; one cannot be both acting as an expert and acting wildly. It is a disciplinary instrument, knowledge made to order, that is, made for one who will order others to build bridges, pay fines, take medicine, or begin work on time. The society founded on expertise would provide the perfect example of Foucault's metaphor of "dressage," whereby the expert minute manipulations of the authorities result in smoothly coordinated movements in the social body performing a series of tasks.[18]

This ideal is the ideal of professionalism that was promulgated throughout the latter nineteenth century. The most obvious example is the address by Henry N. Day entitled "The professions," which urged the lay public to recognize that civilization depended upon the "professional tendencies" and that professional life was entirely distinct from ordinary work.[19] Other examples abound, from Charles William Eliot's use of the public health services to battle promiscuity and protect the white race, to the many self-help manuals stressing that ascetism was essential for becoming a professional.[20] The university presidents were particularly prominent figures in the various reform – that is, control – campaigns and consistently linked reform with expertise. Despite the tendencies of the professions to conserve their privileges once established, they never linked reform to traditional wisdom or received authority, and reform always involved the transference of authority to managers holding an expert knowledge. Professional discourse and social reform were mutually authorizing: for example, the American Psychiatric Association emerged out of the movement to reform prisons and asylums. Knowledge was something possessed by a professional (rather than the learned amateur, the village elder, or the experienced artisan) and something guiding the administration of discrete sectors of society (rather than nurturing the enjoyment of literature, the governance of civil society, or economic independence).

Knowledge bestowed power – but only because it already was constituted by power. As the university increasingly became the central institution in the control of society by the middle class it accelerated the generation of disciplines. Knowledge was declared to be the *sine qua non* of a discipline, although increasingly the opposite also was true: anything not capable of formulation into a disciplinary scheme was defined as something other than knowledge or reformed (deformed) into a body of knowledge. Knowledge was declared to be apolitical and seemed to be so, for no body of knowledge was affiliated with any one political interest, community, or doctrine. In fact, the language of politics could not account for the new system of power, and the language of that system of power carefully precluded identifying the system at all. No discipline is political, yet the disciplinary system is the means for recruiting, training, authorizing, and rewarding the political agents of the dominant class. Knowledge is by definition apolitical, yet the body of knowledge was created as an agency of social control. We have disciplines of economics and political science but not of political economy or popular theodicy. We have been disciplined.

The second point I wish to make is that disciplinary knowledge is produced by a process of spatialization: that is, the basic principle of design is to imagine social reality as a set of contiguous spaces described by separate discourses and maintained by observation. Here Foucault seizes upon Bentham's Panopticon for his representative anecdote to depict "the theme of a spatialising, observing, immobilising, in a word disciplinary power."[21] The Panopticon was a design for a prison consisting of a circle of transparent cells surrounding a central observation tower. It is actually the inspiration for modern prison architecture and is an all too apt metaphor for the fetish with controlled observation found in the social sciences. The basic point, however, is that the establishment of a discipline proceeds by identifying a separate space for inquiry and proceeds best if the investigation is identified with a separate administrative domain in the society, as psychiatry was joined with the asylum, and education with the school, and economics with the government, and management science with the corporation. In every case the knower becomes an administrator – directed to observe in order to maintain the normal condition of the space. Moreover, the spatializing of reality is "immobilizing" in part because it submerges any extensive account of change – because change cannot be comprehended well by a system where each function is located in a distinct space. Thus, any respectable account of social change cannot be sufficiently credible to be used in a critique of the existing system of administration because it is obviously partial and of little explanatory power: the economist can give only a purely economic account, and the sociologist a purely sociological account, and the psychologist a purely psychological account unless each oversteps the certified expertise, and each account is by definition too limited to be powerful. Yet any comprehensive account of change that does not follow the disciplinary boundaries is automatically discredited as being unlearned or popular or partisan or eccentric or radical or utopian.

The second half of the nineteenth century saw the emergence of: the department store, the sports stadium, the great symphony halls, the great public libraries, large city parks, zoos, ghettos, golf courses, floor plans, and breakfast.[22] All of these innovations demonstrate the mid-Victorian conception of space as something that is specialized. Instead of the colonial common room (containing hearth, bed, table, and workshop) the new house contained separate rooms for separate functions – from the maid's pantry to the cook's kitchen to the parent's master bedroom to the children's nursery, and so forth. Instead of eating the same kind of meat and bread and wine in the morning that one would eat at night, the breakfast emerged as a meal requiring special foods (such as breakfast cereal) that had a special nutritional (that is, scientific) rationale and that obviously regulated behavior away from a leisured morning and towards scurrying after one's fortune. Instead of presuming that anything common is public, the public space was created, distinguished by its large, impersonal dimensions, its openness and strong lighting, and the need for special management. "The maintenance of specialized space required the development of a culture with specialized training, uncommon knowledge, administrative ability, and a professional code of ethics and dedication that lent itself to a distinct way of life."[23] The creation of a special management became the most common means for authorizing an institution and regulating a sphere of human behavior. Ultimately all of society could be identified in terms of specific spaces, each having its own specific administration backed by a specific body of knowledge: thus we could account for "the woman in the residential home, the child in the school, the man in his place of work, the dying person in a hospital, and the body in the funeral parlor; the immigrant in the ghetto, the criminal in the prison, the insane in the asylum, the Indian on the reservation, the Negro in his segregated area, the Irishman in the saloon, the prostitute and the pimp in the red-light district."[24] And our account of the separate spaces mentioned here would be known as the disciplines of home economics, education, management science, medicine, mortuary science, sociology, penology, psychiatry, anthropology, and social work.

This comprehensive analogy between specialization and spatialization was sustained through the creation of special vocabularies. "Confined in its space, every serious activity found a literary expression."[25] Sports, cooking, courtship, physical and mental health, all were encased in thousands of articles designed to transform them from pastimes into professions. This expansion of the language was then regulated further by the university presidents, who produced such guides as the Harvard Classics and Webster's Dictionary. The language became the property of the middle class. The professional, epitomizing middle class life, was someone who used a special vocabulary, marking a specific body of knowledge, to administer a specific space in the society. "Legitimate authority now resided in special spaces, like the courtroom, the classroom, and the hospital; and it resided in special words shared only by experts."[26]

The best metaphor for the spatialization of knowledge is found in the university itself. The university is not only the central institution in the disciplinary system but the epitome of spatial definition. Knowledge is categorized by colleges, divisions, and departments, by disciplines and sub-disciplines, by the curriculum and by the arrangement of books on the library shelves. The arts are in one building and the sciences in another. One can take separate courses in the sociology of law, the sociology of religion, the sociology of education, and the sociology of knowledge and never have to refer one to the other. This separation of a common subject is necessary if one is to learn what one is really supposed to learn, which is a basic principle of our mental administration.

The national testing bureau conveniently (and not surprisingly) provides two images of this system with a "map of college majors" and "world of work map" which are administered to high school students. It is interesting that one map imitates the design of the Panopticon, and the other represents the belief that knowledge is coordinate with a distinct space in a master grid. Although the maps are obviously contrived, we must recognize that they exist because they provide images, however crude and self-serving, of the spatialization that is a fundamental principle of design in contemporary academic culture.

Stated otherwise, "spatialization" itself is in part a metaphor for a particular attitude that is an indirect yet powerful determinant of our thinking. "Spatialized" knowledge refers both to our habit of thinking of a subject (say, abnormal personality) as a "field" or "area" having a terrain best managed through a mental procedure similar to the measured observation of surveying, and to our tendency to approach a subject as if it is a territory for exploration and eventual proprietorship. Obviously, no inquiry need be piously free of such motives and any study is likely to contain some tension between its definition of the "field" and its practices of inquiry. It does matter, however, that these tensions are suppressed from consideration within the professional context, and so withheld as means for additional inquiry as well as subjects for evaluation.

The third claim I am advancing is that the power of the disciplinary system to shape knowledge through the university apparatus is also the power to subjugate knowledges, and that rhetoric is one of the subjugated knowledges. "By subjugated knowledges I mean two things: on the one hand, I am referring to the historical contents that have been buried and disguised in a functionalist coherence of formal systemisation. . . . On the other hand, I believe that by subjugated knowledges one should understand something else . . . namely, a whole set of knowledges that have been disqualified as inadequate to their task or insufficiently elaborated: naive knowledges, located low down on the hierarchy, beneath the required level of cognition or scientificity."[27] Foucault's definitions apply powerfully to rhetorical studies, with the tradition of rhetorical "theory" (a term from the university culture) exemplifying one of the "buried knowledges of erudition" unable to fit well into the disciplinary scheme and epistemological rules of university culture, and with rhetorical practice exemplifying one of the "directly disqualified knowledges (such as that of the psychiatric patient, of the ill person, the nurse, of the doctor – parallel and marginal as they are to the knowledge of medicine – that of the delinquent) etc."[28]

There are two ways for a discourse to be subjugated under the disciplinary schema: by not being declared a discipline, and, in some cases, by being declared a discipline. Examples of the first fate are "Marxism," "prophecy," and "oratory"; examples of the second are "economics," "religion," and "speech." In either case this subjugation is the consequence of translating texts into a discipline. Basically, the business of granting degrees presumes, and produces, the activity of certifying texts. Disciplinary certification follows two requirements. First, the subject is spatialized: if oral, it is written; if written, it has its writing checked carefully to produce the immobile text; it is given an index; it is indexed, codified; it receives commentary and the commentaries are indexed; it is made wholly comprehensible, devoid of any secret passages; it is found to confirm the discipline. Second, it is shorn of anything subversive to the disciplinary system. The histories of the individual disciplines reveal how the constitution of each included the suppression of ideas thought dangerous in the Gilded Age. History was cleansed of visionary history, sociology of class consciousness and holistic theory, economics of socialism, medicine of homeopathy, and so forth.[29] In every case properties of manifest interpretation such as nationalism or theism or sentimentality were ordered out of the discipline. Some of these changes will have been rejections of poorly formed ideas badly defended; some of the discarded ideas, however, were found to be bad ideas because they had been discarded.

This shift in intellectual style – from the role of spokesman to that of expert, from the display of copiousness to the cautions of specialization, from an acceptance of obscurity to the pretensions of rationality – was a shift away from the tradition of rhetoric. The nineteenth-century orator had no specific body of knowledge and knew it. But instead of being cast in a struggle with his adversaries, one well entangled in everybody's relation with the sovereignty of the day (as has been the case since the conflict between the Sophists and Plato), the orator in the latter half of the nineteenth century found himself being written out of the script. "As the well-bounded disciplinary communities became the essential model that defined the idea of a profession, public lecturing became unrecognizable as a genuine intellectual profession. Public lecturing vanished as a profession less because the acitivity itself had disappeared than because the cultural lens that had led to its perception as a 'new profession' in the 1850s had been shattered."[30] There was no place in the disciplinary system, no separate space in the disciplinary schema, for the practice of oratory. Only much later could Walter Ong argue that the modality of speech is truncated when spatialized: that much of what is constitutive of the act of speaking, and of the powers of speech, is filtered out by any description of the act of speaking in terms of space.[31]

This disciplinary action was completed by the subordinating of populist oratory to the genteel prose of the professors, in part through the stern exclusion of non-academics from the disciplines of speech and political science. The populist movement occurred outside of and in reaction to the rise of university culture and its growing political power, and the reaction of the professionals to that uprising included the tightening of university control over the knowledges admissable for governance. Populist oratory was disqualified, labeled "amateur" and "unprogressive."[32] Buried with it was "a historical knowledge of struggles. In the specialised areas of erudition as in the disqualified, popular knowledge there lay the memory of hostile encounters which even up to this day have been confined to the margins of knowledge."[33]

Interestingly, a dissenting voice was raised at the beginning: Everett

L. Hunt questioned the professionalization of speech in the first and second volumes of the *Quarterly Journal of Speech*.[34] Hunt asked how the scientific definition of speech could retain the "literature of power" that was the source of public speaking, or how the science could be either as public or as personal as is demanded for the understanding of public speaking.[35] We now can answer him – it can't. Rhetorical studies today exemplify the choice before anyone chafing under the disciplinary system: one can adapt to the system by recognizing its productive power, working to demarcate a separate epistemological space, and articulating a clear usefulness in preparing workers to have the basic competencies for middle class culture – as is done by each discipline's national organization – or one can attempt to explore marginality, that is, to excavate the knowledges interned at the emergence of the university culture.[36]

Conclusions

What, then, are we to do? Unreserved acceptance of professional scholarship as the authoritative learning has several obviously compromising consequences for the rhetoric of inquiry: importing all the fictions of scientism (and the anxieties sustaining those fictions) for an inquiry proven to require better equipment; accepting a slavish relationship with the modern state; losing the capacity for moral assertion; and ultimately abandoning some of the practices and tradition of rhetoric itself.

Yet complete rejection of the modern university would be equally foolish, for professionalism also has been a productive movement producing superb, and superbly coordinated, technical scholarship, as well as advancing democratic access to learning within and without the academy. The contemporary academy resembles the parallel institutionalization of medical science, for each has produced opportune conditions for the good life. The disciplines have produced a large amount of excellent scholarship that otherwise would not have existed, and they have organized an enormously wealthy institution directed to perpetuating knowledge. The professionals do what scholars always are charged to do: conserve and produce knowledge. But, to continue the analogy with medicine, disciplinary study cannot itself provide the good life. For example, the full participation in rhetoric as an important story in the history of ideas must come from an approach to the subject that is not provided by the production of expertise. Perhaps every tradition has to move through but then beyond disciplinary organization; perhaps disciplinary critique and breakdown are signs of successful disciplinary maturation. And to take the analogy to its limit, as medical advances are the product of an industrialization that also represses and kills, so can unchecked disciplinary study support the destruction of literate culture.

It is not enough to recognize that the matter is complicated, however. The following recommendations, conclusions, and caveats are offered in the interest of moving beyond critique towards affirmation of another, more rhetorically active higher learning. As Kenneth Gergen has advised, the rhetoric of inquiry needs to pursue "a metatheory that reconsiders the concept of intellectual progress," particularly as that progress includes the goal of a good society.[37]

1   The rhetoric of inquiry should be pitched in an adversarial relationship with disciplinary knowledge. Disciplinary knowledge is both a claim to know and a means of social control, a productive capability and a rigid system of mental administration, a body of knowledge and a suppression of interpretative thinking. The rhetoric of inquiry is positioned well to identify these silent partners of institutional knowing, for it acknowledges their manifestation as versions of inevitable motives for using discourse, and it is itself situated in the margins of the academic canon. The critique cannot be absolute, for the rhetorical perspective has to allow desire and domination their due in all discourse, but it should be vigorous.

2   If the rhetoric of inquiry is to articulate alternative conceptions of how inquirers can communicate (as, for example, Gergen advises),[38] it must move beyond the disciplinary logic of applying a rhetorical *method* to a *field* of study. Here the representative work is Donald McCloskey's *The Rhetoric of Economics*, a fine study that deserves its influence. But a strong first step is too easily taken to be a completed project. As it stands, McCloskey's analysis offers little more than an alternative expertise and remains subject to the conventional retort that "all a rhetorician's rules but teach him how to name his tools." Thus far, the major statement of a superior communicative relationship for inquiry has been supplied by Richard Rorty's ideal of "conversation," yet much remains to be done. As it stands, "conversation" may be one of the more alienated terms in academic culture, for it remains only a token consideration offering no serious challenge to the academic practices of disciplinary languages, disciplinary forums, and disciplinary rules. Rorty has taken that important second step beyond technical study but he has relied too much on the suggestiveness of his metaphor, and has overlooked its consideration in terms of institutional practices. Now we need to examine alternatives to the norms of expertise, productivity, and social control, including such ideas as commonality, anonymity, and gratuitousness. And any reconsideration of communication relationships and inquiry has to at some point address the question as to whether the alternative proposed can co-exist with the disciplinary system.

3   The rhetoric of inquiry must develop a cultural critique. The first step here is to recognize that disciplinary knowledge is an apparatus of the disciplinary system – or, in Louis Althusser's terms, that it is an "ideological state apparatus"[39] – and so avoid replicating the willed political incapacity of positivism. John Nelson already has argued that the rhetoric of inquiry needs to become more explicitly political, yet current work seems concerned largely with intradisciplinary distinctions.[40] The professional ideology remains firmly in place, allowing each writer both to assume blithely that the politics of his or her discipline are crucial to intellectual progress, and to ignore how they are indeed important to the distribution of power in bourgeois society. It is no accident that as the continental writers figuring prominently in the current revival of rhetoric are incorporated into American academic work they are shorn of their political orientations: such ideas cannot be translated within the disciplinary context.

4   The rhetoric of inquiry must develop a pedagogy. Rhetoric now bears a long tradition of self-constitution as the general science. From the sophists' claims of universality, to Cicero's repeated subordination of specialization to erudition, to Quintilian's institutionalization of the rhetor as a polymath, to the Renaissance repudiation of technical philosophy, even to the subsequent relegating of rhetoric to stylistics (which in one stroke combines universality with marginality) – in each of the major constitutions of the rhetorical art it has been defined as properly articulating those powers of the person that are not amplified by specialized learning.[41] There is a reason for this emphasis, for in each of these incarnations rhetorical instruction was identified as the means for the transmission of literate culture.[42] Specialized learning can either presume or supplant this cultural background, but it is not the means for its reproduction.

Thus, we should recognize that the tension between philosophy and rhetoric contains another opposition as well: the opposition between general education and specialized learning. Branding this second dispute as merely pedagogical is as much a mistake as it would be to deny the true premise sustaining that supposition, which is that rhetoric does have an historical involvement with pedagogy that philosophy has not had to bear. The major presentation of the opposition between the two conceptions of learning is found in Cicero's *De oratore*; it is the major theme of the work. The organization of the dialogue is instructive here: Cicero begins by announcing the theme and presenting his case that erudition is the key to rhetorical achievement and so the proper subject of rhetorical study. The lawyer (professional, if you will) Scaevola argues in favor of specialized learning and a diminished estimation of rhetorical study. Then Antonius intervenes, recalling a debate in Athens about the philosophical foundation of rhetoric, with the options then being a rhetoric that transcribes philosophy or a rhetoric that is no more than the embellishment by practice of a natural aptitude for presentation. The rest of the dialogue is an attempt to extricate rhetoric from this false dilemma. Crassus, who was Cicero's tutor in rhetoric and serves as his spokesman in the dialogue, responds: first, he notes that the prior debate is characteristically Greek – that is, the issue of another culture – and then he begins his reconstruction of a rhetoric both learned and practical by recounting the curriculum of instruction in rhetoric. He has turned to pedagogy, then, both because it is an appropriate concern of his view of rhetoric as enculturation and because it provides a means for recovering rhetoric from the biases of the Greek debate.

The contemporary rhetoric of inquiry could profit from this example. Cicero shows us that sometimes rhetoric is better articulated in terms of an opposition between special and general learning than it is in terms of an opposition between philosophy and rhetoric. The best way to retain his orientation is to elaborate a pedagogy; the best way to conflate the two dialectics is to ignore pedagogy. Pedagogy should be construed less as an uninteresting application of theory and more as a means for reconstructing the arena for intellectual debate. Questions such as: Who is to be taught? What is to be taught? For what purpose? By whom? In what way? should be taken seriously. And taking them seriously means placing one's answers in the context of the critique of professionalism.

5   The rhetoric of inquiry should be used as a means for the recovery of rhetoric, and especially of those versions of the rhetorical tradition squelched by professionalism. We must recognize for a moment, however, what that recovery cannot accomplish. First, the excavation of rhetoric from underneath the disciplinary system will not reveal a rhetoric having all the substance and system and institutional power of an imagined discipline of rhetoric. The excavated knowledges will be found only as fragments, broken vases from a broken civilization. Instead of imagining ideal discoveries we should approach rhetorical criticism with an appreciation of how discourses are distorted when read into the disciplinary schema. Second, rhetoric alone is not going to solve the problems of contemporary philosophy, and especially the philosophy of the human sciences. The study of rhetoric, and especially the study of the rhetorical tradition, and the application of those studies, and especially the application of that tradition's orientation toward *praxis*, all can improve philosophical investigation. But to appropriate rhetoric as a clear, coherent text addressing our problems is to seriously misunderstand rhetoric.

Furthermore, rhetoric must beware its friends as much as its enemies. For the earnest application of technical rhetoric, or a readiness to use "rhetoric" as an all-encompassing rubric for unorthodox philosophies of science, only recapitulates long-conventional definitions of rhetoric as a demi-art either too descriptive or too plastic to sustain serious intellectual labor. It would be a better service to the tradition of rhetoric if we could identify the limitations of a rhetoric of inquiry and use that moment for reflection upon the traditional problems of rhetorical studies. For example, consider how the rhetoric of inquiry might appear to the subject of its analysis: to a Charles Darwin or a contemporary econometrist. The response to the rhetorician's analysis of one's rhetorical activity is likely to be: "Well, yes, of course, but all that is secondary, for what can you say about my subject before I say something?" This retort raises the oldest suspicion about rhetorical study: in classical terms, that the inquiry has no subject and so is a counterfeit knowledge.

Stated otherwise, rhetorical study has long been the primary repository for a mediation upon the question of whether there is a subject necessary for analytical work – what in contemporary terms is known as the attack upon foundationalism. This placement of the problem of the loss of the subject results from the origination of rhetoric as an act of mind – more graphically, from rhetoric's beginning in the fissures of thought. Rhetoric initiates the division of the *logos* into form and content; it ruptures an essential quality of speech – its unity, which gives the world an organic, unified character. (More specifically, the rhetorical analysis of speech into form and content itself displaces a more "original" tension within the *logos* between those linguistic acts that divide the world into parts and those that restore its felt unity.)[43] Yet when one then looks back across this gap between the subject of a speech and the method of speaking, rhetoric cannot be identical with the idea of the subject and so becomes reconstructed as mere method. We then experience the loss of the subject of rhetoric. This profound topic itself then is suppressed by the valorization of knowledge. Professionalization abets this suppression by conditioning scholars to pursue a subject having a presence represented by spatialization, and by determining inquiry so that knowledge can only be the report of the methodical examination of a subject, rather than, say, a form of familiarity with certain habits and difficulties of mental life. Correspondingly, the rhetoric of inquiry provides an opportunity to elaborate rhetoric as a meditation upon the pretensions, limitations, and discontinuities of knowledge.

6 The rhetoric of inquiry should recognize its own place in the history of rhetoric. Two observations are pertinent here, the first regarding the occasion for the current revival of interest in rhetoric and the second regarding its tendency. As other essays have catalogued, the

current turn to rhetoric is a response to a crisis.[44] Frustrated with scientific philosophy, we have looked for other accounts of meaning and knowledge; rhetoric then seems a highly appropriate alternative, for analyzing the literal elements of composition offers an ironic foundationalism. But for most people, rhetoric, like irony, can be at best a way station. Thus, the rhetoric of inquiry, like other rhetorics, is likely to be supplanted by another, more systematic philosophy.

More importantly, the fact that the rhetoric of inquiry is a response to a crisis will determine its own development. We are likely to draw from the rhetorical tradition those ideas and attitudes that suggest promising resolutions to the crisis, rather than enjoying the opportunities that can come from a parting of the ways. Not surprisingly, the rhetoric of inquiry itself demonstrates one of the more grandiose tendencies of the rhetorical tradition: the architectonic motive. Rhetorical studies school one both in the analytic process by which any discourse is broken into its component parts, and in the inventional process of categorizing parts of discourses and then whole discourses into ever more inclusive typologies. Coincidentally, the analytical movement that reduced ideas to techniques is balanced by an inventional movement that generates ideas about the classes of techniques. This inventional orientation, taken to its full expression, becomes the attempt to circumscribe the many discourses comprising one's culture within a single "art of structuring all principles and products of knowing, doing, and making."[45] Historically, the battle cry has been *una est eloquentia* – eloquence is one, regardless of how we have divided up the regions of discourse.[46]

This architectonic motive is stylistically foreign to disciplinary study. The bridge between disciplines is rarely used, because so much power must be left behind. The productive principle of the disciplinary system is that of separating discourses, not of joining them; the more readily one discourse can be bonded to another the more suspect it is of being a popular discourse and consequently unfit for training the professional, that is, for maintaining the division between the expert and the client population essential to power in the disciplinary system.

Yet the architectonic motive is always with us. In this century it has informed such projects as the Encyclopedia of Unified Science (which deconstructed with its last issue, *The Structure of Scientific Revolutions*), General Systems Theory, and General Semantics.[47] The rhetoric of inquiry is another such manifestation of this motive, and perhaps one more promising because it can proceed self-consciously. If a rhetoric of inquiry is to be a successful architectonic project, then it should begin by acknowledging its own interference with the disciplinary discourses being studied. After that, we can develop this tendency by examining those architectonic moments in the classical texts: for example, Aristotle's distinction between the general and special *topoi* (*Rhetoric*: 1358a) considers the proper relationship between the terms of specialized studies and the terms of general inquiry. Pursued too far, however, the search for a master set of inventional terms as the elements of inquiry would lead to the irony Kenneth Burke identified in the motive for perfection: a rhetoric of inquiry formulated in ever more elegant versions of itself would become pure rhetoric, discovering nothing but itself.[48] Perhaps we need to retain our own essential tension between system and discontinuity, authority and marginality, a history of the continuity of inquiry and a history of its discontinuities.

Rhetoric conceived of as a tradition of inquiry is itself highly problematic. The important point here is that they are good problems. The problems of the loss of the subject, of establishing the legitimacy of an art, or of determining the relations between general and special studies are places for understanding the life of the mind. If we are to think about rhetoric as a way of thinking, we must think of it in terms of its problems, especially as they are revealed in its history of suppression and marginality. In our own time, this is a history of a tradition of inquiry at odds with the official doctrine of the institution of inquiry. The rhetoric of inquiry that emerges from the critique of this doctrine of professionalism may create as many problems as it solves, but it will be more than a methodological analysis of expert discourse. Rhetoric's contribution to the higher learning comes in part from its condition as a marginal subject; consequently, it offers the most to one who is admitting to failure. As we are in the historical moment of admitting to a failure of the human sciences (as sciences), rhetoric seems a productive commentary upon that enterprise. If we take the next step and consider the intellectual costs of the modern educational organization, rhetoric can again supply the means for reconsideration. Rhetoric is a discourse that is distinguished by its utility for deception, a tradition of erudition distinguished by the absence of its subject, and a manner of thinking distorted by both its enemies and its friends. The understanding of each mode requires sensitivity to the others, yet none of these are admissable for the trained, examined, certified, expert professional.

Notes

1   John Lyne's report on the Iowa Symposium on Rhetoric and the Human Sciences develops a similar sentiment. He begins by noting the tendency to "methodism with a new face" and concludes by reminding us of rhetoric's function of empowerment: "Perhaps one of the greatest benefits of studying the rhetoric of inquiry in the era of information will be its capacity to explain something of the relationship between power and knowledge" (*Quarterly Journal of Speech*, 71 (1985), p. 71).

2 Paulo Valesio, *Novantiqua* (Indiana University Press, Bloomington, 1980), p. 3.

3 There is considerable overlap between the definitions used by "professionals" themselves and those used by sociologists studying them. This definition was used in a presidential address before the Speech Communication Association: Frank X.E. Dance, Presidential Message, *Spectra*, 18 (Feb.)(1982), pp. 1–3. It is consistent with many of the articles defining professionalism: See, for example, the seminal essay by William J. Goode, "Community within a community: the professions," *American Sociological Review*, 22 (1957), pp. 194–200; Terence J. Johnson, *Professions and Power* (Macmillan, London, 1972), ch. 2; Burton J. Bledstein, *The Culture of Professionalism: The Middle Class and the Development of Higher Education in America* (W.W. Norton, New York, 1976), p. 87. For the inevitable discussion of definitional problems see, for example, Douglas Klegon, "The sociology of professions: an emerging perspective," *Sociology of Work and Occupations*, 5 (1978), pp. 259–83.

4 Bledstein, *Culture of Professionalism*, ch. 1; Magali Sarfatti Larson, *The Rise of Professionalism: A Sociological Analysis* (University of California Press, Berkeley, 1977), ch. 12. Like others writing about professionalism, I am greatly indebted to Bledstein's work.

5 Laurence R. Veysey, *The Emergence of the American University* (University of Chicago Press, Chicago, 1965); Bruce Kuklick, *The Rise of American Philosophy, Cambridge, Massachusetts, 1860–1930* (Yale University Press, New Haven, 1977); Alexandra Oleson and John Voss (eds), *The Organization of Knowledge in Modern America, 1860–1920* (Johns Hopkins University Press, Baltimore, 1979). For studies on academic professionalization, see also, Thomas Haskell, *The Emergence of Professional Social Science: The American Social Science Association and the Nineteenth-Century Crisis of Authority* (University of Illinois Press, Urbana, 1977), pp. 25–6.

6 Robert H. Weibe, *The Search for Order, 1877–1920* (Hill and Wang, New York, 1967).

7 Larson, *Rise of Professionalism*, pp. 145–58; David M. Ricci, *The Tragedy of Political Science: Politics, Scholarship, and Democracy* (Yale University Press, New Haven, 1984), pp. 46–9; Bledstein, *Culture of Professionalism*, pp. 121–8. Each expands on Weibe's account.

8 Bledstein, *Culture of Professionalism*, p. 55.

9 Ibid., pp. 80–6.

10 Ibid., pp. 84–6; Larson, *Rise of Professionalism*, p. 246. For a catalog see Jane Clapp, *Professional Ethics and Insignia* (Scarecrow Press, Metuchen, NJ, 1974).

11 Bledstein, *Culture of Professionalism*, p. 56.

12 Michel Foucault, *Power/Knowledge: Selected Interviews and Other Writing 1972–77*, tr. Colin Gordon, Leo Marshall, John Mepham, and Kate Soper; ed. Colin Gordon (Pantheon, New York, 1980), p. 102. I have selected this collection for its accessibility.

13 Foucault, *Power/Knowledge*, p. 105.

14 Ibid.

15 Talcot Parsons, "Professions," *International Encyclopedia of the Social Sciences*, vol. 12 (Macmillan/Free Press, New York, 1968), p. 142.

16 See, for example, Thomas L. Haskell (ed.), *The Authority of Experts: Studies in History and Theory* (Indiana University Press, Bloomington, 1984); Jethro K. Lieberman, *The Tyranny of the Experts: How Professionals are Closing the Open Society* (Walker, New York, 1970).

17 Magali Sarfatti Larson, "The Production of Expertise and the Constitution of Expert Power," in Haskell, *The Authority of Experts*.

18 Foucault, *Power/Knowledge*, p. 161.

19 Bledstein, *Culture of Professionalism*, p. 178.

20 Ibid., pp. 156–7, 216–17.

21 Foucault, *Power/Knowledge*, p. 160; see also his *Discipline and Punish: The Birth of the Prison*, tr. Alan Sheridan (Pantheon, New York, 1977).

22 Bledstein, *Culture of Professionalism*, pp. 56–65.

23 Ibid., p. 57; see also Richard Sennett, *The Fall of Public Man* (Vintage, New York, 1978), pp. 12–15, 297.

24 Bledstein, *Culture of Professionalism*, p. 56.

25 Ibid., p. 65.

26 Ibid., p. 79.

27 Foucault, *Power/Knowledge*, pp. 81–2.

28 Ibid., p. 82; see also Haskell, *Emergence*, p. 41, for an account of how professionalization attacked the authority of common sense.

29 Relevant essays here include Hayden White, "The politics of historical interpretation: discipline and de-sublimation," in W.J.T. Mitchell (ed.), *The Politics of Interpretation* (University of Chicago Press, Chicago, 1983); Steven R. Cohen, "From industrial democracy to professional adjustment: the development of industrial sociology in the United States, 1900–55," *Theory and Society*, 12 (1983); Bledstein, *Culture of Professionalism*, p. 327; Ricci, *Tragedy of Political Science*; Donald Davie, "Poet, patriot, interpreter," in Mitchell (ed.), *Politics of Interpretation*. See also the long and ragged debate about literary professionalism appearing in *Critical Inquiry*, 10 (1983/4).

30 Donald M. Scott, "The profession that vanished: public lecturing in mid-nineteenth century America," in Gerald L. Geison (ed.), *Professions and Professional Ideologies in America* (University of North Carolina Press, Chapel Hill, 1983), p. 28; see also Ronald R. Reid, "The Boylston professorship of rhetoric and oratory, 1806–1904: a case study of changing concepts of rhetoric and pedagogy," *Quarterly Journal of Speech*, 45 (1959), pp. 239–57, and S. Michael Halloran, "Rhetoric in the American college curriculum: the decline of public discourse," *Pre-Text*, 3 (1982), pp. 245–69.

31 Walter J. Ong, *The Presence of the Word* (Simon and Schuster, New York, 1967), pp. 64ff.

32 See, for example, Robert W. Cherny, *Populism, Progressivism, and the Transformation of Nebraska Politics, 1885–1915* (University of Nebraska Press, Lincoln, 1981). Populist rhetoric still is discredited by the professionals: see, for example, Cal M. Logue and Howard Dorgan, *The Oratory of Southern Demagogues* (Louisiana State University Press, Baton Rouge, 1981).

33 Foucault, *Power/Knowledge*, p. 83.

34 Everett Lee Hunt, "The scientific spirit in public speaking," *Quarterly Journal of Speech*, 1 (1915), pp. 185–93; "General specialists," *Quarterly Journal of Speech*, 2 (1916), pp. 253–63. See also the replies of, for example, James A. Winans, "Should we worry?" *Quarterly Journal of Speech*, 1 (1915), pp. 197–201, and C.H. Woolbert, "A problem in pragmatism," *Quarterly Journal of Speech*, 2 (1916), pp. 264–73. The debate explicitly addresses the advantages and disadvantages of disciplinary specialization.

35 Hunt, "Spirit," p. 187.

36 For an analysis of the role of marginality in rhetorical studies, see Robert Hariman,

"Status, marginality, and rhetorical theory," *Quarterly Journal of Speech*, 72 (1986), pp. 38–54.

37   Kenneth J. Gergen, "The checkmate of rhetoric (but can our reasons become causes?)," paper presented at the Temple Conference on Case Studies in the Rhetoric of the Human Sciences, Philadelphia, April 1986, pp. 11, 12.

38   Ibid., pp. 8–11.

39   Louis Althusser, *Lenin and Philosophy*, tr. Ben Brester (Monthly Review Press, New York, 1971), p. 132.

40   John S. Nelson, "Seven rhetorics of political inquiry: a provocation," in John S. Nelson, Allan Megill and Donald McCloskey (eds), *The Rhetoric of the Human Sciences: Language and Argument in Scholarship and Public Affairs* (University of Wisconsin, Madison, 1987).

41   See Halloran, "Rhetoric in the American College," for an extended discussion of this point.

42   See Bruce A. Kimball, *Orators and Philosophers: A History of the Idea of Liberal Education* (Teachers College Press, New York, 1986).

43   Plato, *Phaedrus*, 265d–266c identifies the two dialectical acts of creating plurality and creating unity. See also Kenneth Burke's meditation upon division and identification in *A Rhetoric of Motives* (University of California Press, Berkeley, 1969).

44   See, for example, John S. Nelson and Allan Megill, "Rhetoric of inquiry: projects and prospects," *Quarterly Journal of Speech*, 72 (1986), pp. 20–37, and Dilip Gaonkar, "The rhetorical turn in the human sciences: limits and models," paper presented at the Temple Conference on Case Studies in the Rhetoric of the Human Sciences, Philadelphia, April 1986.

45   Richard McKeon, "The uses of rhetoric in a technological age: architectonic productive arts," in Lloyd F. Bitzer and Edwin Black (eds), *The Prospect of Rhetoric* (Prentice-Hall, Englewood Cliffs, NJ, 1971), p. 45.

46   Cicero, *De oratore*, 3.5.23. For a contemporary statement: "What I am sure is that as Thomas Kuhn once said, 'we have only begun to discover the benefit of seeing science and art as one.' The main benefit will be the return to a lost impulse in our civilization, last seen wandering off with Leonardo, the impulse not merely to combine the two, which are today considered as distinct, but, as Kuhn says, to see that they are *not* distinct" (Donald N. McCloskey, "The literary character of economics," *Daedalus*, 113 (1984), pp. 114–15).

47   For a related discussion of the architectonic motive, see Robert Hariman, "Putting rationality in its place: a topos for logos," *Explorations in Knowledge*, 3 (1986), pp. 25–32, especially pp. 27–9.

48   Kenneth Burke, *Language as Symbolic Action* (University of California, Berkeley, 1966), pp. 17–18. See also, *A Rhetoric of Motives*, p. 267ff.

Index

conflicting aims, 94; delegitimizing, 111; deliberative, 30; as a demi-art, 227; "empty," 112; as enculturation, 226; eulogistic, 4; excavation of, 226; forensic, 30; history of, 227; inferential function of, 204–5; and legitimation, 110, 208; managerial function, 204, 206; "mere," 3, 112, 114; of possibility, 179; poststructural, 177; preservative function, 204–5; professional, 111; of public service, 111; pure, 229; and the real, 109–17; of reception, 165–6; of rhetoric, 207; role, 198, 203, 208; of self-policing, 111; of social passage, 111; socially ameliorative function, 204, 206; of special expertise, 111; as subjugated knowledge, 221; technical, 227
Rhetoric of inquiry, 1, 62, 119, 195, 196, 203–6, 211–29
Rhetorical analysis, 89, 102, 103, 109, 120; criticism, 46, 213, 226; critiques of science, 207; epistemology, 206; scholarship, 212; theorists, 196; theory, 89
Rhetorical: choice, 2, 42; community, 119; devices, 152; effective practices, 110; form, 6, 120, 124, 130; invention, 6; knowledge, 117; method, 224; rationale, 42; situation, 129; sophistries, 69; *topoi*, 50; tradition, 109; transactions, 89; tropes, 109; turn, 1, 116, 117; vision, 96; voice, 70, 83
Right, common, 99
Ritual performance, 20
Roles, 24
Royal Society, 90, 91, 93, 95, 96, 100
Rules: algorithmic procedural, 136; constitutive, 143, 145; heuristic procedural, 136; mathematical, 186; regulative, 143; situational, 34

Salomon's House, 90, 91, 96
Sampling: methods, 77–8; theory, 73
Scheme, disciplinary, 218; incommensurable, 207
Scholars, 176, 211–29; community of, 206
Scholarship, 170, 223
Science: achievements, 23; anthropological, 121–5; behavioral, 36–45; as cultural genre, 24; and nonscience, 52, 60; politics of, 45; progress of, 28, 92, 101, 102; statistical, 69–84

Scientific: account, 38; advocacy, 34, 38; character, 41; claims, 69; communication, 34; contexts, 193; credibility, 50, 58; debate, 28–46; decision-making, 30; discourse, 30, 119–20; discovery, 89–104; ethos, 48–62; feasibility, 43; justification, 34; language, 1; legitimacy, 56; norms, 48–50; strategic argumentation, 28–9, 30, 45–6; texts, 183, 193; tradition, 196; value, 61; vice, 50; virtue, 50, 57, 59, 60
Scientism, 223
Sebook, T., 50, 53–9
Self-correction, 134
Self-quotation, 185, 188
Semantics, 143; program, 37
Sensory experience, 13
Sermon, in ethnographic writing, 120
Sign system, 154, 157
Significance testing, 73, 79
Signification, at a distance, 20
Signified/signifier, 24
Skepticism, 24–6, 50; Humean, 18; organized, 49, 55; post-empiricist, 21; rational, 24; vicious, 195–8, 207
Skinner, B.F., 30, 35, 36–45
Smith, B.H., 169, 177
Smith, M.L. et al., 111, 113
Social: change, 90, 102, 219; cohesion, 206; control, 215, 218, 224; experience, 215; forces 90, 103; hierarchy, 170; issues, 157; order, 146; organizations, 213; performances, 24; reality, 218; representation, 16; usage, 160
Social construction theory, 166, 170, 178, 180; *see also* Construction
Sociolinguistics, 191
Solvency, in debate theory, 33
Sophists, 6, 14, 116, 197
Source: citation of, 185; credibility, 40
Space, 222; public, 219; separate, 220; specific, 219
Spatialization, 216, 218, 220; of knowledge, 220
Specialization, 215, 220
Spectator, 18, 21
Speech: as complex behavior, 43, 44; face-to-face, 22; professionalization of, 223; public, 223
Sprat, T., 91–3
Stasis: classical, 199; levels of, 198
Statements, progression of, 180
Statistics, rhetoric of, 69–84
Status: academic, 170; disciplinary, 180
Status quo, 33, 39, 145